FINANCIAL TOOLS
for
MARKETING
ADMINISTRATION

FINANCIAL TOOLS
for
MARKETING
ADMINISTRATION

Letricia Gayle Rayburn
PhD, CPA, CMA

amacom

A Division of American Management Associations

Library of Congress Cataloging in Publication Data

Rayburn, Letricia Gayle.
    Financial tools for marketing administration.

    Includes index.
    1. Marketing management. 2. Marketing--Costs.
3. Marketing--Finance. I. Title.
HF5415.13.R349   658.8   76-13897
ISBN 0-8144-5423-2

First Printing

WITH LOVE TO MY PARENTS

Harold Ray and Myrtle Crawford Douglass
whose lives continue to be an inspiration to me

Preface

THE purpose of this text is to provide the manager or business student with financial controls for the administration of marketing cost that will provide a more efficient system for the distribution of products. The development of an effective system is important, not merely to each individual business, but also to the private enterprise system as a whole. Since marketing affects all people every day, improvements in the marketing system will benefit everyone.

Many executives rely on rules of thumb and experience in decision making rather than on the output of the information system. An informal system may be satisfactory for managers with many years of experience in the same company, but the mobile executive in a large company must rely on a formal system. The fact that so many marketing executives do rely on intuition and past experience may indicate a general lack of needed information on vital marketing factors. Many marketing information systems are not geared to the needs of the organization they serve. This prevalent situation is critical because it means that managers are basing their decisions on inadequate and misleading information.

The marketing manager cannot afford to make mistakes since most of the decisions made involve large sums of money. These commitments are often for a long period of time, although the return from a product must be optimized in a much shorter time. Many companies indicate that much of their income today derives from products that were not in existence five to ten years ago. All these factors contribute to a complex environment that requires more efficient marketing management. The future is not definitely clear, but it is certain that change will continue at an accelerated pace, and this prospect makes it imperative that marketing management improve its techniques. The marketing manager must be aware of current trends affecting the firm's products and future marketing operations. The best results come when the accountant and the marketing executive work together as a team in determining what information best fits their needs for the specific decision to be made. It may very well be that some of the traditional ways in which accounting data has been reported are not adequate. If so, the accounting information must be tailored to meet the needs of marketing executives. The object of this book is to provide the manager or business student with a knowledge of these financial controls.

Acknowledgments

I am indebted to Dr. Harold Fox, professor of marketing, De Paul University, who initiated the research that culminated in this book. A special note of gratitude is extended to Peggy McLain for her patience in skillfully typing many of the chapters. I also wish to thank Professor James T. Thompson, chairman, Accountancy Department, Memphis State University, for his interest and confidence in this publication. Finally, I wish to express my appreciation to my husband, Mike, and children, Doug and Beverly, for their inspiring patience, encouragement, and understanding.

LETRICIA GAYLE RAYBURN, PhD, CPA, CMA

Contents

1

Organizing
for
Informational Support

PRESENT-DAY marketing would not exist were it not for the Commercial and Industrial Revolution. Centuries ago marketing was a comparatively narrow activity. This was because consumers produced most of their own goods and trading was largely on a barter basis. The scope of marketing broadened tremendously as civilization developed from a simple pastoral economy through the stage in which village craftsmen supplied a local market to the present economy in which goods from any one country are distributed to the most distant part of the earth. At the simplest level, when the family was the principal producer as well as consumer unit, there were no marketing costs. With each succeeding, more complex stage of development, the expenditures on marketing costs became larger. This breakdown of the self-sufficiency of the feudal system and the beginning of production for the purpose of exchange is often referred to as the Commercial Revolution.

The Industrial Revolution was caused by innovations in technology and management that generated large increases in productivity. Production of specific goods was concentrated in a few favorable areas to gain the advantages from using specialized machinery, labor, materials, and other resources. Production levels had to be high in order to properly utilize the large investment in manufacturing facilities. This specialized mass production increased manufacturing efficiency, but made marketing more complex.

THE MARKETING REVOLUTION

In the 1920s most manufacturing firms had perfected their production techniques to the point of having surplus goods. This created a need for a system of mass distribution. Once the mass distribution system was operating, organizations were faced with yet another problem—that of getting the goods sold—which generated the need for salespeople, sales promotion, and advertising. This sales promotion effort worked well at first, but gradually, in the Great Depression of the 1930s, it was recognized that an effective mass distribution system and aggressive sales promotion were not the answer. The emphasis would have to be shifted from the producer and manufacturer to the customer. Consumers would have to be informed about new products before they would buy them. The increased competition called for increased expenditure on advertising and presentation of the product. It was also recognized that the task of marketing is not merely filling existing demand but also creating and discovering demands for new products.

CONSUMERISM

The ultimate objective of all marketing effort is to produce satisfied customers. The rationale is that satisfied customers will not only buy the product again but will also relay favorable messages to potential customers. Since consumerism is becoming one of the more pressing issues facing management, it behooves marketing executives to consider the interests of the consumer. Consumers today are less concerned with status symbols and more interested in accurate information about the products and services being offered.

MARKETING DEFINED

There is no one definition of marketing that everyone agrees upon. In this book marketing is defined as the broad area of business activity between the time the manufacturing process ends and the time the good reaches the ultimate consumer.

It is a common mistake to regard distribution as a function only of middlemen and retailers, and one that is confined to the finished product. Marketing operations may be part of every step in the entire process. Marketing costs begin with the determination of consumer wants and the delineation of market opportunities. Product design is a marketing function and its costs are marketing costs. Even though costs are often incurred before or during production, the term "after production" is often used to refer to marketing costs.

CLASSIFICATION OF MARKETING COSTS

The generally accepted accounting practice is to charge marketing costs against the operations of the accounting period in which they were incurred. This practice is often followed because there is too much uncertainty about the probable results of marketing expenses in future periods.

There are, however, exceptions to this general rule. Sometimes it is possible to determine objectively the amount of marketing costs deferrable to future periods. Exceptions can be made through prepaid or deferred expense accounts or in the inventory values of stock. Many accountants believe that there should be a deferral of such marketing costs as sales promotion if there is a change in the normal volume of sales during the period under review. Unusual advertising incurred in one period may justifiably be deferred to succeeding periods. For example, if a company advertises this month to publicize a new product to be offered for sale for the first time next month, this advertising campaign cost could be deferred.

When expenditures are made for items that have a life of several years, such as catalogs, they may be charged to a deferred expense account or expensed immediately. Costs of transporting products to warehouses and of handling the product in the warehouse are properly includable in the inventory values of materials at the warehouses. When transportation and handling costs are added to inventory values, they are deferred until the material is sold. The effects on profits of this treatment, however, may not be sufficient to warrant the additional accounting effort required. Unless quantities of product in the warehouse vary considerably from period to period, the effects will be immaterial.

Direct and Indirect Costs

Direct costs can be identified or traced to the specific function or the unit being costed. Indirect costs cannot be traced to specific products, customers, or other cost centers. Indirect costs are incurred simultaneously for two or more activities. Since indirect costs have no measurable relationship to specific units, they cannot be traced directly to the units. These jointly incurred costs must be apportioned to the individual marketing activities. The great bulk of marketing costs are indirect in nature.

The distinction between direct and indirect costs varies with the unit being costed. For example, the costs to operate a district sales office would be direct costs for a district sales territory. A company organized on a product basis would treat salespeople's commissions as direct costs to specific products, while the salary of the general sales manager would be an indirect cost.

Variable, Semivariable, and Fixed Costs

Marketing costs must be further analyzed into variable, semi-variable, and fixed costs. Variable costs of marketing are costs that vary in approximately direct ratio to changes in volume. If any part of the output is sold on the basis of a commission on the selling price or on the basis of a definite sum per unit, these costs will always be variable and will always move in direct ratio with sales. When commissions are calculated as a given percentage of sales, these costs are a variable cost of the direct selling function. Commissions may also vary at an increased rate as sales increase; the change is variable, but the rate of increase of commissions exceeds the rate of the sales increase. Handling, warehousing, and shipping expenses are additional items generally referred to as variable costs.

Many marketing costs are neither fixed nor variable but possess some of the characteristics of both; they are called semivariable costs. Semivariable costs vary with volume, but not in direct ratio because they contain both fixed and variable elements. Any analysis of marketing costs will likely reveal that many costs are fixed for a given range of sales volume but do change in amount when substantial changes in volume occur. For example, within a given sales volume range, salespeople's salaries may be considered fixed, but if sales volume increases beyond this range, additional salespeople will be needed and so total salaries will increase. Another example of a semivariable marketing cost is salespeople's compensation, which is composed of fixed salaries and commissions that vary with sales volume. Statistical techniques such as the scattergraph or the least squares method can be used to separate the fixed and variable elements of a semivariable expense.

Controllable and Noncontrollable Costs

Controllable and noncontrollable costs have sometimes been considered the same as fixed and variable costs; however, these classifications are not synonymous. The distinction between "controllable" and "noncontrollable" is made from the point of view of the person responsible for the expenditures. Controllable expenses are those that are subject to the authority and responsibility of a specific individual; the individual's responsibility can be measured only for controllable costs. Classification of an expense as controllable or noncontrollable must be made within a framework of responsibility and time. For example, expenses such as depreciation are not controllable within the short run, but are controllable in the long run because managerial decisions concerning capital additions determine the amount of depreciation charges.

One of the first major steps in marketing cost analysis is the classification of these costs. It is imperative that an accurate analysis and classification be made of each distribution expense. Unless management is able to distinguish and use marketing costs under such headings as direct, indirect, fixed, variable, controllable, and noncontrollable, much of the analysis is wasted. By using this classification of costs, management can gain an insight into which costs can be reduced and which will remain constant with changes in sales volume.

MARKETING COST ACCOUNTING

Whereas a great deal of attention has been given to production costs, marketing costs have often been neglected. The inventive genius that has been successfully applied to production has hardly begun to be applied to the elimination of distribution inefficiencies. There is much originality in marketing, but most of it has been used to persuade people to buy more goods rather than to reduce prices.

Accountants have not made themselves familiar with the marketing process in the same thorough way they have mastered the production process; they have not completely understood the functions they are attempting to measure or evaluate, nor have they learned what induces consumers to buy or how to evaluate the financial aspects of a new product. Financial people also do not know what motivates the sales staff. They have not learned that the cheapest method of distribution does not always lead to the largest net profit. The effect of the relationship between costs and competition has not been established.

Today, modern management expects pertinent production reports that highlight operational weaknesses; manufacturing inefficiency is viewed as inexcusable. Management has been quick to appreciate the advantages provided by accounting tools in locating areas that need improvement. The establishment of production standards is taken for granted by production management but there has been an attitude of complacency toward marketing costs. Few manufacturers know the cost of selling a product to a specific customer in a particular location. Even fewer producers know how much it should cost to make this type of sale. However, as further decreases in production costs become more difficult, management will likely center its attention on marketing costs.

No doubt real progress has been made in some types of cost analysis of marketing. There has been increased use of power equipment in the physical handling of merchandise. Fork trucks and conveyor belts do much of the work that was once performed by human labor. The operating structure and the division of labor in marketing are being affected by methods of large-scale operations and scientific analysis of distribution processes. Still, there has not been the advancement of large-scale operations in marketing that there has been in production.

Often the progress that has occurred has been made in areas that are comparatively easy to measure. Most of the attention has been directed to minimizing costs and too little attention has been given to evaluating the efficiency of various marketing functions. Because of the lack of accepted techniques, marketing expenditures have not received the critical appraisal necessary for the production of the most effective managerial reports.

Comparison of Marketing and Production Cost Accounting

There is no fundamental difference between the problems involved in cost accounting for production and for marketing. The cost must be located and allocated, and the responsibility for incurring the cost must be indicated for cost-control purposes. The cost accountant must handle company costs through three major stages: costs must be recorded as they are incurred, they must be traced in terms of internal activity, and they must be assigned to periodic revenue. The second and third stages require different treatment for production than for marketing costs. The techniques used in marketing cost accounting are borrowed from production cost accounting, though there are certain fundamental differences between marketing and production costs that make the analysis of marketing costs more difficult. Accountants' inattention to marketing costs has not been due to a lack of concern but rather to the elusiveness of measurable elements.

Numerous and Varied Distribution Agencies

Cost control is more difficult in marketing than in production because of the lack of repetitiveness and consistency in marketing operations. On the whole, the marketing process is not nearly so highly standardized as the production process, either between industries or within the same industry. Each operation of the marketing process is open to a wide variation of methods, with varying costs.

The nature of marketing makes for little comparability between companies. Many complexities are presented in the analysis and control of marketing costs, and it is almost impossible to compare the marketing costs of one company with those of another because the marketing processes probably will be extremely different. Vastly different channels of distribution can be used for similar products. For example, one concern may use a wholesaler-retailer channel of distribution; another may use advertising and house-to-house salespeople to distribute a similar product. In contrast, there are fairly definite limits to the production methods that may be employed by manufacturers producing like products.

Flexible Distribution Methods

The field of distribution is one where courses of action shift quickly. Marketing methods must be flexible enough to adapt to drastic changes and quick revisions in the channels of distribution. Distribution agencies may be quickly readjusted or shifted from one combination to another, or a change in market conditions may necessitate a revision in marketing plans.

Marketing costs are normally subject to more classifications or types of analysis than those of production. Costs presented on a "per product unit" basis are not as meaningful in marketing as they would be in production accounting. The tracing of costs within the firm must be done on the basis of some type of cost unit. The unit for production costing is usually a specific quantity of product such as a pound of sugar or a gallon of oil. In production, costs are also collected by departments, cost centers, and processes. Marketing cost accounting is concerned with determining cost by sales territories, functions, customers, salespeople, products, and size of order. Cost figures relating to specific market functions or sales channels are generally considered more helpful.

Intangible Cost Elements

One reason for the difference in the growth cycles of marketing and production cost accounting is that the latter measures results that are quantitative in character and the former does not. In accounting for manufacturing costs, identifiable quantities are involved. However, marketing cost accounting is complicated by the intangible nature of many of the individual costs involved. Psychological factors are present in distribution that are not involved in production. Marketing costs are associated largely with human effort, and these human activities generally cannot be reduced to mechanical, repetitive operations.

Marketing processes are less easily tested than are production processes; many factory processes are subject to rigid laboratory tests with a fairly predictable outcome. The uncertain factors are more numerous in marketing than in production; among the least predictable factor in marketing is the demand of the consumer. The attitudes of customers and competitors are also difficult to measure.

Uncontrollable Factors

Usually the majority of the conditions surrounding production expenses are entirely within management control. The results of alternative courses of action can be measured with a considerable degree of success, all circumstances are conducive to accurate recording of measurable work, and accurate unit costs can be secured. It is easier to develop efficiency in the plant because facts can be more readily determined and conditions more easily controlled. General business conditions, the weather, and a wide variety of other uncontrollable factors affect the results of marketing activities, and these factors change rapidly. The conditions under which marketing costs are incurred often make costing for control and planning purposes more difficult.

Direct control by one organization over important costly areas of marketing is often absent. In production, the manufacturer is in relatively direct control of the operations he wishes to change. However, in marketing he must work with many operations that are not subject to direct managerial control, such as the dealers who distribute his product. The actions of customers and competitors are also not under managerial control. Concerns have to solicit business where the customers are—which is not necessarily where the concern would like them to be. Customer calls are made at the convenience of prospective buyers, not at the convenience of the company. The size of the market and the conditions under which a customer will give an order are not controllable. Management has little control over what customers will do, since they may respond to various appeals.

Production costs are incurred in and near a specific place (the plant), while marketing activities are spread over the whole marketing area (frequently the entire nation). The setting for marketing functions varies from densely populated cities to sparsely settled rural areas. Within the factory, time and motion studies can be used to measure effort. No such exact measure of selling effort can be achieved in marketing activities because there are no inspectors or timekeepers available when a salesperson contacts a prospective customer.

Economic Factors

Some economic factors are a handicap to scientific management of marketing activities. There is an inherent tendency for marketing costs to rise with expanded selling efforts while production costs tend to fall with increased manufacturing volume. As more products are produced, more effort is necessary to find additional customers and to open new territories. During periods of keen competition management finds it is far more difficult to increase sales without increasing marketing costs more than pro rata.

Historically, most sales managers have considered an increased sales volume as their goal, with little regard to profit. Selling efficiency has usually been measured in increased sales volume, which is taken to indicate increased profitability. Frequently, however, increased sales volume does not mean increased profit, and with the introduction of marketing management, the traditional goal is changing. This managerial attitude has not been prevalent in production because the goal in production has always been decreased cost per unit. Production efficiency is generally measured in terms of decreasing unit costs and there is a constant drive toward the immediate reduction of direct costs. The most effective means of reducing marketing cost ratios is often more effective sales results without any decrease in total costs.

Competitive marketing is often wasteful because the market territory may be so small that one distributor could handle the volume. When a second distributor enters the territory, total marketing costs may double with little or no increased total volume.

Though the public at large is often uncertain as to what benefits it desires from a marketing system, marketers have to consider society's requirements as expressed through public regulatory authorities. These agencies, in an effort to control prices in order to preserve competition, frequently issue rules that hinder the economical distribution of goods.

Joint Cost Allocation

A major problem in both marketing and production cost accounting is the allocation of joint or indirect costs. When an expenditure is incurred for an effort or service that is wholly applicable to one classification for which costs are desired, marketing or production costing is relatively simple. Generally the proportion of the total number of items of marketing costs for a given concern that are direct is small compared with that for production costs. Indirect or joint costs, which are troublesome in production, are even more so in marketing.

Certain marketing costs such as those for labor, material, delivery, and packaging can be traced directly to the cost unit for which the expenditure was made. For example, sales commissions are direct costs and are incurred only in specific cases; these costs are directly attributable to a specific sale. There are also certain marketing services such as credit, return privilege, and servicing of products that can be related to units of product. (However, while these services are related to production units, they are not necessarily incurred by all units of product.) Other marketing costs cannot be clearly identified with units of product because they are incurred by the enterprise as a whole as a necessity of being in business.

One of the problems in marketing cost accounting is the difficulty of allocating the costs incurred to the sales obtained. Since the entire marketing process may extend over a long period, there is often a time lag between effort and result. Frequently a relationship between effort and results is difficult to obtain. During any one fiscal period, for example, the sales may bear little relation to the advertising expense incurred. Thus results obtained from certain marketing efforts such as advertising and sales promotion will not always appear in the period when the cost was incurred. The response to the first advertising campaign may be negligible because successive appeals are often necessary before the prospect becomes a buyer. Institutional advertising is often designed to develop brand recognition or to promote long-range product expansion. It usually represents a capital expenditure insofar as it aids in the creation of goodwill. Advertising expenditures of this type may not only generate sales immediately but also have residual benefits.

Because the majority of marketing costs are indirect expenses and cannot be apportioned to specific cost units, the results that stem from such costs must be determined and separated. A large number of allocations must be made, and made to more kinds of units of measurement than is necessary for similar cases in production. Often a sound and determinable basis by which many of the costs can be allocated is lacking; because these allocations can be achieved in so many ways, a uniform basis of apportionment is generally not established.

Objective of Marketing Cost Accounting

The objective of marketing cost accounting must be to help the organization achieve its overall goals. There are usually many more organizational goals than the two commonly stated ones of growth and profitability. Top management's personal goals influence the organization's stated objectives. In fact, some authorities argue that an organization cannot have goals because it is an intangible thing, and that the goals that are stated as the organization's are really those of the dominant members of the management team. It is unnecessary here to come down on either side of this argument because it makes little difference to the effective operation of financial tools.

Management may want to create and maintain a specific image regarding quality, dependability, or other features of its product. To do this it will have to decide what the company's strategy must be to meet this objective. The strategy will comprise all the different activities and programs the organization undertakes to meet the goals established. Another objective may be to capture and/or retain financial control within a select group such as a family for years ahead.

The individual target goals must be compatible. For example, if one goal is to earn a 30 percent after-taxes profit, management will have a hard time achieving this objective if the organization policies restrict the population segment that sales promotion is designed for. The firm may adopt this restrictive policy because it wants to create an image that the product is so luxurious that only the well-to-do can afford and deserve it, but this policy demands a realistic sales volume goal.

Marketing cost accounting utilizes both cost control and cost analysis; different techniques are used in these approaches. Cost control studies the measurement of the performance of a function against a predetermined goal of performance. This predetermined goal may range from a crude average of past performance to a scientifically determined standard based on time and material studies. The difference between the actual and predetermined performance, usually called the variance, is studied for the purpose of decreasing cost and improving performance efficiency.

Marketing cost analysis is essentially a search for better ways to perform the marketing tasks. Marketing cost analysis is the assembling of marketing cost items into meaningful classifications; these classifications are then compared with alternative expenditures and with related sales volumes and gross margins. This accounting approach is undertaken in order to aid in the selection of products and territories, the channels and methods of distribution, and those quantity sizes in which sale or delivery will yield the largest net income.

Managerial Assistance

The importance of marketing cost analysis has been intensified by the introduction of marketing management. This concept places the marketing manager in a key position in the overall management of a company. Under this philosophy, the marketing man plays an integral part in every phase of the production-distribution cycle. His job does not begin where production ends because he must first establish what products the consumer wants. This is a significant departure from the traditional approach, which focuses on manufacturing and considers the marketing task merely to sell what has been made. The new emphasis on marketing and its expanded functions requires accountants to use their creative talents to develop tools for analysis.

In controlling marketing cost, marketing management must rely upon the accounting system. Organizations cannot avoid the costs of installing and maintaining an accounting system because some reports are mandatory; for example, tax returns and stockholders' financial reports. The additional outlay for recasting this data into information that is useful for marketing management is relatively small in relation to the high potential payoff.

The marketing information system must show the effect on income of changes in volume, mix, cost, and sales price. This will allow executives to make a better selection of the marketing mix, which is important. The marketing mix is composed of a number of devices and marketing activities that are coordinated to meet certain organizational goals. There are a number of these marketing activities that the executive can use. In choosing the marketing mix, the executive has the opportunity to use creativity and artistry as well as a large number of objective financial controls.

The purpose of this text is to provide business people with financial controls for their marketing costs that will help them achieve a more efficient system for the distribution of their products. The solution of this problem is important not merely to each individual business but also to the private enterprise system as a whole. If improvements in the marketing system can be made, then everyone will be better off since marketing affects all people every day—psychologically because it brings satisfaction, and physiologically because it meets the demands for life's necessities.

2

Marketing Information Systems

MOST businesses must keep a watchful eye on external forces in their environment in order to be ready to meet any changes in these forces. Creditors, investors, customers, and government agencies make demands on the organization; competitors' actions must also be predicted. In addition, management must meet the requirements of internal forces. First, it must have an organizational structure staffed with competent executives. They must watch the enterprise's affairs, which range from routine mass production methods to human relations.

With the increase in size and complexity of modern business organizations, the traditional marketing functions are more difficult to perform. The requirements for survival include careful planning, good organization, and effective performance. An organization must constantly be ready to adjust to external forces. Although it should be obvious to all marketing managers that without information the organization cannot survive, this needs to be underscored.

As operations grow and more marketing information is needed, the distance between managers and marketing transactions becomes greater. This means managers have to rely on information from other people and make important decisions on the basis of fragmented information. Marketing managers complain that much of the information they receive is not in the correct form and that it arrives too late. In many cases the information is scattered throughout the organization, so that no executive has the information he or she needs. All too often important information is purposely suppressed to avoid embarrassing personnel. Sometimes employees either forget to relay the marketing data they receive or do not know who could use this information. The result is that marketing managers must hunt for the information they need from these highly scattered places.

In the typical organization, then, marketing research information is not sufficiently supplied. Not only is there a lack of understanding as to what the information objective of the marketing research department really is, but all too often this department does not consider itself a vital part of the information system. While most marketing managers have complaints concerning the information system, too many of them do not take the effort to investigate alternatives to their present system. They hesitate to adopt a new information system.

Yet it is imperative that organizations have a good marketing information system in order to cope with the rapid growth in size and diversity of their marketing operations. The systems approach to marketing functions provides the tools for meeting these complexities in the modern firm, whether the system is computer-based or manual. The systems approach is based on the contention that there is a strong link between the design and management of operating systems and developing information systems for decision making. Obviously the reason for a marketing information system is to assist in decision making concerning the management of operating systems.

CONCEPTS OF MARKETING INFORMATION SYSTEMS

Systems procedures are often identified only with the mechanics of paperwork, though they are an important administrative tool of an organization. The real significance of system work lies in its ability to serve management. Thus the purpose of a marketing information system is not to keep track of shipments and orders but to give marketing managers information that helps them make better marketing decisions. A marketing information system is a set of methods and techniques for the systematic planned gathering, analysis, and presentation of information for making marketing decisions.

The objective of the information system is to supply data to help managers fulfill predetermined organization goals. A marketing information system is a systematic method of accumulating, interpreting, and reporting the data each marketing manager needs for decision making. It strives to provide this timely data in a form that aids his or her understanding. It endeavors to eliminate inconsistent and incomplete data by providing a format for presenting information in a uniform manner.

Information Flow

Every organization must be concerned with coordinating the flow of information from within the firm with the flow from external sources. The internal flow of information must be both vertical and horizontal.

Vertical information flows in two directions: downward—data originating with top management and going to subordinates; and upward—data requested by top and middle management from lower management. There is also a continuous flow of unsolicited data between these three levels.

Horizontal information flows between employees on the same organizational level. It should not be assumed that this communication of information will take place as needed; there must be some planned means for the transfer of data. Management must be constantly aware of the barriers that inhibit the entry and exit of information and provide the means to overcome them.

The environment in which the firm works furnishes information for decision making in marketing. Some of the major sources of marketing information are competition, technology, wholesalers and vendors, the economy, legal and government institutions, cultural climate, trade associations, and customers.

The information in the external environment constantly changes and varies in importance to the firm. At certain times information concerning competition is crucial because a new product is being marketed; at other times a new government regulation will greatly affect the firm's profitability. For example, environmental controls set up by the governmnent concerning the use of some products would be of major significance to certain firms. The marketing information system must be flexible enough to rapidly gather data on critical issues, subject it to analysis, and distribute the analyses to the points of decision making within the organization.

The marketing information system is but one part of the overall system; it connects with other systems such as finance and production. There are two major components of any marketing information system: the part that generates and manipulates data such as marketing research and data processing, and the operations component, which uses the data as an aid to planning and controlling marketing activities. Systems designed for control, planning, and basic research are classified as marketing operations systems. Research systems are designed to test the use and effect of proposed programs and to assess the findings. For example, the nature and characteristics of advertising programs can be related to their effectiveness in increasing sales.

In the study of the marketing information system, every behavioral and mechanical aspect of the organization must be considered. Because of its nature, the marketing information system must be an open system that encompasses several major information flows. An information system may also be thought of as an interrelated set of systems, since it must bridge the gap between the major organization systems.

Each major information system may be comprised of subsystems; for example, there may be marketing subsystems concerned with sales forecasting, market research, and sales analysis by different segments. The future marketing manager will be even more involved in integrating the firm as a system. The information system's goal is to recognize the needs of all organizational units so that they can be met with a minimum of duplication and the corporation as a whole will be served.

The company does not have to be large for the concepts of marketing information systems to be valid. In addition, these concepts will apply even if elaborate electronic data processing equipment is not feasible for the organization. Admittedly, the growing sophistication of electronic data processing techniques has generated increased interest in marketing information systems (an interest that becomes intensified when the organization invests large sums of money in electronic data processing facilities), but the important element in an information system is still the managerial talent that designs and operates it.

INFORMATION NEEDS

Many executives rely on rules of thumb and experience in decision making rather than on the output of the information system. This informal system may be satisfactory for managers with many years of experience in the same company but the mobile executive in a large company must rely on a formal system.

The fact that so many marketing executives do rely on intuition and past experience may indicate there is a general lack of needed information on vital marketing factors. Many marketing information systems are not geared to the needs of the organization they serve.

This common situation is critical because it means managers are basing their decisions on inadequate and misleading information. Many companies maintain sales data only and fail to generate information concerning advertising, pricing, and market segmentation. Feedback concerning trends and alternative marketing plans is needed.

Levels of Management

An information system is essential to every firm, and accounting constitutes an important part of it. The kinds and forms of data that the information system generates should be specified by management needs. Even though top management has the responsibility for making major business plans, often few reports are designed especially for it. Many times marketing reports are only summaries of information given to middle management or copies of the exact report. But top management's information needs differ in quality and kind from middle management's.

A well-designed information system eliminates the need for routing many routine reports to top managers so they can focus all their attention on the few important problems. These items will vary by the firm's size and industry. The background of the top managers should also be considered. If an executive has been with the organization for a long time, obviously he or she will not need as much information as a new executive.

Materiality also enters into reporting. Areas in which the efficiency level of performance will substantially influence revenue and expense should be reported in great detail and in such a fashion that any necessary corrective action can be pinpointed.

Control Information

Executives need various kinds of information, ranging from data for the control and evaluation of daily operations to information for making future plans.

Control systems provide continuous monitoring of operations and furnish management with forecasts of trends, marketing opportunities, and problems. If they receive rapid indications of possible problems and opportunities, marketing managers will be better able to meet these problems and take advantage of available alternatives. This means that the marketing information systems must provide marketing managers with both historical and current data. Historical details concerning past sales by product lines, territories, and other segments are needed. These details will enable management to evaluate and compare past results with planned budgeted results. Historical information will also help forecast future marketing conditions.

This control sometimes takes the form of exception reporting by comparing actual performance with predetermined standards or goals. Deviations from standard can be determined so that corrections can be attempted. The principal value of giving executives important deviations using exception techniques is that it focuses their attention on the areas that need action. In light of these deviations, management may decide that the sales plan is not realistic and may change the standard. Certainly control cannot be achieved by merely establishing standards. Standards are only as worthwhile as the follow-up action that management undertakes.

Information for Planning

Information is needed not only for control purposes but also for planning for the future. The information system must supply regular reports that cover external and internal planning needs. Information from outside the organization about alternative marketing methods that are currently available is needed so that management can analyze the costs and feasibility of changing such factors as warehousing and transportation.

If the organization has the computer facilities, planning systems can allow for the simulation of the effects of alternative plans for the purpose of arriving at better decisions. Planning systems of the future may evaluate alternatives, make decisions, and then take action. Such action may be in the form of placing orders for merchandise and supplies.

The planning system should provide marketing executives with the information required for planning sales and marketing programs. Instead of distributing this information in many regular reports, some companies are combining the basic information a product manager needs for making annual marketing plans and their revisions into one book. This enables all product managers to base their plans on the same data. Their supervisors are then able to review marketing plans on a comparable basis when making approvals.

Many of the external variables are uncontrollable. Tax policies and other government regulations are not controllable; yet they have an impact on marketing functions. Demographic and social trends, as well as the economic environment, affect the level of demand for the company's products. Even the state of the climate is valuable external information for many industries. The marketing manager should not forget the impact of competitors' actions. More of the internal variables are controllable. For example, the advertising budget is determined by management, and policies affecting marketing are internally generated and controllable.

<h2 style="text-align:center">ELEMENTS OF A MARKETING INFORMATION SYSTEM</h2>

Management must create an effective organization and then obtain the personnel who can solve the internal problems as they occur. This requires a constant watchful eye over the enterprise's system of communications.

Company Objectives

With the vast capabilities of current data processing facilities, all functional lines of the organizational structure can be crossed. With the emphasis on the unified organization, the marketing information system must move from a mono-functional approach to a modern multifunctional approach. This requires that top management support the establishment of short- and long-term objectives. It is very difficult for an information system to become operational if there are no established objectives. Certainly the short-term objectives of the firm must be determined first before the techniques of a marketing information system are discussed. These short-term objectives may include plans for conversion to the multifunctional concept. Long-term policies must be established by the executive committee since it alone has an overall view of the needs and objectives of the organization.

Organizational Structure

One of the initial steps in developing a marketing information system is to review the marketing organization, its authority and responsibility, and the policies under which it operates. The spheres of activity for each marketing manager must be clearly defined. In addition, the areas of responsibility and performance evaluation each marketing manager will be held accountable for must be determined. For example, a segment manager must know if his success will be measured by segmental revenue, contribution margin, or net income.

Most companies have information about their organization's policies, goals, assets, and operations. Often the problem is that this information is stored in the managers' minds and is not available for company-wide decision making. This data must be organized in such a fashion that the marketing information system can be designed to reflect the overall company organization. The organization structure must provide for adequate planning and control techniques. The information system should match this delegation of authority within the organization.

Organization charts show how the firm is to function; organizational manuals describe the functions. The organization manual should give in detail the instructions for carrying out the duties and responsibilities involved in company operations. Instructions for the integration of individual subsystems should be specified and available for people to use. However, just because the organization chart and manuals say a firm is supposed to work a certain way is no guarantee that it actually does.

Top Management

If a firm is to have a successful marketing information system, top management must be convinced that the system is absolutely necessary to the growth of the organization. These executives must also consider its development their responsibility, and they must realize that much effort and time will be demanded of them during the development stages. A marketing information system is made up of more than just technology; it must be designed to complement existing systems within the organization. The entire responsibility cannot be given to a group of systems analysts.

Systems Analysts

Sophisticated marketing information systems require the specialized skill and coordination of many groups. In addition to top management support, the talents of systems analysts and designers, programmers, and computer technologists are needed, even though these people must rely on management to define their information needs.

Within business circles it is questioned whether the employment of outside professional systems analysts is a better choice than using internal systems personnel. Public accounting firms have specialists in their administrative services or management services departments who are qualified to design both accounting and nonaccounting systems. In performing audit procedures, public accountants often find opportunities for system improvements. Likewise, management consultants may undertake system assignments after studying an organization's markets or transportation network. The outside consultant's opinion is usually respected and his or her word carries authority. The consultant brings to the organization a new viewpoint; only time will prove if it is a better one.

In larger companies system design is usually the responsibility of a systems specialist who serves as "staff" and has no responsibility for operating activities. Under these circumstances, systems personnel must guard against interfering in line authority while studying the organizational cost center. In smaller companies system design is not a large enough task to occupy a person full time; thus the work is assigned to a line official.

Development Approaches

Leadership is needed in developing a marketing information system since there is reluctance to change existing patterns. There are several approaches that can be used, from operating within the present organizational structure to drawing up a new organizational chart. There may be a total lack of coordination between the financial data supplied by the accounting department and the market data supplied by the marketing research department. This places management in the incorrect position of having to correlate the data. While some authorities would argue that the ideal approach would be to abolish these two departments and establish a management information department, this would not ensure a successful marketing information system because the management information department could not supply all the marketing data needed such as field sales information.

A committee may be charged with the responsibility for developing the marketing information system. This is a good means for sharing ideas and joint learning. Committee discussions can lead to an awareness of potential areas of compatibility and the coordination necessary to reconcile them. The committee approach does require a great deal of time for meetings and discussions, and it is difficult to get a busy line manager to carry out additional assignments. Because the committee usually lacks authority, leadership is often missing.

Some organizations have assigned the development of a marketing information system to a junior member of the research department staff. This is not a good approach because of the complexity of the tasks involved. An inexperienced junior staff member usually cannot exercise the authority necessary to overcome resistance to the development of something new. Adoption of this approach reflects adversely on top managers because it indicates they don't understand the importance and functions of a marketing information system.

Another approach is to assign a top-level executive, probably the vice-president of marketing, the responsibility for the development of a marketing information system. This vice-president and his top-ranking executives would define the objectives that are to guide the system, and coordinate and review the efforts of the people working on the system.

Additional people would be required under this approach because top-level executives would not have the necessary skill or time to commit. The actual work would have to be done by a group composed of individuals such as the firm's computer center specialists, the marketing research director, a representative of the sales force, the economic research director, and the chairman of the accounting department. In addition, a director of marketing systems would be appointed. He would have the authority to control costs and would be responsible for the overall budget, which would include compensation for the services of systems analysts and programmers.

This approach is the one most likely to secure top management support. It also has the advantage of using the special talents and training available within the firm.

Functional Cost Records

There is no complete agreement on whether structure or function should be the beginning point in the study of operating systems. The current view leans toward functionalization; however, the structure of an organization cannot be ignored because it affects the method of operation and determines the limitations of the performance of each function.

Business organizations are normally organized along functional lines. This is an outgrowth of the specialization of skills. Marketing managers must think in terms of the work that must be conducted on a daily basis—marketing functions. To build an information system for marketing purposes, the marketing functions must be defined and the information required be determined. Each marketing function requires and/or generates information. The nature and level of operating expenses are determined by the functions performed.

Functional-cost records recognize this assignment of responsibility and authority along lines of specialization. If responsibility has been clearly assigned for marketing tasks, functional-cost records enable managers to hold various persons accountable for the results. Reasons for changes in expense or deviations from standards can be traced to the factors causing them.

Natural Expense Classification

A proper system of accounts for recording marketing cost is an essential prerequisite in cost control and analysis. The criteria used for choosing expense classifications are very important. The items in a ledger account should be homogeneous and large miscellaneous classifications should be avoided. At the other extreme, classifications should not be so detailed that the accounting costs are excessive.

Frequently the chart of accounts provides information for tax, audit, and internal control purposes but is not designed for management control. Most business organizations record marketing costs by nature or object of expenditure. This basis is often called the primary expense classification since it is usually made a part of the ledger accounts. Such traditional classifications as wages, repair expenses, and advertising expenses describe the kind of service the company secured for the expenditures. The particular natural expense classification for a firm depends entirely upon the nature of the enterprise's activity. The number of accounts depends on the extent and detail of the information desired by management.

Functionalization

Since there is no distinction between production and marketing activities under the natural expense classification, it has little value for managerial planning and control purposes. In addition, this method of accumulating costs has no value in market segmentation. Because the natural expense classification does not allow for the accumulation of data to permit proper analysis, another approach is necessary so that the cost of the marketing functions can be determined. Distribution of the individual natural classifications to the various functions is the same process as that used in distributing manufacturing overhead costs to departmental accounts.

The term *function* is defined in this study as any separate and distinct marketing activity carried on by a business concern. Personal exertions that are merely part of another activity are not separate marketing functions; each function should represent a distinctly different activity.

A more dynamic portrayal of company performance can be achieved when expenses are classified by functions. Functionalization of distribution activities also leads to a consideration of cost responsibility and control since the responsibilities of individuals in a business organization generally follow the specific lines of a function. Whenever possible, distribution functions should coincide with an organization setup under an official responsible for results. This organizational setup may be a department, a division, a branch sales office, or another unit. Regardless of the scope of this unit, the administrative head is usually delegated authority and is held responsible for the efficiency of performance under him.

Major Functional Classifications

The functions comprising the marketing distribution task are variously described and many different ways of organizing distribution cost are suggested in the pertinent literature. However, each company must prepare its own list of activities on the basis of a careful study of the exact work done. Since the selection of functions depends on the degree of cost control and cost responsibility desired, marketing executives and accountants should determine the functions jointly. The best breakdown may be the one that already exists for conducting the company's business.

The number of functions will vary from one company to another, depending upon such factors as size, method of operation, and the internal organization. The following examples illustrate how some of these factors affect the scope of distribution activities assigned to marketing departments. A manufacturer of a broad product line that sells the product nationally requires an extensive field organization. If the products are sold through several channels of distribution, an even wider range of functions is assigned to the marketing department. This case may be contrasted with a manufacturer of a narrow product line that sells through a single channel of distribution. A field force is responsible for personal selling and for providing information concerning products.

The approaches to functionalizing marketing costs vary concerning the degree of functionalization—the homogeneity of the marketing activities classified within categories. Functionalization may be integrated completely in the chart of accounts or made independently of the books. Marketing expenditures with one major functional group may require further breakdown into small classifications of responsibility. A greater degree of control can be achieved if major marketing functions are detailed.

The chart of accounts can provide for accumulation of sales and marketing distribution costs by control units through the use of digit codes. Digit codes can be incorporated for both analysis by function and analysis by manner of application, with charges coded at the source of the expenditure. In some cases the accounting classification can be set up on a functional basis with the major functions further subdivided by detailed functions. The incorporation of location or territorial codes into functional codes provides for the accumulation of major and detailed functional costs by territories. Segmental codes such as product codes, customer codes, and sales personnel codes can also be added to simplify additional analysis by manner of application.

If possible, the chart of accounts should be so designed that each function receives most of its charges directly, rather than through allocation, because this incorporation in the general ledger obviously facilitates periodic cost analysis and control. However, such refinements in the official account classification should be carried only to the point where they are feasible. For example, direct identification of an expense item to functions and to application would be neither desirable nor feasible if it caused accounting costs to be excessive. Consideration must also be given to responsibility accounting that dictates cost accumulation along organization lines. In cases where a single responsibility center performs more than a single function, or where production responsibility centers perform some marketing distribution functions, functionalization cannot be incorporated in the chart of accounts.

Internal Control

One of the most important features of an information system is internal control. While accounting is an important instrument in maintaining this feature, internal control is basically a management function. Each system should be studied to determine the type and levels of control required because a control procedure adequate for one phase of a system may not be feasible for another. The characteristics of the information involved in the system and its relationship to other systems should be determined. The objective of internal control is adherence to established goals while minimizing fraud and waste and promoting effectiveness. Certainly internal control cannot guarantee the total prevention of fraud; its task is to help achieve efficient operations. The marketing manager should check his or her system for these features of internal control. This checklist applies to both computer and manual systems.

Separation of duties and responsibilities. Responsibility must be fixed in order to ensure the maintenance of high-quality control. In addition, record keeping and operations must be separated. One employee must not be responsible for the accounting records and at the same time have control of the operations giving rise to the transactions to be recorded in these accounting records. No one employee should be in complete charge of a business transaction. For example, computer programmers or systems analysts should not be allowed to conduct the physical operations of the computer for any program written by them. The console operator must not be allowed to modify or change any program or system. Very often this separation of duties is not practiced. Some managers permit their machine operators to modify programs, which is an open invitation for a dishonest operator to freely engage in fraud.

The record-keeping function and the physical handling of assets should not be performed by the same individual. The accounting function should be separated from the operating departments so that unbiased, independent records may be maintained. The organizational plan should also allow responsibility to be fixed since this promotes care and efficiency. Management can expect a higher level of performance if individuals are held accountable for their inefficiencies.

Responsible personnel. The marketing manager must understand that the marketing information system is only as good as the personnel operating it. Each employee should be given duties and responsibilities that match his or her training.

Employees should be carefully chosen and trained. If enough attention is given to this training, the results will be better performance, reduced costs, and more alert employees. Employees in key positions in the information system should be bonded.

Rotation of duties. The basic pattern of rotation is to reassign personnel periodically to different applications of information processing. This provides for flexibility and limits the chances for a dishonest employee to alter information or mishandle assets. Many organizations frown upon this practice because, they argue, it forces them to retrain personnel constantly. Without rotation, however, there is a lack of flexibility, which becomes obvious when an employee is absent from work or leaves the organization and there is no one else who is familiar with his or her part of the system. Rotation prevents placing so much reliance upon one person for the processing of information.

An organization is mismanaged if it cannot allow its employees to take vacations. Certainly employees handling cash, vital information, and other valuable assets should be forced to take vacations. Vactions are a control technique because they allow for the rotation of duties at least for a limited period of time.

Prompt transaction recording. If as soon as a transaction occurs a record is made, there will be less chance that errors will occur. Source documents should be prenumbered and accounted for.

Physical protection. Adequate physical protection of assets should be provided through the proper use of locks, safes, and watchmen. Incoming and outgoing mail should be controlled, especially when it contains checks and customer statements. Information should be considered a valuable asset and protected and controlled.

Manual of instruction. Organizational policies and instructions should be reduced to writing. This promotes efficiency by promoting compliance with regulations and policies.

Independent check. There will be fewer personal irritations and errors if the information system allows for self-checks. All available checks and proofs of accuracy should be utilized.

Both external and internal auditors should be used in periodic reviews. Internal auditing by a staff that is completely independent of the operations materially strengthens the internal control of a system. The effectiveness of internal control should be appraised.

Equipment

The modern marketing information system must consider the utilization of computers because this equipment offers opportunities for improvements. Computers make it possible to integrate large volumes of information that was formerly separated. Many marketing activities that previously were functionally and geographically separate can now be combined. If decisions can be made upon the basis of formal rule or policy, decision rules can be programmed for computer application. Computer-based decisions can be made better and with more economy than those based solely on human judgment. Examples of decision rules that have been programmed for computer solution are purchasing and inventory control.

The adoption of a computer system requires a large sum of money because hardware must be available for storage, processing, and retrieval of information. Investments in systems equipment and changes should be made only when they will be more than recovered by the savings the change creates. It should also be determined how long it will take to recover the investment. Each marketing information system will have its own computer requirements, depending upon what specifications management has made. Technical assistance will be needed in choosing the hardware but it is management's responsibility to be certain that the equipment will meet the system's requirements.

A large number of people will be engaged in clerical operations and information-generating jobs even if computers are used. It must be remembered that the computer is not the central element in an information system. The managerial know-how that designs and operates the system is the most important element. However, marketing managers must be willing to take an active part in the installation of marketing information systems.

Feedback

In designing the marketing information system, the concept of an information feedback system must be prevalent. A good information system presents predetermined standards for each operation. Actual performance is then compared against these goals. Information received from the system should allow the executive to focus attention on any important variance from established objectives. There should be a self-correcting interplay between parts of the system. The inventory control system is an example of an information-feedback system.

A good marketing information system employs exception techniques by sending only information that is needed and requested by the recipients. Management by exception should be practiced so that managers do not waste time pouring over reports trying to find the deviations that deserve their attention. Excessive preparation and distribution of data causes executives to doubt the usefulness of such information. If only key data are presented, the manager's attention is more likely to be focused on the activity requiring action.

Flexibility

Systems methods must be flexible enough to change with business practice. The introduction of a new product or the opening of a new territory affects the information system. A marketing information system also affects the planning function since it provides managers with better techniques and information for planning and forecasting. With the introduction of a marketing information system, it may be necessary to make major changes in corporate communications. Because these changes will affect staff and operating personnel relationships (employees' status and security may be threatened), resistance can be expected. Preparation for the introduction of a marketing information system is a top management responsibility, and this is the level at which the education process should start. Top management should inform the new lower management level how it will be affected and the opportunities that are inherent in the change. Each management level will then inform the personnel below it, down to the lowest level of employee affected by the change. This type of educational process will go a long way in paving a path for the smooth conversion from the old organizational structure and system to the new one.

The successful systems designer is the one who convinces managers and employees that it is *their* system, because unless a system is accepted by the people who use it, it will not work. There is often a communication gap between a system's designers and its users. Managers should learn more about the capabilities of the information system so that they will make reasonable demands on it. Conversely, the systems analysts and computer technicians need to understand what is involved in the management process so they can design systems that fill management's needs.

Relevant Economic Data

There is great emphasis today on performance measures. At the same time, since modern computers can print a large amount of management information, this often results in an abundance of reports. At one time marketing managers had difficulty obtaining enough control information; now their problem is sorting out the valuable data and interpreting and organizing this information. If it is passed on to them without proper interpretation, executives will have to refine the data themselves and search for significant facts. Often they are pressed with administrative duties and consequently make only limited use of the reported data. Thus much of the cost of gathering the data is wasted, and management still may not have adequate information to direct operations successfully.

The design of the information system is crucial to future costs and work flows. A system that produces more than management can or will use is too involved or expensive to adopt. Unnecessary reports, records, and work motions will be eliminated if the correct system methods are installed. There will be less chance of error if simple, straightforward procedures are used. If only necessary reports are prepared, there will be less occasion for overtime, less working space for the storage of the paper flow, and a lower consumption of materials and supplies. Timely, more useful records create a better environment in which to operate. Employees will feel pride in their work when they see that it serves a purpose.

Therefore it is necessary to determine what price a user should or is willing to pay for accurate data. The greater the need or desire for accuracy, the greater the number of controls that must be installed, which increases costs. While there is still no method that can exactly correlate these factors, if managers are encouraged to consider them, the final results will be improved. The system should omit irrelevant data and provide relevant data on a timely basis. The information users, not the systems analysts, must make the final evaluation of cost-benefit relationships because they are aware of the internal and external constraints affecting their needs.

The content and form of cost accounting reports should be adapted to the executives who will use them. Some executives prefer tabular reports, while others prefer narratives. Reports generally are broader for high executives than for first-line foremen. Functional executives should receive general summaries of the operation and performance of their respective cost centers. Long-term relationships and trends also should be presented.

FUTURE TRENDS IN MARKETING INFORMATION SYSTEMS

It is expected that attention in systems design will shift from the automation of routine clerical tasks such as accounts receivable and payroll to more sophisticated applications intended to give managers information needed for decision making. More emphasis will be placed on evaluating current systems in order to incorporate improvements. The information system should be designed so that it leads people to accept company goals as their own personal goals. This will allow them to make decisions that are not only in their own interest, but also congruent with the organization's goals.

Level of Sophistication

In deciding how complex the marketing information system should be, a review of the organization's needs and the costs of meeting these needs should be considered. Attention should also be given to the abilities of the managers involved. A balance between management sophistication and marketing information sophistication should be maintained. In the past there were not enough people knowledgeable about sophisticated marketing information systems to take advantage of the equipment's computational ability and storage capacity, and when people do not have a basic understanding of the complexity of a system, it is unlikely that better decisions will result. The information generated from the sophisticated system will probably not be used; instead, it will be met with confusion and resentment.

Information quality can be upgraded more easily and more rapidly than management quality. It is an easy matter to throw the management system into a state of confusion by installing a complex marketing information system whose capabilities no one appreciates. Very little can be accomplished under this approach. A more positive approach that introduces improvements gradually should be used. As the competence of the personnel designing and operating the computers improves, the technical developments already in existence will be better utilized. If managers take advantage of computer-related courses for the purpose of increasing their knowledge of this tool, they will feel more confident in participating in the design of the system.

An organization should not try to develop a complete marketing information system initially because the probability of failure is high under this approach. A more desirable procedure is to build subsystems one at a time. The participation of not only top management but also line managers should be solicited. Line managers should be involved in developing the specifications so that a consensus regarding the overall program can be reached.

The information needed for planning and controlling marketing functions should be identified, as should the critical decision points. Flow charts of the system should be studied so that each person sees how the system fits into the overall environment. Once people see for themselves the cost of certain alternative information requested, they may be more sympathetic if it is decided that the benefit of the data is not worth the cost involved. Their participation in design should result in a better and more effective information system.

While some people question whether managerial planning and control systems require the speed of real-time systems, it is forecasted that the use of real-time systems will increase. Improved technology is allowing managers to send inquiries into a control data bank and obtain responses in a short time.

There will likely be increased emphasis on time sharing as more small organizations use a terminal connected to a commercial time-sharing service bureau. Organizations with branches will probably adopt systems with small computers at the branches for payroll and billing, which will act as satellites to the larger central computer. Future data processing costs will likely be cut under time-sharing plans. In addition, this arrangement offers access to canned programs.

SUMMARY

The marketing information system is a means for gathering and transferring the necessary data for the control of present and future activities to the decision makers. Despite the need for marketing information systems, very few companies have developed sophisticated systems. Instead, most of the marketing information systems in operation could be classified as subsystems because they relate to only a portion of the marketing decisions made. Marketing information systems have not developed to the same extent as production and accounting systems. The state of computer technology and model building does not explain this slow development because they are both sophisticated enough for effective marketing information systems.

As a business increases in size and complexity, appropriate changes must be made in the information system so that it continues to provide adequate data for control and planning purposes. Without doubt, the basic reason for a marketing information system is the better decisions it allows. The reporting of information is not the critical step; it is the *use* of this information by managers that provides the return. The marketing manager of the future must be highly skilled in logical decision making, and he or she must have the necessary information to perform this process.

3

Management/
Marketing/
Accounting Interactions

COMPLEXITY in business communications under centralization leads to slower decisions because the decision maker is far removed from operations. The employee in a large impersonal environment often feels unimportant to the organization. His or her supervisor may also be deprived of the contact with organizational goals that is necessary for success. In addition, full centralization results in a large volume of decisions that have to be made at the top managerial level. To solve some of these problems, management often turns to decentralization as a means of dividing authority and responsibility.

DECENTRALIZATION

A company is said to be decentralized when certain related activities are grouped together for administrative direction and control and the responsibility for this segment's operation is delegated to an executive. The optimal amount of decentralization distributes decision making so that top management is freed from having to control the details of current operations and is allowed instead to concentrate on planning. This division of the workload also enables segment managers to receive on-the-job training for higher levels of management.

Decentralization and Motivation

Another purpose of decentralization is to increase overall corporate profitability by making managers on low and middle levels aware of the organization's goals. The organizational structure of a firm is very important for motivation. With the large mass of communications necessary in centralization, it is difficult for managers to be aware of the needs of the employees under them. Consequently, employees often feel unimportant and their morale is low. Workers do not have the "feeling of belonging" if their work group is large.

With a decentralized organizational structure, managers and employees are in direct daily contact. Managers are better able to assess their employees' relationship to the operation and recognize their needs. Managers in a decentralized organization have the authority to provide the specific rewards that are effective motivators, and are better able to achieve goal congruence because they can persuade employees to accept the goals of the organization and work toward fulfilling them.

Responsibility accounting facilitates effective motivation. Operating decisions are made on a lower level in a decentralized organization. By assigning controllable costs to the individual segment, managers are encouraged to properly use the authority they have to motivate the workers under them. However, there are many factors that affect morale, and the size of the work group is not the most important. Even if the worker has a "feeling of belonging" to the group, there is no assurance that he or she will accept and try to achieve the goals of the the overall organization. In fact, small informal groups can increase or decrease productivity, depending upon whether or not the workers accept the company objectives as their own. Employees are more likely to accept company objectives if their supervisor understands and is working toward them. Operating in a less restricted environment under decentralization, the segment manager has the necessary authority to encourage employees to work effectively.

How decentralized an organization is depends to some extent on management's attitude toward delegation of responsibility. The nature of manufacturing and marketing activities also determines how easily decentralization can be accomplished. Complete decentralization seldom occurs since it is usually not practical to give maximum decision-making freedom to managers. Full decentralization implies an assortment of separate businesses, and this does not work because even in decentralized organizations there will usually be centralization of such activities as research, advertising, and computer processing.

In deciding how much decentralization should be attempted, an organization must take a cost-benefit approach.

Profit Centralization

Decentralization can be achieved in different forms; for example, geographical decentralization, functional decentralization, or profit decentralization. Profit decentralization is based on a division of activities according to profit-oriented centers; the manager of the center has the responsibility of generating profit from the segment's assets. Company-wide financial statements do not serve all the data needs management has for individual segments, so profitability analysis by segments is needed. This will make it easier to identify the areas requiring remedial action. There are a number of segments that may be used in gathering costs. Among the principal ones are customers, territories, sales personnel, products, distribution channels (retailers and wholesalers), methods of solicitation (mail, telephone), methods of delivery, and warehouses.

Profit and Cost Centers

Cost and profit centers should be established congruent with the decision-making points within a firm. If the business firm is organized around territories, this segment becomes the primary cost or profit center. A cost center is any component of the organization to which it is practical to trace costs. A cost center is the smallest segment of activity for which costs are accumulated. Rather than organizing segments into costs centers, the decision units can be organized as profit centers that operate somewhat as individual units within the organization. A profit center goes one step further: it is a business segment that is responsible for income but also for relating this income to its invested capital. A single individual may be responsible for several profit or cost centers but the responsibility for one center should not be divided.

Some organizations refer to their segments as profit centers, but their managers have little authority in decision making. In other organizations managers of cost centers may have much authority in purchasing materials, labor, and capital goods. The number of profit centers and cost centers does not indicate whether decentralization exists or would be beneficial. For example, a small retail department store can effectively decentralize its individual departments into profit centers.

RESPONSIBILITY ACCOUNTING

The reason for decentralizing the decision-making process is to give segment heads authority and responsibility for their divisions. While it is recognized that their decisions will affect the total performance of the organization, management cannot specify completely the consequences of every action of the segment heads. The accountant cannot completely overcome this problem in organizational design, and the system of responsibility accounting will only be as detailed and as accurate as the organizational design permits.

Before costs can be controlled, it must be known where they are incurred and who is responsible for them. No new accounting techniques are introduced into a responsibility accounting system. The attention is focused on people rather than on the collection of data for product costing. The concept of responsibility accounting involves accountability for the activities of a unit—the person with authority over a unit must answer for the expense of his or her activity. The beginning point of a responsibility accounting system is the delegation of authority. Certainly the authority to control expenditures must accompany the responsibility for their incurrence. Basic to responsibility accounting is the construction of an organization chart that clearly shows definite lines of authority and responsibility.

Control systems should be structured around the areas of responsibility that exist in an organization. The responsibility accounting system represents an attempt to classify the results achieved according to decision centers within the organization. Responsibility accounting helps measure the performance of managers of cost centers by focusing attention on the cost items subject to an individual's control. Responsibility accounting can be extended to cost centers, profit centers, and investment centers. The exact number and nature of responsibility centers or cost centers used depend upon the nature of the firm and its organizational structure. So many different techniques are practiced under the name of "responsibility accounting" that it has become synonymous with management accounting. These techniques apply to organizations of all sizes, whether centralized or decentralized.

Responsibility accounting is based on certain assumptions concerning organization design and human behavior. One of the basic assumptions is that managers should be held accountable only for items within their control. In addition, the principle of management by exception should be in operation, budgets should be set at a level that is reasonable and attainable, and segment managers should be able to participate in the development of plans for their portion of the organization.

Responsibility accounting requires cooperation among all members of the organization. Certainly top management should consider the establishment of management accounting controls to be of prime importance. However, the establishment of a responsibility accounting system does not guarantee control since reporting information is only one aspect of control within an organization. There is no assurance that the individual receiving this information will take the necessary corrective steps.

Responsibility Reporting

The essence of responsibility reporting is that the accounting reports are designed to measure how effectively a person has fulfilled his or her responsibility. Responsibility reports emphasize the association of economic data with the persons responsible for it. The various levels of management need different types of information. Operational management is interested in data directly affecting its sphere of responsibility, such as hours worked, units sold, and budget deviations. Top management is concerned with long-range plans and needs data to help formulate policy.

It is fairly easy to discuss the theory of responsibility accounting; however, its implementation in actual operations is difficult. Often there is dual responsibility for cost incurrence, and controllability rests in more than one place. Mixed responsibility creates a problem— the final answer, though not a completely satisfactory one, may be the assignment of responsibility to the person who seems to be in a position to exert the strongest influence on costs.

Responsibility accounting is not a substitute for good management; it is only a tool that is of no use unless it is applied. Responsibility accounting is an integral part of the management process because the accountant's role is technical and supporting. Unless it has support from operating personnel, the responsibility accounting system will likely fail. This is why it is so important to have managerial participation in designing the system.

FUNCTIONALIZATION

The natural classification of expenses into wages, materials, and so forth creates inputs for the responsibility unit. Most traditional charts of accounts emphasize these natural classifications. A chart of accounts based on natural classification may be inadequate, however, because the major functions in each responsibility unit are not distinguished. Usually the chart of accounts must be redrawn to accumulate costs for each major function; the natural expense classification is retained in a secondary or subsidiary position in the chart of accounts.

Some natural expense items will have to be apportioned among several functional-cost groups since the items relate to more than one functional activity. Expenses directly allocable to a functional activity are prorated directly. Expenses not directly allocable to functional activities must be prorated on equitable bases. The bases chosen should reflect most clearly the benefit derived from the indirect costs by the various functions. The procedure is similar to the accounting procedure for production costs, in which the total of the burden is analyzed according to departments or other functional subdivisions of the production process.

Many marketing activities are organized on a segmental basis so that each segment can be charged directly with the expenses incurred within its area, which minimizes the proration of expenses. This is especially apt when different marketing segments are served by different sales staffs.

A review should be made of each of the functional costs in order to determine if it is a direct or indirect cost to the segment involved. For instance, three types of expenses might be included in the advertising and sales promotion costs: direct territorial advertising, national advertising, and indirect advertising expenses. Advertising that could be definitely identified with expenditures within a specific territory should be allocated directly to each territory. National and indirect advertising covering all territories should be allocated on the unit of variability that appears most appropriate.

Once direct functional costs are determined and allocated, the application of indirect costs to territories, products, or other market segments can be on a unit fractional cost basis, using the factor of variability that appears most appropriate. This procedure appears elementary; however, units of variability may need to be redefined for certain functions. The unit of variability in the functional analysis may not be related to the objective of the applied analysis. The same factor can be applied to some distribution expenses for use in various types of analyses. For instance, the factor of variability for warehousing is weight, and this same work unit can be used in analyses by territories, products, and customers. Other distribution expenses require different factors—traveling expenses, for example, are applied on a per mile basis to territories and a per call basis to customers and products. Different conditions may even necessitate different units of variability for allocating the same indirect expenses to segments.

Decentralized organizations present some major accounting problems. Management needs an accounting report that evaluates the effectiveness of the segment managers in meeting the goals of the organization, and this requires the allocation to the different segments of their share of the input and output measures reported by the firm. It is difficult to determine this basis of allocation since it should reflect the extent to which the decisions of the different department heads affect the total performance of the organization.

Controllable and Noncontrollable Costs

A responsibility accounting system requires that costs be separated into controllable and noncontrollable categories. If this separation is made clearly, responsibility can be determined and an efficient system of cost control established. The controllability of cost items depends upon the level of management under consideration. A cost that is noncontrollable at one level of responsibility may be regarded as controllable at some other, usually higher, level. All costs are controllable by top management in the short run; however, many fixed costs are noncontrollable at the middle and low management levels. Those costs that vary with the amount of effort exerted in a marketing function tend to be more controllable. If this concept is properly applied, it helps avoid confusion in the area of cost control.

MARKETING COST CONCEPTS

While there is a desire to measure the performance of marketing segments, the attempts to do so have been confused because there is no agreement concerning the proper cost concept to be used. Marketing cost analysis can take many different forms, using either a full-costing approach or a contribution-margin approach. The analysis can be made by segments and broken down into controllable and noncontrollable costs.

Full-Costing Approach

Accountants have been predisposed by financial reporting, in which a net income is determined, to choose the full-costing approach. Advocates of full costing feel that all costs that bear a relationship to the units in question should be assigned to the units for purposes of measuring their profitability. They believe that each unit must bear its share of the company cost of doing business in addition to its own direct costs. They argue that many of the indirect costs can be assigned to the unit being costed on the basis of demonstrable cost relationship. Where a strong relationship does not exist, the cost must be prorated, but the basis is still reasonable. Those who present this case believe that there is merit in computing a net profit by business units because, in the long run, each unit must produce profits, and all costs that bear a relationship to the units in question should be assigned to them for purposes of measuring their profitability.

The full-costing approach assumes that each segment of operations should bear an equitable share of both indirect and direct costs, and this does present a problem. Costs that can be traced to each segment are called direct costs and, of course, need no allocation. But what is an equitable share of overall company costs for each marketing segment? These indirect costs require the selection of a base on which allocations can be made.

Full-costing advocates argue that many of the indirect costs can be assigned to the segment being costed on the basis of demonstrable cost relationship. Where a strong relationship does not exist, the cost must be prorated. If arbitrary bases are chosen, the resulting allocations will also be arbitrary. Therefore the allocation base chosen should be examined closely.

Often marketing costs are allocated on the basis of sales dollars or percentage of gross profit. This is a convenient method, but only those costs that show a close relationship to changes in sales volume should be handled this way. For example, assume that sales salaries are allocated to product lines on the basis of sales dollars. This allocation would correctly reflect actual conditions only if more sales effort is devoted to the product lines with a higher sales price or larger total sales dollars. However, if more time is spent on product lines that have small orders, this unprofitable situation will be hidden.

A direct relationship between sales orders and costs often cannot be established. These activities are a cause rather than a result of sales; the volume of orders obtained may depend on the amount of money spent for these costs. An increase in sales promotion and advertising may increase sales volume, but not necessarily at the same rate as the cost of promotion. It is particularly important to recognize that allocations may be arbitrary because marketing managers tend to think only in terms of sales volume and gross profit percent. Profit potential is not revealed under this approach.

Marketing managers often feel that full costing contains a safety valve for pricing. There is a danger that lower management might price just to cover variable costs. However, it is not necessary to give lower management complete information concerning variable and fixed costs. Instead it can be given levels below which it cannot reduce sales prices without permission.

Contribution-Margin Approach

Other analysts believe the only reliable way to evaluate business activity is to measure the contribution of each unit to the indirect costs that exist for the benefit of all. Advocates of this opposing view think that any effort to allocate or prorate costs is confusing and misleading. They feel that allocating common costs to segments may lead to the incorrect conclusion that the removal of a territory would lead to the elimination of the common costs allocated to it.

Methods that require allocating all costs are potentially misleading and require further analysis because they allocate costs that are not affected by changing the alternatives under consideration. For instance, if a market segment shows a net loss, this loss cannot be avoided simply by dropping the market segment because, the fixed costs allocated to the discontinued market segment would then have to be borne by other segments of the organization. If a segment has a net loss, the organization may decide to keep it anyway because some of the costs cannot be avoided merely by closing the segment. The contribution margin provides a measurement of the effects of keeping operations. If a segment's contribution margin is negative, the organization would do better to drop this division.

The objection to the full-costing approach expressed above is that there is no objective way to assign certain indirect costs; as a result, the final analysis is only a reflection of the way that management wants the costs to vary. Instead, the contribution of a segment should be determined; this is the segmental revenue less the direct costs that attach to its operations. Expressed in a slightly different way, contribution margin is the difference between revenues and discretionary costs specific to the segment, which management can change during the involved period. This approach avoids controversy over the fairness with which allocations of indirect costs have been made. Often disagreements over expense allocations prevent management from correctly analyzing the costs that are affected by the action proposed.

While many direct costs are variable, these two terms are not interchangeable. For example, suppose the segment being analyzed is a territory. The straight-line depreciation on the equipment used within the territory, then, is a fixed direct cost. A better definition of direct costs is those costs that exist because the segment is in operation, and which would no longer be incurred if the segment were eliminated.

Contribution margin is a better indicator than sales of the amount available for recovery of fixed expenses and income. This approach can be used in evaluating alternatives such as meeting competition, pricing, special orders, and changing marketing methods. Contribution margin data aids management in determining which segments should have attention in order to improve a weak situation or to make the most of a favorable one.

Segmental Reports

Two forms of segmental reports are illustrated in Exhibit 3-1 and Exhibit 3-2. Normally such reports would contain actual, budget, and variance data. They are excluded in this chapter in order to concentrate on concepts. (A more detailed analysis appears in Chapter 12.) The segmental revenue would be the value of goods transferred.

The approach used in Exhibit 3-1 is to assign all expenses to each segment analyzed. Exhibit 3-1, which allocates full costs broken down into controllable and noncontrollable costs, has serious limitations. The inclusion on a financial statement of a cost that management cannot control often detracts attention from the data that should be focused on. There is some merit in including in reports noncontrollable costs such as allocated costs, but they should be grouped separately and labeled accordingly.

Exhibit 3-1 emphasizes the excess of the segment's revenue over controllable costs. This concept is similar to that of the contribution of a profit center illustrated in Exhibit 3-2. However, differences will exist to the extent that there are fixed costs that are controllable

Exhibit 3-1. XYZ Company segmental income report for period ending ____.

Revenue	$10,000
Less costs from other segments	4,000
Excess of revenue over costs assigned	6,000
Less controllable segment costs	2,000
Excess of revenue over controllable costs	4,000
Less controllable costs of segment	1,000
Segmental net income	$ 3,000

Exhibit 3-2.   XYZ Company contribution analysis by marketing segment for period ending ____.

Revenue		$10,000
Less: Variable manufacturing costs	$3,000	
Variable marketing costs	1,000	4,000
Variable margin		6,000
Less nonvariable costs traceable to segment		1,000
Segmental contribution margin		$5,000

at the segment level. In fact, the final figures listed on Exhibit 3-1 and Exhibit 3-2 will be equivalent only if the controllable costs also represent the variable costs of producing the output of the segment.

The net profit approach has the advantage of centering management's attention upon problem areas calling for long-run remedial action. Net profit is also an indispensable management tool for judging the profitability of individual segments. Management is familiar with and accustomed to using net profit figures, and the same techniques can be applied to all segments of the business. Management often believes that no income is realized unless all expenses have been recovered. If a segment does not include its share of all expenses, management may overlook the need to recover all expenses.

The full-costing approach emphasizes segment profitability, while contribution reporting places more concern on cost responsibility. Most authorities feel that complete allocation should be made only if management insists upon it. Instead, management should be encouraged to use contribution reporting.

TRANSFER PRICING

Transfer pricing is a requirement that arises from interactions between decentralized segments. The shift from a centralized to a decentralized organization increases the role of transfer pricing because some of the revenue of one responsibility center becomes part of the cost of another. The finished or partly finished unit from one division often becomes the raw material of another division in a decentralized organization. This in turn makes it difficult to appraise managerial performance. Obviously the price at which these units and services are transferred has an important effect on the profitability of both centers involved, the supplying as well as the receiving one.

Since management has multiple objectives, it is difficult for a company to establish logical and sound transfer prices for these goods and services.

The transfer pricing problem is greater where there is much interdependence among major divisions. There would be little problem with transfer prices in a firm that diversifies into different basic industries. However, in a vertically integrated firm there is usually a large volume of intracompany transfers.

It is often an unhealthy situation if the division manager feels assured of a market for his or her product. This assurance is not conducive to effective cost control and can create inefficiencies within the segment that are expensive to detect and correct. In addition, less attention will be given to the development of methods for reducing costs in order to meet the competition on each sale. Internal competition is one way of making segments pay attention to current developments. Management often focuses attention on uneconomic activities in the process of determining transfer prices.

The organization should establish a policy regarding the outside purchase of products and services. The normal policy is to expect internal procurement when the organization's product is equal or superior in quality and performance to others in the field. (This assumes that delivery can be made as required.) The policy may also state that outside procurement may be made if the internal source of supply is not competitive. Certainly segment managers should be allowed the freedom to purchase externally if the price is lower and the quality comparable. However, in justifying any outside purchase, the segment manager should produce evidence that an effort was made to bring the internal supplier's terms into agreement with those of the outside source.

Much consideration should be given to the price at which goods and services should be transferred from one organizational segment to another. There are several bases available such as full cost, market prices, negotiated prices, and variable or incremental costs. Whatever basis is used, it should be established before the transfer is made rather than afterward. With this information available, segment managers will know in advance what price they will pay or receive for transfer goods.

Full Costing

A very common method used for transferring goods and services is full costing; this includes actual manufacturing cost and portions of distribution, administration, and research costs. This method is convenient and has been firmly established in centralized companies. The full-costing method is not appropriate for companies with decentralized structures that need to measure the profitability of autonomous units.

Under the full-costing method, segment performance cannot be easily evaluated since this approach does not permit an income to be shown on intradivisional sales. The full-costing basis does not show a return to the supplier. Each primary and intermediate processing segment is guaranteed the recovery of its costs on each product transferred to another department.

Standard full costing has some advantage over the historical average costing because the segment manager knows in advance what price he or she will receive or pay for transferred goods. The use of standard full costing also eliminates the effect that fluctuations in production efficiency in one division can have on the reported income of another segment. The full-costing method's greatest weakness is its lack of usefulness in evaluating planning and motivation; it does not provide a guide for decision making.

Market Price

The use of market prices as transfer prices is essentially an opportunity-costing approach. Under this measurement procedure, products or services are transferred at whatever cost would be realized in an "arm's-length" transaction occurring in an unrestricted market—that is, each producing department should receive whatever price the product would command if sold to an outside customer.

Market prices are established objectively rather than by individuals who have an interest in the results. Each segment is regarded as if it were a completely separate organization. Even though income centers are not independent organizations and some transfers could not go .through the market, it may be possible to maintain the self-regulatory conditions of the market by pricing these internal transfers at market prices. If a segment cannot afford to pay market prices, it should not be permitted to buy internally at less than market. If it can sell outside at the market price, it should not be required to sell internally for less. Pricing intermediate goods according to market price has the advantage of motivating the supplying center to reduce its costs as much as possible. Research and development will be emphasized, using a market-based transfer price.

A market-based transfer price system has several drawbacks. One is that no dependable market price exists for some products. In addition, market prices based on a very small number of transactions are not usually valid. And often, even if a market price is available, it may represent a contract that could not be renewed under present conditions. Since the products are not actually being sold in the market, assumptions must be made concerning the sale, such as the degree of existing competition.

Negotiated Price

Very often an organization uses a compromise transfer price that gives weight to competition as well as a fair return to the supplying division. A price could be negotiated between the supplying and receiving departments. Top management may serve as arbitrator in order to avoid time-consuming and inflammatory negotiations. The disadvantage of using negotiated prices as the basis for transfer pricing is that it diverts the efforts of key personnel from activities affecting the welfare of the overall organization to those affecting segments only.

Variable and Incremental Costs

Pricing transfers at variable costs assures the best short-run use of overall facilities and maximizes short-run income. Sometimes a shortcut is taken and it is assumed that incremental cost is equal to the variable costs. While incremental and variable costs are not the same thing, there is a close parallelism over a wide operating range. Incremental costs are the increases in total company cost if an alternative is added to the present organization. They can also be calculated by determining how much total company costs will be reduced if an activity is dropped. This approach ignores changes in efficiency and opportunity costs connected with fixed costs.

If the incremental cost is readily available, management can examine the additional cost of further processing an intermediate product in deciding whether a product should be sold to a related division and processed further or sold externally. This incremental cost should be compared with the probable increase in sales value of the final product over that of the intermediate product. In an incremental or variable transfer pricing system, each segment manager is given a schedule representing the incremental cost of each of his or her supplying divisions at various volumes of operations. With this information, the manager has a basis for calculating the price for additional quantities of the intermediate products to his or her division. To these costs the manager will add his or her own incremental cost figures to determine a composite incremental cost schedule for the final product. The segment manager then should adjust the division's volume to the level at which the additional revenue from the sale of an additional unit of the final product is just adequate to cover the total incremental cost.

Solution to Transfer Pricing

An argument can be made that full-cost, market, and negotiated transfer prices are all irrelevant and lead to a lack of goal congruence. Goal congruence is highly desirable. When all persons in the firm are working toward the same organizational goals, conflict between individuals and corporate goals will be at a minimum. Using incremental costs as transfer prices will promote goal congruence more readily than any of the other methods.

No available transfer price scheme is likely to serve all possible purposes equally well. A transfer pricing method will be most useful if it is uniform and consistent. It should be easily administered without undue delay or bargaining, and it should be applied without bias. Periodic review of the method used should be made by people who thoroughly understand the limited significance of transfer pricing, and who are impartial—that is, are not responsible for the performance of any segment.

SUBOPTIMIZATION

As companies become more complex and operations more decentralized, segments sometimes operate at cross-purposes. Decentralization may lead to suboptimization, meaning each profit center makes decisions for its own benefit without regard to the overall organization. Decisions are made that increase the current segmental income but hurt the overall organization. Suboptimization often occurs because segmental boundaries are inadequately designed and various segments compete with each other rather than with outside firms.

Suboptimization can occur when a segment manager has the alternative of buying outside when prices are lower. Interplant facilities may in turn become idle and overall company income be reduced. This situation can develop easily when the total full cost at the transfer point is greater than the outside purchase price available to the purchasing segment. Certainly the segment manager buys from the outside source in order to maximize his or her division's income. Since the organization is committed to its fixed-capacity costs, the total income of the firm is decreased if the difference between the full-cost transfer price and the outside purchase price is less than the difference between the incremental cost in the selling division and the full-cost transfer price. Stated another way, suboptimization can arise if the outside purchase price is greater than the variable or incremental cost in the supplying division.

While it is recognized that some degree of internal competition is good because it leads to providing better service to the company's customers, proper steps should be taken to prevent this competition from resulting in suboptimization. A more elaborate information system is required under decentralization to help alleviate this problem. More attention will have to be given to ensure congruence between the goals of the dominant members and managers of the organization and those of the overall organization.

SUMMARY

Transfer pricing and segmental income measurement are intended to serve several purposes. An organization is departmentalized so that a manager can be placed in charge of each department. Responsibility accounting is then feasible, and the results should be used as a partial basis for the evaluation of segment performance as well as for guiding managers in decision making. Certainly transfer pricing policies must be carefully established so that segments will not purchase products outside when they can obtain them from high-fixed-cost internal facilities that would otherwise remain idle, because this would be detrimental to the overall company.

Management needs to recognize the conflicts of interest inherent in decentralization and in turn in any transfer pricing system. It should avoid creating situations where segment managers, who are held responsible for their segments' performance, labor under restrictions on their purchasing functions. It is important that the system provide measures of segmental income that are objectively determined and as free from administrative bias as possible. The objective should be to remove, insofar as possible, the transfer price as an alibi for poor income performance. Responsibility accounting aids decentralization and promotes effective motivation.

4

Decision-Making Costs

THE accounting system normally makes these financial statements available: a balance sheet, an income statement, a retained earnings statement, and a statement of changes in financial position. These are considered broad-purpose statements and are designed for a variety of external users. Certainly some companies find it necessary to prepare special-purpose statements that are directed to specific external or internal users.

FINANCIAL STATEMENTS DEFINED

A *balance sheet* is sometimes referred to as the statement of financial position because it reports the financial condition of a business at a certain date. It includes all the accounts with balances remaining in the general ledger after the closing process has been completed. In the past the balance sheet was considered the primary statement and was used extensively by creditors to evaluate the liquidity of the company. Accountants have shifted attention from the balance sheet to the income statement.

The *income statement* is sometimes called the earnings statement and summarizes business activities for a given period. An income statement shows the changes in owners' equity for a specific time period. Accountants normally use the matching principle to determine net income. The matching principle involves determining the amount of revenue that has been earned by an organization during a given period of time, and the amount of expired costs that are applicable to that revenue.

This income is then reflected in the *retained earnings statement.* In addition, the retained earnings statement shows an analysis of all changes in stockholders' equity that have been recorded in the retained earnings account during a specified period.

A *statement of changes in financial position,* often referred to as a fund statement, describes the changes in the financial resources that have taken place since the position of the enterprise was last stated. This statement covers a period of time and reports increases and decreases in the flow of funds. It also provides information as to the effectiveness with which management has handled working capital during the period of the statement. The adequacy of present funds is indicated and stockholders and investors are told something of management's plans for the future.

Balance Sheet

The balance sheet is an expansion of the basic accounting equation Assets = Liabilities + Owners' Equity. Assets are defined as property to which an individual or business holds legal title. Assets include those costs that have not been matched against revenues in the past and represent economic utility in the future. Both monetary assets such as cash and nonmonetary assets such as inventories are included. The assets are valued in conformity with generally accepted accounting principles and arranged in the order of their probable availability in liquid form.

Liabilities measure the debt obligation of the organization to its creditors. Owners' equity is more difficult to describe than assets or liabilities; it is referred to as stockholders' equity, capital stock, retained earnings, and net worth. The owners' equity of a single proprietorship or partnership is evidenced by the capital accounts in the ledger. A corporation has more owners' equity accounts, some of which reflect the earnings retained in the business after dividends are declared. Owners' equity measures the interest of the ownership group; this interest arises from investments by the owners and changes in net assets. Net income increases owners' equity. The accounting equation Assets − Liabilities = Owners' Equity expresses this relationship. This equation, however, does not express what the owners might realize if the business were sold or dissolved.

Exhibit 4-1.   XYZ Company balance sheet, December 31, 19___.

ASSETS		
Current assets:		
Cash		$ 35,000
Marketable securities and other short-term investments, at cost or less, plus accrued interest (approximates market)		212,000
Receivables	100,000	
Less allowance for uncollectible accounts	5,000	95,000
Merchandise inventory		115,000
Other current assets		10,000
Total current assets		$ 467,000
Special funds and investments:		
Factory equipment deposits (Note)		$ 180,343
Other		60,000
Total special funds and investments		$ 240,343
Property and equipment:		
Factory equipment, at cost (Note)		$1,540,000
Less accumulated depreciation (Note)		40,000
Factory equipment—net		$1,500,000
Other property and equipment, at cost		605,000
Less accumulated depreciation (Note)		5,000
Other property and equipment—net		$ 600,000
Property and equipment—net		$2,100,000
Deferred charges:		
Unamortized debt expense		$ 15,000
Long-term prepayments and other deferred charges		10,000
Total deferred charges		$ 25,000
Total		$2,832,343

There are two common forms of the balance sheet: the account form and the report form. In the account form the assets are listed on the left side and the liabilities and the owners' equity on the right side. Thus it is designed to represent a ledger account. This arrangement makes for easy comparison of current assets with current liabilities.

In the report form of the balance sheet, which is illustrated in Exhibit 4-1, assets appear first, followed by liabilities and shareholders'

Exhibit 4-1 (continued).

LIABILITIES		
Current liabilities:		
Current maturities of long-term debt		$ 130,000
Accounts payable and accrued liabilities		40,000
⌐Accrued income taxes		43,000
Total current liabilities		$ 213,000
Long-term debt, less current maturities (Note)		$ 900,000
Deferred credits:		
Deferred federal income taxes (Note)		$ 30,000
Other		5,000
Total deferred credits		$ 35,000
Total liabilities		$1,148,000

	Number of Shares	
Shareholders' equity:		
5% preferred stock, without par value, stated value $2.50, liquidating preference $50 per share		
Authorized	100,000	
Issued and outstanding	40,000	$ 100,000
Common stock, par value $5 per share:		
Authorized	150,000	
Issued and outstanding	80,000	400,000
Contributed capital from common stock transactions		68,343
Retained earnings (Note)		1,116,000
Total shareholders' equity		$1,684,343
Total		$2,832,343

equity. (The notes to financial statements are indicated but not described.) This form is most often used for comparison purposes with other accounting periods. It is also the most common form published. The preferences of management, as well as the nature and type of business of a particular firm, will determine the type of balance sheet form used.

Certain assumptions are operative in the preparation of financial statements. It is usually assumed, for example, that the firm is a going concern, which means it will continue to operate. Obviously if the business is involved in bankruptcy proceedings, this assumption must be discarded and another form of balance sheet must be designed to meet this specific need. The statement of affairs shows the financial position of an insolvent company. The assets that have been pledged to creditors are identified and the realizable value is estimated and listed for each asset. Liabilities are classified as prior or preferred, fully secured, partially secured, and unsecured creditor claims.

Another form is a pro forma balance sheet, which gives effect to the anticipated changes in assets, liabilities, and owners' equity. The effects of proposed transactions such as reorganizations, recapitalization, new financing, and consolidations are projected in pro forma statements.

Income Statement

A single-step income statement has no classifications except that revenue and income are separated from costs and expenses. It is a simplified form of the income statement, compact and uncluttered, and its advantage is that all costs and expenses are treated as deductions from revenue. No intermediate profit is recognized at different stages such as gross margin or income from operations (which appear on a multiple-step income statement).

The multiple-step income statement is illustrated in Exhibit 4-2. Normally a series of sections is presented in this format. The sections for a merchandising firm include: (1) revenue from the sale of merchandise and services; (2) cost of goods sold and the expense of providing the services sold; (3) operating expenses; (4) other revenue and expense items; (5) income taxes related to income before extraordinary items; and (6) extraordinary gains and losses net of income taxes.

Retained Earnings Statement

Though there is evidence of a trend toward combining the income statement and the retained earnings statement, published annual reports still often include separate retained earnings statements. Each major category of changes in retained earnings during an accounting period is shown on the retained earnings statement. Exhibit 4-3 illustrates that changes in appropriated retained earnings are separated from free or unappropriated retained earnings. Restrictions on a specified portion of accumulated earnings can be made by appropriating retained earnings so these amounts are not available for distribution as dividends. Appropriations can be made for specific purposes; for example, to fulfill a contractual agreement of a bond issue stipulating a restriction on retained earnings. When the need

Exhibit 4-2. XYZ Company income statement for year ending December 31, 19___.

Revenue:			
Gross sales			$667,000
Less: Sales returns and allowances		$ 1,500	
Sales discounts		1,000	2,500
Net sales			$664,500
Costs and expenses:			
Cost of goods sold:			
Merchandise inventory, January 1,		$118,000	
Add: Merchandise purchases	$300,000		
Freight-in	1,000		
Cost of purchases	$301,000		
Less: Purchase returns and allowances	$500		
Purchase discounts	600	1,100	299,900
Total goods available for sale		$417,900	
Deduct: Merchandise inventory December 31,		150,900	
Cost of goods sold			267,000
Gross margin on sales			$397,500
Operating expenses:			
Selling expenses:			
Commissions	$ 4,000		
Freight-out	950		
Salaries	10,000		
Advertising	18,000	$ 32,950	
General and administrative expenses:			
Bad debt expense	$ 100		
Rent	200		
Office payroll	3,210	3,510	36,460
Income from operations			$361,040
Deduct:			
Other expenses:			
Interest on notes payable	$ 800		
Bond interest expense	500	$ 1,300	
Other incomes:			
Dividend income	1,100		
Interest income	700	1,800	500
Net income before income taxes			$361,540
Less: Provision for income taxes			173,540
Net income for the year			$188,000
Earnings per share of common stock: $2.29			

Exhibit 4-3.   XYZ Company statement of retained earnings for year ending December 31,19__.

Retained earnings appropriated:		
Balance, reserve for bond sinking fund, January		
1, 19__	$360,000	
Appropriation for current year	40,000	
Total appropriated balance, December 31, 19__		$ 400,000
Retained earnings unappropriated:		
Balance, January 1, 19__	$600,000	
Add: Net income for year per income statement	188,000	
	$788,000	
Less: Appropriation to bond sinking		
fund reserve	$40,000	
Dividends declared	32,000	72,000
Total unappropriated balance,		
December 31, 19__		716,000
Retained earnings, December 13, 19__		$1,116,000

for an appropriation ceases to exist, the amount is transferred back to unappropriated retained earnings.

The principal increases in unappropriated retained earnings result from net income, transfers back to unappropriated retained earnings of amounts previously appropriated, and prior-period adjustments resulting in an increase in net assets or a decrease in liabilities without a corresponding change in other assets or liabilities. The main decreases in free retained earnings would result from net losses, dividend declaration, transfers to appropriated retained earnings, and prior-period adjustments opposite to those just described.

The Statement of Changes in Financial Position

The statement of changes in financial position is a direct descendant of what was formerly called a statement of source and application of funds, or fund statement, or funds flow statement. This statement was usually developed from either an analysis of cash flow or of working capital flow. Working capital is defined as the difference between current assets and current liabilities.

For several years accountants included this statement at their option in the firm's financial statements. Now, however, its inclusion is mandatory, and an "all-resources" concept must be applied rather than either a working capital or a cash concept. The objective of using a broad all-resources concept is to provide the missing link in reporting all changes in financial position between two consecutive balance sheets. Exhibit 4-4 illustrates a statement of changes in financial position prepared in part on a working capital basis. It

Exhibit 4-4. ABC Company statement of changes in financial position—working capital basis for the year ending December 31, 19__.

Financial resources generated:		
Working capital generated:		
Income before extraordinary items	$20,000	
Add: Expenses not requiring working capital in the current period:		
Depreciation expense	3,000	
Amortization of bond discount	1,000	
Working capital generated by operations exclusive of extraordinary items		$ 24,000
Extraordinary items:		
Building sold	$ 5,000	
Machinery sold	4,000	
Working capital generated by extraordinary items		9,000
Other sources of working capital:		
Bonds payable sold		11,000
Total working capital generated		$44,000
Financial resources generated not affecting working capital:		
Bonds issued for land acquired	$40,000	
Preferred stock issued to retire bonds payable	20,000	
Common stock issued to acquire other assets	10,000	
Total		70,000
Total financial resources generated		$114,000
Financial resources applied:		
Working capital applied:		
Cash dividend payable	$32,000	
Land purchased	11,000	
Total working capital applied		$ 43,000
Financial resources applied not affecting working capital:		
Land acquired by issuing bonds payable	$40,000	
Bonds payable retired by issuing preferred stock	20,000	
Other assets acquired by issuing common stock	10,000	
Total		$ 70,000
Increase in net working capital during the period		1,000
Total financial resources applied		$114,000

Exhibit 4-4 (continued).

Changes in working capital accounts:	Account Balances 12/31/19B	Account Balances 12/31/19A	Working Capital Increase (Decrease)
Current assets:			
Cash	$10,000	$ 9,000	$1,000
Marketable securities	500	1,000	(500)
Accounts receivable (net)	4,500	2,000	2,500
Inventory	6,000	9,000	(3,000)
Prepaid expenses	1,000		1,000
Total current assets	$22,000	$21,000	
Current liabilities:			
Accounts payable	$ 4,100	$ 4,000	(100)
Dividends payable	1,000	1,100	100
Total current liabilities	$ 5,100	$ 5,100	
Total working capital	$16,900	$15,900	$1,000

should be emphasized that depreciation is added back to net income not because it generated working capital but because it had been deducted from net income although it did not require working capital.

LIMITATIONS OF FINANCIAL STATEMENTS

Financial statements have definite limitations despite their appearance of completeness and exactness. Most financial statements are for annual periods; as a result, the net income or loss shown on the income statement for each period is an educated estimate. The only accurate net income or loss figure that can be determined is for the entire life of the business, and this can be stated only when the firm ceases operations. Obviously management cannot wait this long for a net income or loss figure. Financial statements are needed at relatively frequent periods and should be prepared periodically.

Accounting Period

For internal purposes statements are usually prepared at least as often as once a month. For external purposes an annual net income or net loss must be determined. Many businesses adopt the calendar year as their fiscal year. Some organizations adopt a fiscal year of

52 weeks divided into 13 equal periods of 4 weeks each. This approach overcomes the weakness of preparing monthly financial statements using irregular calendar months, which vary in their number of days. In addition, the day of the week that a holiday falls on has an effect on sales and in turn marketing costs. Retail stores traditionally do the bulk of their business at the end of the week. Marketing managers should determine in advance the precise number of holidays in each period as well as the day of the week on which the holidays fall.

Other business organizations adopt the natural business year for their accounting period. The natural business year is determined by the annual cycle of the firm's operations. The cycle ends at a time when business activities are at a nadir and when inventories and receivables have been reduced to a small amount. This is the time when the business is in its most liquid state, prior to the replenishment of inventories that will begin a new cycle. Financial statements prepared under the natural business year approach have the advantage of being more reliable and complete since incomplete transactions are at a minimum. Statistical data obtained at this time should present a truer picture of existing conditions. Since the financial statements would likely represent a more liquid financial position, a more favorable and reliable credit rating can be established. In addition, the cost of taking a physical inventory should be low since there is less inventory to count.

Cost Principle

The basis of the cost principle is that cost is the proper concept for the initial recording of all assets and service acquisitions, expenses, debt, and owners' equities. This concept is opposed to the current-cost and replacement-cost concepts. The cost principle can be defended as an objective method that does not introduce subjective values. However, readers of financial statements have argued that the cost figure is often of little meaning because it does not reflect the market value at which the asset could be sold or the replacement value (the amount that would have to be expended to replace the asset).

Mixed Dollars

Since accountants use the objective measure of cost to record assets, both the balance sheet and the income statement reflect dollar values of many different dates. The general price level has increased markedly within the last several decades. However, plant assets are recorded and depreciated at their cost. Often this depreciation is only a margin of the depreciation appropriate on a replacement cost basis.

It is especially important to remember this limitation when comparing sales between periods. An increase in sales dollars may or may not mean a larger number of units has been sold. All or part of the increase may represent increases in selling prices.

Omissions

Financial statements do not reflect many factors that affect the firm's profitability because these factors cannot be expressed in dollars. Such factors as the firm's reputation and prestige, its credit rating, and the efficiency and integrity of its management are not given a dollar value and shown on the statement because it is too difficult to assign them an objective figure. For years accountants argued that it was not necessary to consider these intangible factors because their influence would be felt through higher or lower sales and expenses than normal. For example, a firm enjoying an excellent reputation in a community would have higher sales than the average firm.

Even though most corporate annual reports state that the company's employees are its most valuable assets, an interested reader is unable to find this most important asset on the accompanying financial statements. Managers also cannot find answers concerning the condition of their firms' human resources or determine if these human assets are changing.

Managers often hesitate to incur funds for building human assets (recruiting, training, and so on) because these expenditures are treated as periodic costs and are charged against the revenue for the year in which they are incurred. This results in an improper matching of revenue and expense, especially in years when the firm is investing heavily in creating new human capabilities. If assessments of human resources within organizations were included in the accountant's role, managers would be encouraged to give more serious consideration to human resource investment decisions.

In recent years accountants have been giving much more consideration to these factors. Much attention is being devoted to measuring and quantifying the efficiency and loyalty of company employees. Multiple measurements of human resources are utilized in research efforts. Human resources are being measured in terms of their acquisition cost, replacement cost, and economic value. Acquisition cost refers to the firm's expenditure to obtain its human resources. Replacement cost is a measure of the expense necessary to replace the firm's existing human resources. It should indicate what the firm would have to spend to recruit, hire, train, and develop people to its present employees' level of technical proficiency and familiarity with the organization and its operations. The economic value of human resources is the present value of the organization's future profits that can be traced to human resources.

The conventional approach of expensing all human resource investments has hindered management from giving close scrutiny to expenditures in this area. Human-resource information will enable management to determine criteria regarding the optimum magnitude and mix of human capital expenditures. Capital budgeting procedures can be applied to human capital investments for the purpose of increasing the payoff of human-resource investment expenditures. Management can become more selective in making investments in human resources. Though generally, continuing training of employees is a sound investment, some employees are not responsive to efforts to increase their capabilities. Others may show no evidence of increased value to the firm after being exposed to training. These are cases in which the investment is not paying off and management should take remedial action.

Human-resource data can redirect management's thinking and action toward a broader and more realistic concept of the contribution being made by segments of the firm. All too often managers are encouraged to meet cost, revenue, or income goals without regard to the changing condition of human resources.

New behavioral patterns of management should emerge as employees are treated as valuable assets rather than as operating expenses when personnel problems arise. For example, suppose an employee loses optimum effectiveness because he or she is unable to adjust to changes in role and responsibilities. If the firm adheres to the traditional view of the worker as an operating expense, management might consider replacing or terminating the employee. If, on the other hand, management considers the employee a valuable resource, its line of reasoning might be different. It would realize that the employee is, say, a $500,000 human asset, and that this asset is not yielding an acceptable return. The next logical step would be to correct the condition so that a maximum return on investment could be realized.

Wartime Conditions

The limitations of the financial statement under peacetime conditions are accelerated when abnormal or wartime conditions prevail. During a worldwide war firms are engaged directly or indirectly in war production. Goods of a different type are produced than in peacetime; in addition, the use of plant facilities is increased. Management is faced with the problem of converting plant facilities to war production, and later with reconverting these facilities to peacetime or normal activity. Under these environmental conditions the accountant may be uncertain as to what costs should be allocated to the various accounting periods involved. This is especially difficult in such expense areas as depreciation, repair and maintenance, and the amortization of war production facilities.

ALTERNATIVE ACCOUNTING METHODS

Very little accounting information is 100 percent accurate; accounting data is a mixture of facts, educated estimates, and professional opinions. All accountants understand that accuracy in accounting is relative. One accountant operating under certain presumptions and following certain procedures will arrive at $X net income. Under alternative methods, another accountant might just as accurately arrive at $Y net income. alternative methods exist particularly in the areas of depreciation accounting and inventory costing.

Depreciation Accounting

Depreciation accounting takes into consideration the foreseeable factors that tend to limit the usefulness of a tangible fixed asset to the organization. Both physical and functional factors require that depreciation be recognized as an expense. Physical factors include the wear and tear over time from operations and from deterioration. Inadequacy and obsolescence are examples of functional factors. A change in market value is not recognized as depreciation according to generally accepted accounting principles. There are several correct methods of determining depreciation expense; some of these relate primarily to the passage of time and others to production output. Instead of depreciating the individual assets, group depreciation may be used. This procedure treats a collection of similar assets as a single group. The depreciation rate is based on the average life of assets in the group. When an item is retired from the group, no gain or loss is recognized.

Straight-line method. The straight-line method of depreciation is simple to apply, as can be determined from Exhibit 4-5, where the depreciation on a machine costing $220 with an expected residual value of $20 and an expected life of five years is illustrated. Since this method relates depreciation directly to the passage of time rather than to use, it is appropriate if the decline in economic service potential of the asset is approximately the same between periods, and if this

Exhibit 4-5. Depreciation schedule, straight-line method.

YEAR	DEPRECIATION EXPENSE	BALANCE OF ACCUMULATED DEPRECIATION	UNDEPRECIATED ASSET BALANCE (BOOK VALUE)
0			$220
1	$ 40	$ 40	180
2	40	80	140
3	40	120	100
4	40	160	60
5	40	200	20 (residual value)
	$200		

decline is related to the passage of time rather than to use. This method gives more accurate results if the production and the sales volume do not change materially from one accounting period to another.

Service-hours method. The service-hours depreciation method is based on the theory that a purchase of an asset represents the purchase of a number of hours of direct service. This method relies on the assumption that the decline in service is caused by the actual use of the asset rather than by the passage of time. An estimate of the asset's life in terms of service-hours is required.

The depreciation for a machine costing $220 with a residual value of $20 and an estimated life of 1,000 hours is illustrated in Exhibit 4-6. Depreciation is calculated as follows:

$$\frac{\$220 \text{ cost} - \$20 \text{ residual value}}{1{,}000 \text{ estimated hours}} = \$.20 \text{ per service-hour}$$

For simplicity, Exhibit 4-6 assumes that the actual number of machine-hours used over the 5 years is 1,000.

For each period the use of the asset must be determined and applied against the depreciation rate in arriving at the depreciation charge. If production output changes between periods, depreciation expense will also change. In periods of increased production, depreciation expense will be larger. This ensures a proper matching of costs and revenue because it is assumed that the asset would not be in operation unless there was productive output.

Productive-output method. Productive-output depreciation is based on the theory that an asset is purchased for the service it can render in the form of a finished product. An estimate of the

Exhibit 4-6.　Depreciation schedule, service-hours method.

Year	Service-Hours Worked*	Depreciation Expense		Balance of Accumulated Depreciation	Undepreciated Asset Balance (Book Value)
0					$220
1	250	(250 × $.20) =	$ 50	$ 50	170
2	200	(200 × $.20)	40	90	130
3	100	(100 × $.20)	20	110	110
4	225	(225 × $.20)	45	155	65
5	225	(225 × $.20)	45	200	20 (residual value)
	1,000		$200		

*It is assumed that the asset was actually used in this manner and that the original estimate of useful life was confirmed.

Exhibit 4-7.　Depreciation schedule, productive-output method.

Year	Units of Output	Depreciation Expense (Debit)		Balance of Accumulated Depreciation	Undepreciated Asset Balance (Book Value)
0					$220
1	1,500	(1500 × $.04) =	$ 60	$ 60	160
2	2,000	(2000 × $.04)	80	140	80
3	750	(750 × $.04)	30	170	50
4	500	(500 × $.04)	20	190	30
5	250	(250 × $.04)	10	200	20 (residual value)
	5,000		$200		

total unit output must be made and divided into the depreciable costs to arrive at a depreciation charge to be assigned to each unit of output, as illustrated in Exhibit 4-7. The illustrative asset costing $220 with a residual value of $20 is estimated to produce 5,000 units of output over the five-year period. The depreciation is calculated as follows:

$$\frac{\$220 \text{ cost} - \$20 \text{ residual value}}{5,000 \text{ units}} = .04 \text{ depreciation per unit}$$

Again it is assumed that actual output agrees with the volume of output estimated.

The expense varies as volume of production changes. This method recognizes, as does the service-hours method, that some assets such as machines will always depreciate more rapidly with higher usage.

Accelerated methods. There are several methods of depreciation that result in reducing charges: one is the sum-of-the-years-digits method, another is the declining-balance method. Under these methods, the periodic depreciation charges are higher in the early years and lower in the later years of the life of the fixed asset.

Accelerated methods of depreciation are reasonable when the benefits provided by the asset decline as it grows older. This approach to depreciation is also appropriate when the maintenance and repairs over the asset's life increase as the asset gets older. This means that in the first years, when repairs are lower, depreciation charges are higher. In addition, these methods are frequently used for tax purposes. While the total depreciation taken over the life of an asset cannot exceed the depreciable basis, the accelerated methods have the advan-

Exhibit 4-8. Depreciation schedule, sum-of-the-years-digits method.

Year	Depreciation Expense		Balance of Accumulated Depreciation	Undepreciated Asset Balance (Book Value)
0				$220.00
1	$(5/15 \times 200.00) =$	\$ 66.67	\$ 66.67	153.33
2	$(4/15 \times 200.00)$	53.33	120.00	100.00
3	$(3/15 \times 200.00)$	40.00	160.00	60.00
4	$(2/15 \times 200.00)$	26.67	186.67	33.33
5	$(1/15 \times 200.00)$	13.33	200.00	20.00 (residual value)
		\$200.00		

tage of recognizing higher depreciation in the early years of an asset's life and thus permit the firm to postpone income taxes.

The sum-of-the-years'-digits method provides decreasing charges by applying a series of fractions that decrease each succeeding period during the life of the asset. The reducing fraction is multiplied by the cost to be depreciated. The weights for the purpose of reducing fractions are obtained by using the years' digits listed in reverse order. The denominator for each fraction is obtained by adding these weights; the numerator is the weight assigned to the specific year. Exhibit 4-8 shows the depreciation for an illustrative asset costing $220, with a residual value of $20 and a life of five years. If the life of the asset is long, the denominator, which is the sum of the digits, can be easily computed using the following formula:

$$SYD = N\left(\frac{N+1}{2}\right)$$

There are several variations of the declining-balance method. In applying this method, the book value of the asset is multiplied by a percentage rate. Since this rate is applied to a declining base, each subsequent depreciation charge is lower. One variation of this method allows for a constant rate that is twice the straight-line rate.

This variation is illustrated in Exhibit 4-9 for the illustrative asset having a five-year life costing $220 with a residual value of $20. The straight-line rate is 20 percent, and gives a 40 percent double-declining-balance rate. This 40 percent rate is applied against the depreciable basis of $200.00. In year 5 the depreciation expense is the remaining depreciable basis of $10 rather than 40% × $30 = $12.

Exhibit 4-9.   Depreciation schedule, fixed-percentage-on-declining-base method.

Year	Depreciation Expense (Debit)		Balance of Accumulated Depreciation	Undepreciated Asset Balance (Book Value)
0				$220
1	(40% × 200.00) =	$ 80	$ 80	140
2	(40% × 140.00)	56	136	84
3	(40% × 84.00)	34	170	50
4	(40% × 50.00)	20	190	30
5		10	200	20 (residual value)
		$200		

Inventory Costing Methods

The selection of an inventory-flow method should be a major policy decision because it affects not only financial income reporting but also important income tax considerations. Inventory costing refers to the sequence in which recorded costs are transferred through inventory accounts to cost of goods sold or cost of material used in manufacturing. It is the pattern in which goods physically move through inventory and the dollar cost patterns associated with this movement of goods. The acceptability of a particular inventory flow does not rest upon the physical flow of goods but upon the proper matching of cost with revenue. When an inventory method is chosen, a decision must be made as to the assumed flow of costs that is to be used in costing. The recent trend, which is to emphasize the income statement rather than the balance sheet, suggests that the primary point is the matching concept.

Inventory can be valued by a number of acceptable methods; most of them are based either on cost or the lower of cost or market. The term *market* as used in the phrase *lower of cost or market* is defined as current replacement cost. Market has reference in most cases to the invoice price plus transportation and other necessary expenses of replacing the goods on the date of the inventory and in the volume usually produced or purchased by the business. Cost as used in inventory valuation refers to either the actual cost of a specific item or a cost based upon an assumption of the order in which the inventory is sold or used. In using an inventory method it is important that consistency from period to period be maintained.

Accountants have developed several approaches to determining what ending inventory balance figure will be shown on the balance sheet. The following actual cost inventory methods are available to accountants: specific identification, simple, moving, or weighted average, *FIFO, LIFO*. Rather than use an actual costing method, standard costs can be used for inventory valuation purposes. There are other inventory valuation methods, but they are all closely related to these. Illustrations of each method follow, so that comparisons between the various inventory valuation methods can be made.

Specific-costing procedures identification method. Under the specific-identification approach, each item that flows through inventory may be separately identified and matched as an expense with the revenue obtained from its sale. Each item is valued at its actual cost. The cost flow is identified with the specific flow of physical goods; either the periodic or perpetual inventory procedure may be used.

The specific-cost method is difficult to use because each item issued must be carefully identified; consequently, detailed bookkeeping is required. If the product involved is large in size or has a high cost and small quantities are handled, specific costs may be feasible. This method is not practical, however, when the inventory contains a large number of low-priced items purchased at different prices. This approach would have more practical application to a low-volume seller. A multiproduct firm selling high-volume standardized merchandise would find the detailed record keeping that is necessary burdensome and very expensive.

Average-cost method. There are several variations of the average-cost method: the simple average, the weighted average, and the moving average. These variations assume that the cost of goods on hand at the end of an accounting period is the average of the cost of the inventory on hand at the beginning of the period and the cost of the goods purchased or produced during the period. A form of the average-cost method is often used by organizations that hold goods for a long period of time because it tends to "even out" the effects of net increases and decreases on costs.

The *simple average* is not theoretically sound because each unit purchase price is given equal weight regardless of the quantity involved. This method is illustrated in Exhibit 4-10. If a perpetual inventory system is used, the pricing of the units issued cannot be completed until the end of the accounting period. At that time the simple-average cost is determined. This deferment of costing precludes the use of a simple average when perpetual inventory procedures are employed.

Exhibit 4-10.   Inventory record, simple average.

	UNITS	UNIT PRICE	TOTAL COST
Jan. 1 Inventory	10	$1.00	$10.00
10 Purchase	5	1.20	6.00
20 Purchase	6	1.50	9.00
25 Purchase	9	2.00	18.00
Issues	30	5.70	$43.00
Jan. 8	2	$1.425*	2.85
18	10	1.425*	$14.25
			17.10
Final Inventory	18		25.90

*Simple average unit cost $5.70/4 = $1.425 approximately.

Under periodic inventory procedures, the *weighted-average* unit cost is based upon data from beginning inventory and current period purchases. The number of units involved is considered along with the unit purchase price. This method is illustrated in Exhibit 4-11, which uses the same data as Exhibit 4-10. The weighted average is theoretically and mathematically correct and can be used easily under periodic inventory methods. However, this method is not satisfactory if unit costs must be available during the accounting period. When perpetual inventory records are used, the pricing of the units issued can only be considered at the end of the period when the

Exhibit 4-11. Inventory record, weighted average.

	UNITS	UNIT PRICE	TOTAL COST
Goods available:			
Jan. 1 Inventory	10	$1.00	$10.00
10 Purchase	5	1.20	6.00
20 Purchase	6	1.50	9.00
25 Purchase	9	2.00	18.00
	30		$43.00
Issues at weighted-average cost:			
Jan. 8	2	$1.433*	$ 2.87
18	10	1.433*	14.33
			$17.20
Final inventory at weighted-average cost:			
Jan. 31	18	1.433*	$25.80

*Weighted average unit cost $43/30 = $1.433 approximately.

weighted-average cost is determined.

If perpetual inventory procedures are used, the *moving-average* method is more appropriate than the weighted-average method because it permits issues to be currently costed. The inventory is withdrawn at the average unit cost of the goods on hand as of the withdrawal date. As illustrated in Exhibit 4-12, a new unit cost is calculated after each purchase. To simplify the illustration, the calculations have been rounded to even cents. The theoretical weakness inherent in the simple-average method is overcome with this method; in addition, cost computed under the moving-average method is more current than under the weighted-average method. This approach tends to level off short-term price fluctuations. As new purchases of goods are made

Exhibit 4-12. Perpetual inventory record, moving average.

	RECEIVED			ISSUED			BALANCE		
DATE	UNITS	UNIT COST	TOTAL COST	UNITS	UNIT COST	TOTAL COST	UNITS	UNIT COST	TOTAL COST
Jan. 1							10	$1.00	$10.00
8				2	$1.00	$ 2.00	8	1.00	8.00
10	5	$1.20	$ 6.00				13	1.07*	14.00
18				10	1.07	10.70	3	1.07	3.30
20	6	1.50	9.00				9	1.35*	12.30
25	9	2.00	18.00				18	1.68*	30.30

*New average computed.

at lower or higher prices, the established unit costs move downward or upward. However, it is necessary to use perpetual inventory records under the moving-average cost method.

FIFO method. The first-in, first-out (FIFO) method is based upon the assumption that the cost flow should be the same as the physical flow of products; consequently, issues are costed at the oldest unit costs and the remaining inventory is costed at the most recent unit costs. The ending inventory as illustrated in Exhibit 4-13 is assumed

Exhibit 4-13. Perpetual inventory record, FIFO.

	RECEIVED			ISSUED			BALANCE		
DATE	UNITS	UNIT COST	TOTAL COST	UNITS	UNIT COST	TOTAL COST	UNITS	UNIT COST	TOTAL COST
Jan. 1							10	$1.00	$10.00
8				2	$1.00	$2.00	8	1.00	8.00
10	5	$1.20	$ 6.00				8	1.00	8.00
							5	1.20	6.00
18				8	1.00	8.00	3	1.20	3.60
				2	1.20	2.40			
20	6	1.50	9.00				3	1.20	3.60
							6	1.50	9.00
25	9	2.00	18.00				3	1.20	3.60
							6	1.50	9.00
							9	2.00	18.00

to be from the most recent purchases. This method follows the orderly outflow of goods in an organization. FIFO is widely used for inventory costing since it is adaptable to either periodic or perpetual inventory procedures because the same dollar results occur whether FIFO is applied under periodic or perpetual inventory. The FIFO method also produces an inventory valuation that approximates current replacement cost and does not suffer from the theoretical weakness of being a nonrepresentative cost as does the simple-average method. When the FIFO assumption is used, a rise in price will tend to inflate income, and a decline in price deflate income.

LIFO method. The last-in, first-out (LIFO) method assumes that the last items purchased are the first to be used or sold. LIFO goods issued are priced at the cost of the material most recently acquired. Goods in ending inventory are costed at prices in existence at a much earlier date. The advantage of this method is that it allows for a matching of current costs against current revenues. The LIFO inventory method is becoming more widely adopted as its advantages becomes more evident.

LIFO can be used either with periodic or perpetual inventory records. Exhibit 4-14 illustrates the periodic LIFO inventory method, while Exhibit 4-15 illustrates the perpetual inventory method. There is some variation in the results under these methods; for example, the issue on January 8 resulted in costing out units that were not purchased until January 20.

Exhibit 4-14. Periodic inventory record, LIFO.

	UNITS	UNIT PRICE	TOTAL COST
Jan. 1 Inventory	10	$1.00	$10.00
10 Purchase	5	1.20	6.00
20 Purchase	6	1.50	9.00
25 Purchase	9	2.00	18.00
Issues			$43.00
Jan. 8	2	1.50	$ 3.00
Jan. 18	9	2.00	18.00
	1	1.50	1.50
			$22.50
Final Inventory	10	1.00	10.00
	5	1.20	6.00
	3	1.50	4.50
			$20.50

Exhibit 4-15. Perpetual inventory record, LIFO (costed currently).

	RECEIVED			ISSUED OR SOLD			BALANCE		
DATE	UNITS	UNIT COST	TOTAL COST	UNITS	UNIT COST	TOTAL COST	UNITS	UNIT COST	TOTAL COST
Jan. 1							10	$1.00	$10.00
8				2	$1.00	$2.00	8	1.00	8.00
10	5	$1.20	$ 6.00				8	1.00	8.00
							5	1.20	6.00
18				5	1.20	6.00			
				5	1.00	5.00	3	1.00	3.00
20	6	1.50	9.00				3	1.00	3.00
							6	1.50	9.00
25	9	2.00	18.00				3	1.00	3.00
							6	1.50	9.00
							9	2.00	18.00

Standard-cost method. Instead of actual costs, standard costs may be used for valuing inventory. This produces a saving in the clerical cost of accounting for inventory. Cost standards are scientifically predetermined costs of production or processes used as a basis for measurement or comparison. The difference between what the costs should be and what they actually are is noted and the causes for this difference are found. Standard costs are usually entered in the accounts to aid in the evaluation of actual performance.

The establishment of correct standards for a business firm's manufacturing expenses is of great importance and requires considerable insight into the complexities of business management. Year-to-date totals of material quantity should be studied and used as guides in setting the physical quantity of materials needed. However, the accountant will need assistance from the manufacturing supervisor who is thoroughly familiar with the raw materials composing the finished article. The accountant and the manufacturing supervisor should establish a "specification sheet" for each finished product listing the raw material components. This theoretical material weight must include factors for scrap, shrinkage, and waste.

The engineering department may be used extensively for setting material standards. The operation schedule and bills of material established by this department should be forwarded to the purchasing department. On these operations schedules will be listed the materials and the quantities required for the expected volume of production. The purchasing department will place an expected material price on these raw materials and this will determine the material price standard. Often it is not sufficient to base material quantity standards on engineering specifications. The accountant can enlist the help of the plant foreman to conduct tests under controlled conditions. A quantity of material is put into process and the results are carefully analyzed. The best principle to keep in mind in establishing material price standards is that the standard must be based on the best information possible.

COST-BEHAVIOR PATTERNS

Before marketing managers can use accounting data in planning and control, they must understand the behavior pattern of the organization's costs. This information is imperative in forecasting the impact of their decisions on future revenue and expenses. Cost analysts must recognize that income tax regulations exert much influence on accounting practices. Accounting methods such as accelerated depreciation are used to reduce taxes, but they also change cost-behavior patterns.

Variable and Fixed Costs

Variable and fixed costs are usually determined in relation to how a total cost changes when there is a change in the volume of the activity base. Activity bases are various; for example, the number of product units manufactured or sold, man-hours worked, or miles driven by salespeople can be used. If the total cost changes in direct proportion to changes in activity, the cost is variable. Variable costs are considered the cost of doing business and are related to utilization of available capacity. Even though direct labor is usually considered a variable cost, this expense will not stop automatically with decreases in volume unless management exercises control over it. Employees will be reluctant to admit that they are not needed when orders are slack and they may spend their time in nonproductive work in the hope that they will not be discharged.

Conversely, if the total cost remains unchanged when the activity base changes, it is considered fixed. Since fixed costs are related to the provision of a capacity to do business, they are often referred to as committed costs. The amount of committed costs is not controllable in the short run because it results from past decisions. In cost-behavior analysis committed costs present no problem since they remain unchanged until a decision is made to change capacity.

Some fixed costs are related to the volume of activity planned and are referred to as programmed costs. Once the planned level of activity is set, the programmed cost tends to remain at a constant amount even though the level of activity actually attained differs from the level planned. Advertising and market research are typical programmed costs. While programmed costs do not vary with changes in volume, they can be changed from one period to another by management.

All costs are variable in the long run and too great a significance should not be placed on an arbitrary classification of costs into variable and fixed. Many semivariable costs increase and decrease with changes in volume but do not vary in direct proportion. They present the biggest problem in cost analysis because often there is no discernible relationship between cost and volume.

Since a given period of time and a given range of volume are assumed in defining fixed and variable costs, the distinction is often dependent upon the activity base chosen. For example, salespeople's salaries should be considered a fixed cost if the activity base is a territory. However, if the activity base is product lines, sales salaries could be considered a variable cost. Separating these costs into two categories is strictly impossible because many costs have both fixed and variable components. Even separating the two components of certain semivariable costs will be arbitrary because many will fall into a borderline area.

It is not enough merely to define fixed and variable costs according to the rate of output, for whether a cost is fixed or variable usually depends on the terms in which output is measured, the time period allowed for adjustments, the degree of flexibility, and the extent to which certain costs are calculated ahead of time. Even the most fixed costs have some variable characteristics. Since the behavior of certain costs, especially overhead, is exceedingly complex, occasionally certain parts of the separation process will be decided on on the basis of practicability or expediency rather than on strict adherence to an established accounting principle. There is also a strong temptation to include only those costs that are obviously variable as product costs. In extreme cases variable overhead may be eliminated from product cost, thus producing misleading profit contribution data.

THE DIRECT-COSTING AND ABSORPTION-COSTING APPROACHES

Since the behavior of fixed and variable costs has great significance in decision making, an approach to inventory costing called direct costing has been developed. Many people are still uncertain as to what direct costing is, what its purposes are, and how a system is developed. One cause of this uncertainty derives from the terminology. *Direct costing* is by no means the best name for the concept because the word *direct* implies a high degree of traceability. *Variable costing* is a more appropriate term since it suggests that the distinction is between fixed and variable costs. Direct costing may also suggest that this is a concept that can be used only where there are systems of cost accounting; however, this concept can be very effectively used in small businesses where there are no cost accounting systems. Despite its disadvantages, the term direct costing will be used here because it is consistent with popular terminology.

Essentially, direct costing is a concept under which only prime costs and variable overhead are treated as product costs; all other manufacturing costs are treated as period costs. Since the only costs assigned to inventories are variable costs, the unit cost assigned is uniform. Under direct costing, fixed costs are considered as the costs of providing a level of capacity and are charged in their entirety against the revenue of the period.

The difference between direct and absorption costing seems to lie primarily in the treatment of fixed factory overhead—whether it is charged off against income when the cost is incurred or when the goods are sold. Absorption costing gives effect to both sales volume and production volume, while direct costing gives effect primarily to sales volume.

Development of Direct Costing

Historically, direct costing is an outgrowth of management's increased need for quantitative data analyzing the effect of cost-volume-price relationships on the firm. The antecedent of direct costing is the principle of burden application that was developed around the turn of the century. Because charging certain actual manufacturing expenses to production must be delayed until the end of the fiscal period, accountants decided to estimate overhead in advance and create a predetermined overhead rate. The burden application concept recognizes not only that certain costs defy identification with certain outputs but, in addition, that some of these costs may have service potentials that extend beyond a single accounting period. At the end of the fiscal period the disposition of the over- or underabsorbed balance resulting from the differences between actual and applied expenses still presents a problem. Often the variances are treated as periodic costs and are not allocated to inventories. This type of adjustment is generally more valid on annual statements than on short-period statements.

Flexible budgets containing estimated expenses for all possible levels of output do not completely overcome the influence of fixed cost. A favorable or unfavorable volume variance will result when actual production differs from the production used in the budget to compute the standard overhead rate.

Another serious controversy of absorption costing concerns the distribution of the financial statement. Readers are confused by a statement showing a loss for some products when the firm is still in business and solvent. Many times management finds it necessary to make special studies in order to obtain the needed information for decision making. These supplementary reports involve extra work, are often inefficiently prepared, and, when used, frequently confuse the managers who ordered them.

With automation on the increase in American industry, burden becomes an even larger element of the cost of products. A large portion of this burden is fixed in nature. The spread of guaranteed annual wage contracts also changes (increases) the portion of a firm's costs that are fixed. Such a shift in the cost characteristics of a firm emphasizes how important it is for management to understand the impact of fixed costs. A firm will have less flexibility in altering decisions because more dollars will be invested in machinery and plant. More adequate information will be necessary because management will have to deliberate very carefully before expanding the firm's labor force and production facilities.

With an increase in the portion of costs that are fixed, seasonal variations in production and sales tend to cause a distortion in the income reported on the income statement. Absorption costing assumes that the existing facilities and management were set up to make and sell an average volume of goods over a period of years. This approach supplies a base for price determination and avoids great fluctuations in inventory values, but it also distorts income and it is difficult to justify this income distortion to management. Under absorption costing, when production volume is increased, fixed costs are built up in inventory and are not charged off until the inventory is sold. If there is a lag in sales, absorption costing may show high profits during this period of heavy production even though sales are low. The opposite would be true during the reverse cycle.

Advantages of Direct Costing

Many companies that have converted to direct costing to obtain the advantage of a certain aspect have found many other unanticipated advantages. Ease of understanding by management is vital and is one of the most important merits of direct costing. Accountants must provide information that is accurate, complete, and timely, but the information must also be understandable. If top managers find their company reports too complex, they will have no faith in the figures and will not realize their importance.

Managerial decision making and control. The clarity of the cost-volume-price relationship has been listed by many as the prime advantage of direct costing. The cost-volume-profit relationship provides a valuable tool for planning without any additional information. Direct costing improves the collection and presentation of information in regard to the relationship between cost, pricing, profits, volume, and product mix. Profits move in the same direction as sales under direct costing; this effect is more logical than under absorption costing, where profit is affected by changes in inventory. This information is very useful to management in selecting product lines, in deciding upon which line to emphasize more, in pricing, and as a basis for decisions on other problems involving alternatives. Direct costing is especially important to companies that have the opportunity to indulge in make-or-buy decisions. Comparisons of company costs with costs of buying from outsiders have certain features when the company is operating under direct costing.

Management is able to find the cost-volume-profit ratio without working with two or sometimes several sets of data. If this information is given to managers other than the top executives, they will be encouraged to improve their departments. They will no longer plan the month's report out of focus because sales will vary directly with production. Direct costing removes the confusion and provides a stimulus for prompt action in the future.

Decisions can be more easily made if fixed expenses are separate rather than buried in production cost. Since the total fixed expense for the period appears in the income statement, the impact of fixed expenses on profits is emphasized. Direct-costing advocates stress that fixed costs are by definition sunk costs because the commitment has been made. Variable costs are the only production costs that require current managerial decisions in regard to working capital because fixed costs are beyond the control of management in the short range. Since variable costs are controllable, they are the crucial costs for decision-making purposes. It is highly desirable in many situations to classify costs in terms of their behavior patterns.

One of the important purposes of direct costing is to help management control operating costs. Separating the fixed and variable costs automatically centers attention on cost reduction. Executives who have had experience with direct costing find that simple procedures are employed for showing what costs actually are as compared to what they should be. Responsibility accounting is more easily accomplished under a system of direct costing than under conventional absorption costing, because by not allocating fixed costs to products, the tracing of costs by lines of managerial responsibility is simplified.

Pricing policies. Direct costing provides more relevant information concerning pricing policies than does absorption costing. Often it is assumed that no product should be kept in business lines for any substantial length of time unless its price is higher than its average full cost. However, in the long run it cannot be assumed that competitive conditions will be the same for all products because market conditions will vary. Pricing to cover average full costs may not be the most advantageous method for a company either in the long or short run. When making any pricing decisions, the effect of prices on volume and of volume on cost must be considered. Under direct costing, management has the data to determine when it is advisable to accept orders or make orders in certain periods of the year. In this way management can take advantage of doing business that may contribute only partly to the carrying of the fixed expenses.

Direct costing highlights the often serious results of price cutting. A common error is to cut prices by a certain percentage and then assume that all that is needed to compensate for the loss is an increase in volume by the same percentage. In trying to gain volume from a competitor, management must understand just how much a price can be cut before the company is selling below costs. Once management understands how price cutting to gain volume seriously affects profits, it will be more cautious in cutting prices just for the sake of underselling a competitor. It will know that sometimes a company can cut itself out of business.

Direct costing is of considerable assistance in the appraisal of marginal products or marginal volume. Direct costing, in effect, corresponds closely with the current out-of-pocket expenditure for a product. When this figure is available, management can see what contribution the product has made to fixed overhead. The problem of product-line simplification is not always easy; yet an important aspect of the appraisal is made available by the use of direct costing. The relative importance of a product's contribution can be determined by obtaining the gross margin percent and volume of the item.

After all the variable costs have been subtracted from net sales, the remaining figure is the contribution to fixed costs and income. This figure is usually called *marginal income* and is very useful to management. A sharper focus is reached on the profitability of products, customers, and territories. Management can evaluate marginal income and more easily find where unprofitable items should be eliminated. This is true because the data is not obscured by the allocation of fixed costs.

Dangers of Direct Costing

The simplicity of direct costing is advantageous because management can understand the resulting figures more easily. However, there may be dangers if the principle is misapplied.

Intangible factors must also be considered. A product with a low contribution rate may be handled for the convenience of customers. If this item is dropped, the loss in customer goodwill could well offset any gain from products with high contribution rates.

Long-run pricing. Eliminating the danger in fixed overhead costs from inventories should be recognized. Recently there has been an increasing trend to automation in manufacturing, resulting in more overhead and a lower direct labor cost. It is possible to foresee a time when direct material will constitute the only variable item of manufacturing cost. Thus the company with the largest fixed expenses would have the smallest unit inventory costs. This looms as a serious threat to the usefulness of direct costing and does not follow the accepted theories of inventory valuation. This is one reason why the American Institute of Certified Public Accountants and the Internal Revenue Service have not recognized direct costing as acceptable for inventory costing. Also, management has to face the reality that all expenses must be met by sales—regardless of how inventory is valued.

Direct-costing income is higher than absorption-costing income when sales substantially exceed current production. The sales department may ask permission to lower sales prices or demand higher fringe benefits or sales bonuses after evaluating the higher direct-costing income. For long-range policy decisions, especially those concerned with pricing, an allocation of fixed overhead on some volume base must be made. Direct costing provides product figures that give little basis for long-range pricing policies.

Direct Costing versus Absorption Costing

Accounting figures are used by those outside and inside the company and by people other than accountants. These people have become accustomed to the normal relationship of certain figures to other figures. Management, for example, is accustomed to using net income figures. A change to another accounting method that gives a completely different picture under similar labels is therefore confusing, even though the purpose of the change is to provide better information and bring about more understanding.

Both the absorption- and the direct-costing approaches have advantages and are useful to management. What use management wants to make of the information involved will determine whether absorption costing or direct costing is more proper. The use of direct costing alone would be improper if new products that require the use of existing facilities are under consideration. The net profit approach under absorption costing also has the advantage of centering management's attention on problem areas calling for long-run remedial action. If a unit does not include its share of all expenses, management may overlook the need to recover all expenses. It is impossible to say whether a unit is profitable or not, or how profitable or unprofitable, unless it is bearing its share of the fixed cost. Management should endeavor to set long-run prices to recover full costs as well as provide a profit.

Standard costing and direct costing are compatible and should be used together. By adopting direct-costing standards, the company will have an excellent tool for managerial decision making. Unit costs and departmental costs will be separated according to fixed and variable overhead.

Whether or not fixed manufacturing costs are deferred in inventory, management should have different types of cost information to meet its needs. With an aborption-costing method that uses flexible budgets and standard costs, fixed- and variable-cost information should be prepared so proper use can be made of all cost information. Both direct-costing and absorption-costing systems depend upon a thorough knowledge of cost behavior classified by type of cost and by function.

Exhibit 4-16.   Income statement.

	ACTUAL	STANDARD	VARIANCE
Sales	X	X	X
Less cost of sales:			
Direct material	X	X	X
Direct labor	X	X	X
Variable factory overhead	X	X	X
Total variable manufacturing costs	X	X	X
Sales less variable manufacturing costs	X	X	X
Less variable operating expenses:			
Variable marketing expenses	X	X	X
Variable administrative expenses	X	X	X
Total variable operating expenses	X	X	X
Marginal income	X	X	
Less:			
Fixed factory overhead	X	X	X
Fixed marketing expenses	X	X	X
Fixed administrative expenses	X	X	X
Total fixed expenses	X	X	X
Direct costing income	X	X	X
Variation for fixed-cost influences of Inventory (units produced—units sold × fixed factory overhead per unit at normal capacity)	X	X	X
Absorption-costing net income before income taxes	X	X	X

Since each approach has its own area of usefulness, a combined approach is suggested. The income statement presented in Exhibit 4-16 is based on standard costs, flexible budgets, and a division of all costs into their fixed and variable components. Variable costs are first subtracted from sales to give a net contribution to fixed cost and income, and then fixed cost is subtracted to give net income. The income statement should be supported by schedules showing the variances due to such factors as price and quantity.

Having both sets of profit figures enables the executive to form a judgment with much greater facility than would be the case if only one profit figure were available. Responsibility accounting is facilitated because it is possible to have accounting by organizational level. This approach provides the additional information that management needs for making decisions and still complies with accepted accounting principles. The system combining direct costing and absorption costing with standard costs and flexible budgets provides for more effective cost control since each tool can be used where it best serves.

There is no need to divide the client's accounting system into either absorption costing or direct costing because both approaches must be understood and used when appropriate. For a business to reach its full potential in a mature business economy, management must have all the information necessary for the various decisions it must make. In evaluating the effectiveness of individual and departmental performance, the accountant needs to use direct costing as a tool. Answers to some problems would be destroyed if absorption costing were used—for example, in evaluating the effect on overall profits caused by a new item.

There is fairly general agreement concerning the value of direct costing for internal reporting. However, much discussion remains concerning the application of direct costing for external purposes. Reporting for external uses is normally expected to conform to generally accepted accounting principles, but financial data prepared for internal uses need not be prepared in accordance with generally accepted accounting principles.

Neither the Internal Revenue Service nor the American Institute of Certified Public Accountants has recognized direct costing as acceptable for inventory valuation. Many managers believe that direct costing has no value since it has not been completely accepted for financial reporting. However, the invalidity of the direct-costing technique for external reporting does not impair its unique usefulness as an analytical tool for management.

Relevant Costs

Relevant costs are those that are valid or pertinent to the decision to be made; they are the costs that would be changed by a decision. Precision or accuracy is not the same concept as relevance. By giving single emphasis to relevant costs, irrelevancies may be eliminated and the manager's thinking focused on costs for decision making. Even though variable costs are more likely to be relevant than fixed costs, it is not a foolproof approach to assume that all variable costs are relevant and all fixed costs irrelevant.

For example, the book value or unrecovered costs of equipment that would be scrapped at no salvage value if a territory was closed would be irrelevant in trying to decide the future of that territory. The depreciation on this equipment would be a direct cost of the territory; yet it would not be used in deciding whether to keep the territory or not. The relevant costs are the out-of-pocket costs that will change with the decision. Costs that apply to a certain decision are not properly used in other circumstances.

Sunk Costs

Sunk costs are historical costs that cannot be changed; they are irrevocable in a given situation. They are irrelevant in decision making because the decision was made in the past to incur these costs and no decision in the present or future can change them. Investments in plant assets are an excellent example because as soon as the physical facilities are installed, their cost becomes sunk. At this point management can sell the plant or equipment and realize whatever the market value is, or it can use the asset and attempt to recover the costs through the revenue generated by the asset.

Escapable Costs

Escapable costs are those that will be eliminated if the segment is discontinued. These costs are directly related to the segment. Nonescapable costs are the indirect costs that will not be eliminated if the segment is discontinued; instead they will be reassigned to other segments. In considering the elimination of a business segment, only escapable costs are relevant. For example, if an organization is trying to decide if it would be more profitable to eliminate a product line, escapable costs would include inventory carrying charges of the product line. The cost of the warehousing and delivery facilities not eliminated by discontinuance of the product line would be nonescapable costs.

Incremental Costs

Another useful cost concept in planning and decision making is incremental costs. These are the additional costs incurred between two alternatives. Another name for this is *differential costs* (marginal costs refers to the same concept, but on a per unit basis). The marketing manager will find incremental costs helpful in determining the effect on income of changing sales volume; it is also a valuable aid in making pricing decisions and changing product mix. Even though the majority of incremental costs will be variable and semivariable, fixed costs may also be included when there are certain changes in activity.

Opportunity Costs

There are other cost concepts that marketing management should use in comparing alternative courses of action and in arriving at a decision. The accounting records do not provide the data for all costs that should be used in decision making. According to correct accounting theory, expenses are recorded only when an outlay of cash or its equivalent is required or will be required in the future. Opportunity costs do not involve cash outlays, and accordingly are not used to determine the accounting net income. Instead opportunity costs are the earnings that could have been made if the resources available had been channeled into other uses. Once a decision has been made to utilize a certain facility, the opportunity for alternative uses is lost.

Opportunity costs are often valuable to decentralized organizations where management determines the profits made by each operating division within the company. This approach has the advantage of placing each individual organizational unit in the same position as if it were an independent business instead of an operating division of an enterprise.

The explicit introduction of opportunity cost figures into profitability calculations is helpful for short-term decisions. Successful business management often is a matter of finding and exploiting opportunities that other managers have overlooked. These opportunities arise at different times, such as when an increase in capacity is proposed or when the company has superfluous funds and seeks to employ them. As an example, suppose a business organization has $1 million to invest. The investment alternatives must first be identified. The respective payoffs of each alternative must be established and assessed in light of the organization's objectives.

A company ordinarily does not increase plant size or make any other fixed investment just because it has surplus funds. Sometimes it must move ahead to meet future demand, or competitors' actions, and such efforts may not be profitable for a time. If normal expansion is the only motive, a fixed investment must be justified on a profit basis. If the return is very low in view of the risks, then alternative investment of surplus funds in securities or other forms must be considered.

All of these determinations must be carefully made and checked by management and supplemented by independent experts as needed. The conclusions are then set up in a schedule, such as Exhibit 4-17, for study and decision.

In Exhibit 4-17 management has established payoffs for four alternatives. This process has the advantage of forcing management to search until it finds as many available alternatives as possible. It is doubtful if management can ever be certain it has identified *all* feasible alternative courses of action. Obviously, the search cannot be allowed to take so much time that action is unduly delayed.

Exhibit 4-17.   Payoffs of alternative actions.

ALTERNATIVES	ENVIRONMENTAL CONDITIONS		
	EXCELLENT	AVERAGE	POOR
Advertising campaign for present Product X	+$100,000	+$ 60,000	−$40,000
Open new territory in which to sell Product X	+$300,000	+$100,000	−$10,000
Produce Y	+$120,000	+$ 75,000	−$30,000
Produce Z	+$ 80,000	+$ 80,000	—

The payoffs from each of the four strategies depend upon the state of the environmental conditions. Since management does not know which of the three states of market conditions will prove to be true, the payoffs of each alternative should be projected and analyzed. Management should then choose the dominant strategy that will produce the best payoff regardless of which market condition proves to be true. Exhibit 4-17 shows that the alternative of opening a new territory will be dominant in excellent and average market conditions, but not dominant in a poor market since it results in a loss of $10,000. The strategy of producing Z would be the best decision if poor market conditions exist; however, it will not produce the best payoff in an excellent or average market. Since the payoff table contains no alternative that is clearly dominant over all other alternatives, a decision problem exists.

Exhibit 4-18 is a quantified regrets table showing the return foregone. For example, assuming excellent conditions, Exhibit 4-17 shows that an advertising campaign for Product X would yield a $100,000 net income, while opening a new territory for the product would result in a $300,000 net income. If management chooses to open the advertising campaign instead of the territory, it will have chosen to lose $200,000, the difference between the projected net incomes. This is the maximum regret figure in Exhibit 4-18. Since opening a new territory yields the highest payoffs under excellent market conditions, all alternatives in Exhibit 4-18 are compared to the $300,000 net income.

Management would naturally want to select the alternative whose maximum opportunity cost is a minimum. Thus opening a new territory to sell Product X would be dictated since its maximum regret is $10,000, while the maximum regret is $200,000 for an advertising campaign

Exhibit 4-18. Opportunity cost of alternative actions.

ALTERNATIVES	ENVIRONMENTAL CONDITIONS		
	EXCELLENT	AVERAGE	POOR
Advertising campaign for present Product X	$200,000	$40,000	$40,000
Open new territory in which to sell Product X	—	—	$10,000
Produce Y	$180,000	$25,000	$30,000
Produce Z	$220,000	$20,000	—

for Product X, $180,000 for producing Y, and $220,000 for producing Z. Since the opportunity costs listed in Exhibit 4-18 are conditional and depend upon the occurrence of a specific market condition, management must gamble on which future environmental condition is most likely.

Marketing managers should hesitate to make a decision involving a large outlay of funds solely on the basis of the information contained in Exhibit 4-18. Instead it should have some data on the probability of each possible event. The alternative of opening a new territory in which to sell Product X might not be preferable if there is only a small chance that this higher net income (and lower net loss in comparison with an advertising campaign for Product X and the production of Y) will occur.

For instance, suppose the marketing manager estimates that the chance of a poor market condition existing for an advertising campaign for Product X is 50 percent, for an average market 40 percent, and for an excellent market 10 percent. The expected value of the outcome of each alternative is found by multiplying each possible payoff by its probability and adding the products as follows:

Excellent environmental conditions	$.1 \times \$100,000 =$	$+\$10,000$
Average environmental conditions	$.4 \times \$ 60,000 =$	$+\$24,000$
Poor environmental conditions	$.5 \times -\$ 40,000 =$	$-\$20,000$
Expected value		$+\$14,000$

Applying probabilities. Once the marketing manager is able to study market conditions, he or she may be able to attach fairly reliable probabilities of occurrence to each state or condition. The alternative selected should be the one that produces the largest income, as long as the organization is not exposed to a high probability that a large net loss will result. By weighing the payoffs according to the relative probabilities that the various marketing conditions will occur, the payoff under each alternative can be reduced to one figure. This figure is known as the expected value. The payoffs for all four alternatives are weighted and the expected values of each alternative are computed in Exhibit 4-19. The higher the expected value, the more favorable the alternative. An "opportunity gain"—the difference between the highest expected value and that of other alternatives—can be determined. In order to maximize profits, the marketing manager should produce Y.

Risk factors. In choosing the proper alternative, the marketing manager must determine what risk the organization is willing to assume. The organization's willingness to assume risk may be reflected in determining the payoffs listed in Exhibit 4-17. Suppose an advertising campaign for Product X was chosen and a poor market condition was encountered which resulted in a net loss of $40,000. If a net loss of this amount would throw the company into bankruptcy or, less seriously, cut working capital considerably, marketing management should be cautious and weigh the possible loss by a factor much larger than its relative probability. Conversely, if a net income of at least $120,000 is needed to pay off a pressing debt or to satisfy another important objective, the decision may be to open a new territory in which to sell Product X or Product Y, with the hope of operating in an excellent environment.

Exhibit 4-19. Probability of the payoffs of alternative actions.

ALTERNATIVES	ENVIRONMENTAL CONDITIONS			EXPECTED VALUE
	EXCELLENT	AVERAGE	POOR	
Advertising campaign for present Product X	.1 × $100,000 = +$10,000	.4 × $ 60,000 = +$24,000	.5 × −$40,000 = −$20,000	+$14,000
Open new territory in which to sell Product X	.2 × $300,000 = +$60,000	.1 × $100,000 = +$10,000	.7 × −$10,000 = −$ 7,000	+$63,000
Produce Y	.5 × $120,000 = +$60,000	.2 × $ 75,000 = +$15,000	.3 × −$30,000 = −$ 9,000	+$66,000
Produce Z	.3 × $ 80,000 = +$24,000	.5 × $ 80,000 = +$40,000	.2 × 0 = 0	+$64,000

SUMMARY

As long as marketing management must operate in a world of uncertainty, there is little hope that any accounting method or any decision-making cost analysis can do much more than make a partial contribution to problem solving. Yet when these methods and analyses are used in the right perspective—that is, with an awareness of their limitations—they are useful tools. None of these accounting methods will solve all the problems of historical costs or of an absorption-costing system; however, they should be used *in addition to* generally accepted accounting methods. Determination of the type of cost analyses to be prepared should be made on the basis of the needs of management and the problems to be solved.

5

Evaluating Marketing Segments

MANY different means of evaluating marketing segments are available for use by the marketing manager. The manner of application a firm chooses to use will vary, depending upon its potential market, competitive strategy, and organizational structure. Certainly a thorough appraisal of past activities should be made because market conditions change continually. Plans that were most appropriate last month may need revising for the coming period.

METHODS OF EVALUATING MARKETING SEGMENTS

Some of these methods have inherent weaknesses because of either the dissimilarity between marketing segments involved or the difficulty of establishing objective standards for nonrepetitive marketing tasks. Despite these weaknesses, however, information can be helpful in pointing out areas where additional investigation is needed. Moreover, areas where planning should be improved may become evident.

An organization needs performance standards so that personnel at all levels will know what is expected of them. Various standards are used to evaluate divisional performance. Standards for marketing activities can be expressed in different ways. They may be a measure of ideal performance or they may represent a normal or average level of accomplishment. Standards may be expressed as a quota for a product line or customer grouping. Return on investment (ROI) and gross margin expressed as a percentage of sales are also currently used. Scientifically predetermined standards may also be adopted for work units within each function.

Cash Payback

Every segment can be considered as a separate investment so that the payback period can be calculated for each. The cash payback of an investment is the time required to recover the original outlay. The expenditures necessary to get the marketing segment established would be considered the original outlay. The segments chosen could include territories, product lines, salespeople, projects, channels, and market tests.

Exhibit 5-1.   Cash payback.

	INITIAL OUTLAY PERIOD 0	CASH PROCEEDS PERIOD 1	CASH PROCEEDS PERIOD 2
Investment in Segment X	$ 5,000	$ 3,000	$4,000
Investment in Segment Y	10,000	5,000	5,000
Investment in Segment Z	15,000	15,000	7,000

For example, assume the limited information given concerning three marketing segments in Exhibit 5-1.

Under this approach, the investment in Segment Z would be the most desirable since it would be recouped in one period, while more than one period would be required to recoup the investment in Segment X and two periods would be required for Segment Y. The cash-payback method has inherent weaknesses. It gives no consideration to the timing of the cash proceeds, a dollar earned in period 1 has the same significance as a dollar earned in period 2. In addition, the life of the investment after the payback period does not enter into consideration.

Return on Investment (ROI)

Often marketing managers become preoccupied with volume of sales dollars or marketing expenses. The amount of income or the relationship of income to sales is not an absolute test of profitability. It is the relationship of income to invested capital that should be determined and evaluated. An important ratio for marketing managers to watch is ROI. Return on investment focuses on the optimum asset investment, whether this be cash, receivables, inventories, or plant assets. Long-run profits will be maximized if the optimum level of investment in each asset is achieved.

The following realtionship outlines ROI:

$$\frac{\text{Sales}}{\text{Invested capital}} \times \frac{\text{net income}}{\text{sales}} = \frac{\text{net income}}{\text{invested capital}}$$

This formula may be expressed in another way:

Margin percentage on sales × capital turnover
= return on investment

By observing the factors of the formula, it can be seen that any action that increases sales, reduces costs, or reduces invested capital while holding the other factors constant is beneficial. An improvement in capital turnover or margin percentage without changing the other factors will increase ROI.

The traditional return on investment for the same marketing investments is shown in Exhibit 5-2. The computations reveal that while Investment Z had the shortest payback period, its return on investment was less favorable than that for Investment Y. If the rate of return on investment is larger than the rate desired by management, the investment may be accepted. Conversely, if the rate of return is less than desired, it may be rejected. Before deciding that Investment Y is the best alternative, the limitations of ROI should be considered.

In computing ROI management must decide if it wants to use undepreciated cost or net book value (cost less accumulated depreciation). If gross assets are used, a decline in earning power will be more evident if income decreases as the plant ages. A constantly decreasing net book value will reflect a possibly deceptive higher rate of return in later years. Net book value has the advantage of being less confusing because it is consistent with both the total assets

Exhibit 5-2. Return on investment.

	Outlays	Total Cash Proceeds	Net Income	Average Income	Average Investment	Return on Investment
Investment X	$ 5,000	$ 7,000	$ 200	$100	$2,500	4%
Investment Y	10,000	10,000	1,000	500	5,000	10%
Investment Z	15,000	22,000	750	375	7,500	5%

shown on the conventional balance sheet and the net income computations, which include depreciation expense as a deduction. Replacement cost is sometimes used as a base by employing appraisal values of specific price indexes.

Limitations of ROI. Some marketing managers are convinced that the use of ROI for divisional performance evaluation is misleading and destructive. The measurement is difficult because tangible and intangible assets are allocated to the investment and these are often difficult to value. Furthermore, the amount of the investment base is arbitrary because such expenditures as research, patent costs, recruiting, and development of customer loyalty have residual values beyond the accounting period and these are not capitalized. Segments that are concerned with marketing often have a small investment base; as a result, their ROI reported on divisional profit statements is large. Since assets can appreciate or depreciate in value, original cost and current economic value do not have a direct relationship. The original cost is the result of decisions made by different people many years ago, while the economic usefulness today depends on such facts as the current market and technology. Both numerator and denominator in ROI are the result of and/or subject to wide ranges of arbitrary decisions.

If the segments are completely independent of one another, return on investment serves an important purpose. However, if the segments are closely interrelated and produce a large volume of goods for one another, it is questionable if a valid return on investment can be attained. This is partly because the transfer prices used are often arbitrarily determined.

Designing performance reports that measure departmental performance becomes more complex as higher degrees of decentralization are encountered. Reliance must be placed on indirect performance measures. Analysis using a single rate of return is an indirect measure of performance since the effects of so many decisions are combined into one calculation. This calculation can be most effectively applied when it is used to evaluate segments whose operations are quite independent of other segments and whose output can be objectively valued.

Some managers feel that if they give close attention to ROI the other ratios will not need much attention. However, the true calculation of ROI cannot be determined until year-end, and business organizations need current information on operations. Since ROI has such severe limitations, it cannot fulfill the entire needs of top management, though it should be used along with other performance measurements.

Present Value

A difficulty with the ROI method is that some investments may have more than one rate of return. For example, there may be periods of positive proceeds followed by periods of negative cash flows. It is easier to reach a decision using the present-value method than the ROI method. The present-value method assumes that the proceeds from the investment can be invested at the same rate of interest as the cost of money.

Under the present-value method, cash flows out and cash flows in are discounted back to the present period, using an appropriate discount rate. If there is a positive net cash flow, additional analysis should be made. Otherwise, the investment would usually not warrant additional investigation. The present value of the cash flows of two investments is given in Exhibit 5-3, which assumes a cost of money of 6 percent. The present value for alternative Investment Z is greater

Exhibit 5-3. Present value.

	INVESTMENT X		
PERIOD	CASH FLOWS	PRESENT VALUE FACTOR	PRESENT VALUE
0	($5,000)	1.0000	($5,000)
1	3,000	.9434	2,830
2	4,000	.8900	3,560
			$+1,390

	INVESTMENT Y		
PERIOD	CASH FLOWS	PRESENT VALUE FACTOR	PRESENT VALUE
0	($10,000)	1.0000	($10,000)
1	5,000	.9434	4,717
2	5,000	.8900	4,450
			$- 833

	INVESTMENT Z		
PERIOD	CASH FLOWS	PRESENT VALUE FACTOR	PRESENT VALUE
0	($15,000)	1.0000	($15,000)
1	15,000	.9434	14,151
2	7,000	.8900	6,230
			$+5,381

than the present value of the cash flows for Investments X and Y. Assuming that its life is only two periods, Investment Y should not be considered because it has a negative present value. Investment X has a smaller positive present value than Investment Z, and if a decision must be made between these two alternatives, Investment Z should be chosen.

Residual Income

An investment center may be evaluated by its residual income instead of its ROI or present value. Residual income is the operating income of the investment center after the inputed interest on the assets used by the center has been deducted. This approach encourages managers to concentrate on maximizing dollars of residual income rather than on a percent, as is the case in the return-on-investment approach. In trying to maximize ROI managers of highly profitable centers may reject projects that would be profitable to the overall organization. The cost of capital must be specified in both the ROI and residual-income methods. There is a danger in using a uniform rate if different segments are earning different rates. The better approach is to use different rates for each segment.

Contribution Reporting

Another approach is to evaluate divisional managers on the basis of their controllable performance. Some marketing segments will continue to be poor profit performers regardless of the efforts of the manager. A contribution approach can help distinguish between the performance of the segment and the performance of the manager.

The full-costing approach should not be used in segment evaluation. It is unfair to hold a segment manager responsible for corporate-level costs because he or she has no control over the incurrence of these costs. However, this does not imply that each segment should not be expected to contribute toward these indirect costs.

There are many theories in regard to the proper allocation of costs to time periods. The net profit reported can be significantly affected by the type of depreciation used and the estimated life of the investment. The net income is also affected by whether an item of expenditure is capitalized or treated as an expenditure. Over a long period these differences in treatment cancel out, but the effect is usually significant in the short run. The reported net income can be different for two divisional managers with identical performances.

Only the overall organization can make a profit; all that each segment can do is to make a contribution toward that profit. A segment's contribution is the revenue it has earned less the direct costs that are traceable to its operations. Both variable and nonvariable costs are deducted from the revenue. Organizational profits will be maximized when marginal contribution is maximized. Therefore it is very important that management be provided with approximations of marginal contribution at each point when a decision must be made.

An analysis using the contribution concept is presented in Exhibit 5-4. The statement is condensed for illustration purposes. Each of the two territories is assumed to have two salespeople. No attempt is made to allocate any joint costs of the organization. If there are some nonvariable costs that can be traced to the territories but not to the salespeople, a segmental contribution margin can be separately determined for the territories and the salespeople.

The greatest usefulness of the contribution approach is as a tool for making decisions concerned with meeting competition, short-run pricing, special-order pricing, and other problems that admit of alternatives. Usually material joint or fixed costs are involved in these alternatives. The contribution-margin approach assumes that these costs will not be changed in total by the decision.

Breakeven Point Analysis

The level of sales at which the company will recover all its expenses and show neither an income nor a loss is referred to as the breakeven point. Breakeven can be determined mathematically or by means of a chart. Assume that the following conditions exist for XYZ Company:

Variable expenses are 60 percent of sales.
Total fixed costs are $120,000.
Maximum sales volume at full capacity is $600,000.

If breakeven is determined by mathematical formula, the following results are obtained:

$$
\begin{aligned}
1.00S &= .60S + \$120,000 \\
1.00S - .60S &= \$120,000 \\
.40S &= \$120,000 \\
S &= \$300,000
\end{aligned}
$$

Thus the organization will break even with sales of approximately $300,000 (it is impossible to find the precise sales volume at which there will be no income or loss). Exhibit 5-5 is a breakeven chart on which fixed and variable expenses and sales revenue are plotted.

Exhibit 5-4.   XYZ Company contribution analysis for Territories X and Y by salespeople.

	Company Totals	Territory		Territory X		Territory Y	
		X	Y	Mr. A	Ms. B	Ms. C	Mr. D
Revenue	$20,000	$12,000	$8,000	$7,000	$5,000	$3,000	$5,000
Less variable manufacturing costs	10,000	$ 6,000	$4,000	$3,500	$2,500	$1,500	$2,500
Variable marketing costs—salespersons' salaries	3,000	1,800	1,200	800	1,000	500	700
	$13,000	$ 7,800	$5,200	$4,300	$3,500	$2,000	$3,200
Variable margin	$ 7,000	$ 4,200	$2,800	$2,700	$1,500	$1,000	$1,800
Percent of sales	35.00%	35.00%	35.00%	38.57%	30.00%	33.33%	36.00%
Less nonvariable costs traceable to segment	4,000	2,000	2,000	1,500	500	700	1,300
Segmental contribution margin,	$ 3,000	$ 2,200	$ 800	$1,200	$1,000	$ 300	$ 500
percent of sales	15.00%	18.33%	10.00%	17.14%	20.00%	10.00%	10.00%
Nontraceable costs	500						
Net income	$ 2,500						
Percent of sales	12.50%						

Exhibit 5-5.   Breakeven chart.

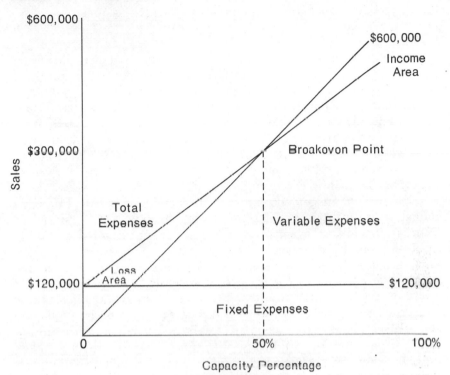

The chart illustrates that breakeven will be achieved at 50 percent capacity.

Breakeven information is useful in forecasting the effect upon earnings of an increase or decrease in sales volume. The effects of plant expansion and increased sales can be determined. The breakeven point could be ascertained for each marketing segment; however, since fixed costs must be considered, there must be an arbitrary allocation of fixed costs. Thus breakeven point analysis has strong limitations when applied to segments.

Breakeven point analysis also has some inherent limitations. It assumes that selling prices will remain constant at all volumes; this is the reason sales revenue is plotted as a straight line in Exhibit 5-5. It further assumes that all costs and expenses can be separated into nonvariable and variable categories; variable costs are drawn as a straight line, which indicates that they fluctuate in direct proportion to volume. If the segment sells more than one product line, a predetermined mix of the products must be assumed.

Ratios

A limitless number of ratios can be computed for marketing operations in total or for each market segment. For example, direct selling expense to sales dollars can be computed for each individual segment as well as for the total organization. Many trade associations collect and make available to their members information in ratio form for comparative purposes. These figures are often classified by sales volume. However, it is not easy to compare total distribution costs between any two companies in the same industry because of the wide variation in classifying items as marketing costs.

Different management concepts in companies within the same industry also militate against valid intercompany cost comparisons. There is, in addition, a lack of uniform agreement on both distribution methods and the methods of charging items to distribution costs. One firm may employ account titles identical to those used in the rest of the industry but charge different cost items to the titles.

Industry figures, therefore, may represent an average firm whose characteristics differ significantly from those of any concern employing the analysis. Thus the value of this analysis depends upon the ability of the firm's analysts to interpret differences between their company and the industry average. If the quality of the industry figures is not very high, of course, these differences will have little meaning.

STANDARDS FOR MARKETING COSTS

Control cannot exist without standards against which actual results can be compared. All business managers use some kind of standard in controlling operations under their direction, though it may be only a plan, idea, goal, or past performance. Just because a standard is not engineered and recorded does not mean that it does not exist.

Standards make executives cost-conscious because a standard-cost system makes them aware of cost variances. The variances between standard cost and actual cost should be studied and the physical causes of each variance determined. Once standards are determined, they should not be frequently adjusted in an attempt to keep them in line with actual results because this will destroy a valuable device for examining cost.

Too often the standard-cost principle is considered a set of procedures for cost finding only. The principles of standard cost are much broader. A good standard-cost system rests upon sound modern organization, budgets, standards of performance, and control of cost variances. Standard cost includes the concepts of planned performance and timetable scheduling. It avoids the hit-or-miss approach, for standard costs are based on data that is backed by knowledge of current happenings.

Effects of the Environment on a Standard-Cost System

In considering the adoption of standards for distribution, it is important to determine if the surrounding conditions are conducive to a successful use of standard costs for cost control. First of all, management should be interested in controlling costs. In order to achieve maximum utilization, distribution-cost analysis must be sold to both top management and marketing management. There will be little difficulty in selling the latter because the data supplied by the program can be of invaluable assistance to them in accomplishing their objectives. Top management is usually interested in any program that promises to improve net profit in the distribution operations, but it also wants assurance that this improvement will not be offset by increased costs in other company operations, particularly in accounting procedures.

Management and operating personnel must have confidence that the standards established are both correct and fair. In order to build and keep this confidence, standards should be established on a current basis, and the rates should be reliable and represent attainable performance.

Timing is very important in a standard cost system. Its effect on controlling costs must come before or at the time the costs are incurred. The person responsible for a cost should know the standard in advance and should be promptly informed of any variances. Many times the accounting system fails in this respect, for the variance is compiled only on long reports, which arrive long after the cost has occurred and are of little value for cost control.

Setting of Standards

The establishment of correct standards for a business firm's marketing expense is of great importance and requires considerable insight into the complexities of business management. Since standards serve as measurements, they promote efficiencies. They have the effect of controlling and reducing costs. Management executives and supervisors become cost-conscious as they work through the process of setting standards. The effectiveness of this control, however, depends largely on the quality of the standards established. Standards should be reliable and accurate, and all pertinent factors should be considered in their establishment. Marketing executives can be of valuable assistance to accounting personnel in setting standards.

A fundamental principle in setting standards is that those responsible for meeting them should have the opportunity of passing upon them before they are finally set. The people whose activities are controlled by the standard-cost system are naturally interested in the methods followed in setting the standards. They can be of great assistance to the accountant because they are eager that the problems of distribution be given proper weight and they have an insight into day-to-day problems that is valuable for formulating standards.

When selecting standards for distribution costs, the program should be explained fully to the supervisors of cost centers in order to solicit their support. These supervisors should have an honest desire to meet the standards. They should believe they are accurate and presented in terms that the employees under them will understand.

If maximum effectiveness is to be obtained, standard costs should also be explained to the employees. The labor force in the cost center to be measured should participate in setting the standards so they will believe the standards are accurate, reliable measurements of performance.

Functional Factors of Variability

The factors that cause marketing costs to vary must be identified. Such a measure is known as the unit of variability or the work or service unit. The validity of the functional-unit costs depends upon the reasonableness of the cost unit. If the work unit is not reasonable to begin with, the resulting functional-unit standard cost will not be valid. Thus care must be exercised in the selection of work units if the standards based upon the work units are to be meaningful and if variances from the standard are to be accepted in the measurement of performance. The work unit should be readily measurable, produce results that are reasonably accurate, and be economical to apply. There should be a demonstrable relationship between the work unit and the marketing activity. The factor chosen must fluctuate concomitantly with the activity that is the source of the cost. Attention should also be focused on the objectives that management had in mind when the expenditures were authorized. The work unit selected for an operation must be a common denominator for all work done in that operation.

The cost accountant should avoid the pitfall of accepting the work units supplied by the marketing department without first analyzing them. Marketing personnel concentrate on the selling aspects and often do not understand how to prorate the time and effort they spend on functional activities.

Sometimes the work unit is chosen merely because of its ease of computation, regardless of the logic. Work units such as percentage of net or gross sales, percentage of marketing costs, or percentage of gross profit are often not appropriate. Frequently a total operations standard is set for the branches that have been in operation for some length of time. This standard is expressed as a percentage of sales. A segment is considered profitable if its expenses are less than a certain percentage of gross sales. If segmental expenses exceed the designated percentage of gross sales, an unprofitable situation is indicated because either sales volume is too low or segmental expenses are too high. A direct relationship between sales volume and many marketing costs often cannot be established. Sales promotion activities are a cause rather than a result of sales; the volume of sales obtained may depend on the amount spent on advertising. This is particularly important to stress because distribution managers have tended to think only in terms of sales volume and gross profit percent.

Another reason for not using sales as the work unit on which to establish marketing cost standards is that there is an element of fixed costs in some of these expenditures. In many types of advertising and sales promotion expenses there is no straight-line relation to sales. For example, stores that are open for business need money for displays even though sales may not immediately result from these displays.

The simplest method of allocating functional costs to segments uses a single measurement unit to apportion the entire costs of a function. This approach is similar to factory cost allocation methods employing labor-hours or machine-hours to apportion a cost center's overhead to products. Its shortcoming is that it fails to recognize that some functional expense elements may vary with, and be most accurately allocated through, more than a single basis.

This is why it was earlier suggested that the more precise functionalization is generally preferable so that the work units can reflect the tasks performed. The selection of a reliable work unit is difficult if discordant elements are combined into a single classification. Analysis of each functional activity to identify the various tasks that must be performed facilitates the selection of valid work units.

The work unit used by other companies for allocating cost is not necessarily a guide to the work unit that should be chosen in a specific case because conditions differ. For this reason no attempt has been made in this study to tabulate all the various work units that could be applied to each function. Since there is no one work unit for each functional operation, it is also difficult to make any intelligent generalizations as to the most appropriate work unit for each function. The examples given in this chapter are for illustrative purposes only.

Order-getting Costs

There are some differences between standards as applied to production operations and as applied to marketing operations. Standards adaptable to production measure a direct relationship between effort and result. This relationship may not exist in some marketing costs, especially those concerned with order getting. In this analysis the two principal marketing functions, direct selling and advertising and sales promotion, are considered order-getting costs, those costs incurred in activities concerned with persuading the customer to buy. Direct selling differs from advertising and sales promotion in that the activities it includes represent primarily personal presentation of the service or product to the prospective buyer. Standard costs for order-getting activities are often based on units that measure effort expended rather than results obtained.

Order-filling Costs

Other distribution costs incurred for executing the sales order are designated as order-filling costs. Many order-filling activities relate to the physical handling of goods and to clerical operations. Order-getting activities include mainly nonrepetitive operations, while order-filling costs more often involve repetitive operations.

Many executives believe that marketing functions vary so much between time periods and between companies that it is impossible to establish and use standard costs. However, close examination will reveal that many marketing activities are uniform and are susceptible to techniques for setting standards on a physical basis. The same basic techniques and methods used to determine production standards may be used to determine many marketing standards. Standards should be established for each of the functional factors of variability on the basis of past experience, industrial engineering studies, or judgment. The determination of a standard sales volume is the starting point in the setting of standards for distribution costs. A standard function-unit cost should always be established for each marketing activity on the basis of a normal capacity.

STANDARDS FOR REPETITIVE OPERATIONS

Marketing functions can be divided into repetitive and nonrepetitive functions. A job audit or analysis may be prepared for all functions; all the operations performed in each function are listed as completely as possible on this analysis. The object of a job analysis is to measure time apportionment among the tasks comprising a function. Once jobs are determined, each operation should be studied to discover if the procedures are repetitive and routine in nature and can be standardized.

For each marketing distribution function in which there exists a fairly regular work routine it is possible to study the routine and record the time that each operation should require under normal conditions. Information can be obtained from the supervisor and the employees performing the operations. Previous time and motion study reports may also be examined. However, overall averages of past performance should be avoided because they may conceal unnecessary delays and thus not reflect good performance.

The number of observations required will vary according to the task. If any one of the observations deviates radically from the majority, this deviation should be investigated in order to decide whether it should be included in determining the standard performance rate or discarded. In choosing the number of observations to be included in computing the standard for a distribution element, the human element must be recognized. However, the margin of error that can be ascribed to fatigue and other personal factors is usually small and insignificant.

An adjustment to the standard should be made for nonproductive time lost through rest, interruptions, fatigue, and other factors affecting production time in a normal working day. Before final acceptance, the rate should be tested by a standards committee. A time standard can then be applied to each operation element that reflects a fair performance expectancy for a worker of acceptable skill functioning at a reasonable pace. Once a standard time per operation has been set, the standard number of operations that could be performed in any given time period can then be computed by dividing the total working time in that period by the standard time per operation.

Standard time may then be converted into standard unit costs by applying the costs expected to prevail during the period for which standards have been set.

Materials

An accountant familiar with standard costs should be in charge of the procedure for establishing standards for distribution materials. Year-to-date totals of material quantities should be studied and used as guides in setting the physical quantity of marketing materials needed. Work sampling can also be used in determining the standards for materials used in distribution. The engineering department may conduct tests under controlled conditions. A quantity of material can be put into the distribution process and the results can be carefully analyzed. The accountant will also need assistance from marketing supervisors who are thoroughly familiar with the materials used in each marketing function. Together they should establish detailed information regarding the standard material components needed in each distribution function. This theoretical material quantity must include factors for scrap, shrinkage, and waste.

The best principle to keep in mind in establishing material price standards is that the standard should be based on the best information possible. An ideal standard should take into consideration both past prices and anticipated prices. All foreseeable factors such as strikes, wide fluctuations in prices, weather conditions, and new discoveries in material must be weighed in setting material price standards. The purchasing department should place an expected material price on the distribution materials and use this in determining the material price standard.

Warehousing and Handling

Warehousing expenses are incurred from the time finished goods are received from the production process or another concern until they are ready for shipment or delivery. In wholesaling and retailing organizations the cost of the receiving function is usually included in these expenses. The warehousing and handling operations performed are largely of a repetitive nature and lend themselves to standardization and cost control in a manner similar to that used for production operations. Industrial engineering methods and personnel can be utilized to set operation standards because warehousing consists largely of physical handling.

If each territory has its own warehouse, handling facilities, and clerical employees for processing orders, these costs are direct charges to the territories. If, however, the company centralizes such facilities, the cost must be allocated to the territories and shipping clerks must be required to ascertain and report the amount of time they spend on each territory.

Shipping forms may indicate the type of packaging used in shipment by codes so that the standard allowed for each order can be determined. This permits the charging of each order for warehousing cost and a comparison of actual costs of warehousing with the standard cost of the activity.

Where all products are approximately the same in size and weight, product units can be used to develop warehousing and handling standard costs. However, if the effort required to move and handle the various product lines differs because of disparities in size and weight, a table of unit equivalents for the products should be computed. For instance, the smallest item can be assigned a value of 1 unit, the next largest $1^1/_4$ units, the next $1^1/_2$ units, and so forth. This weighting factor compensates for the differences in packing and handling time. In order to determine the number of units put into stock, the actual number of product units is multiplied by the proper unit equivalent.

Standard and actual unit costs can be developed using the most applicable of the following units:

Function	*Work Units*
Sorting	Physical unit stored
	Dollar of average inventory
	Order
Assembling stock for shipment	Order
	Order line
	Item
	Shipment
	Sales transaction
Packing and wrapping	Order
	Order line
	Physical unit shipped
	Shipment
Handling returns	Return
Receiving	Purchase invoice line
	Weight or number of shipping units
	Shipment
	Dollar of merchandise purchased

Function	*Work Units*
Pricing, tagging, and marking	Warehouse unit handled Invoice line
Taking physical inventory	Warehouse unit Dollar of average inventory
Clerical handling of shipping orders	Order Item Shipment Sales transaction Order line

Total warehousing and handling	Shipment
	Order line
	Item handled
	Physical unit of goods handled
	    (product, weight, or weighted
	    factor)

Transportation

Transportation expenses, as used in this chapter, begin at the point where the products are packaged for shipping and delivery, and consist of the shipping and delivery costs incurred in getting the products into customers' possession. Traffic routings should be carefully designed by competent traffic personnel to produce economical physical distribution costs for the required distribution pattern.

Transportation costs are directly charged to territories if each geographical unit has its own delivery equipment. When the transportation facilities are centralized, the cost must be allocated to the territories. Transportation costs can be identified as to territories by invoice numbers.

Because the transportation function consists largely of physical operations, the same type of techniques that are applied in production operations to develop standards can be used. The technique that is used in time studies of manufacturing operations can be employed, but the times noted are for a broader operation than the elements or motions observed in shops. For instance, the standard may be developed on day-long studies with the time-study observer watching all operations and noting the time required to perform them during the entire day.

If the delivery trucks carry different types of products, different weightings representing relative space requirements in the hauling can be assigned to the products. It costs more to ship larger containers, but smaller containers may have a certain minimum cost. The business concern should consider giving small containers a fixed minimum charge even when the weight factor is used in allocation. Rather than being used to establish standards for each shipment, this technique is more useful when the number of shipments is rather small and each shipment is large.

In establishing standards for transportation costs data should be compiled for like units of equipment. For example, the standard operating cost of a gasoline-operated truck is not the same as that of a diesel-operated truck. A set of functional-unit costs should be computed for each class of automotive equipment. A separate set of functional-unit standard costs should also be computed for line-haul equipment and pickup and delivery equipment. City delivery trucks make a great many stops, whereas trucks on long-distance hauls make a minimum number of stops. The mileage accumulated by each vehicle class should be recorded so that an actual expense per mile can be calculated and compared with the corresponding standard.

Transportation costs may be controlled by establishing standards and determining actual costs on such bases as cost per work unit, as shown in the following list:

Function	*Work Units*
Gasoline, oil, repair, and maintenance	Mile Truck-miles
Drivers' and helpers' wages	Truck-hours of operation Truck-miles Cubic floor space
Loading and unloading	Pounds loaded
Transportation clerical work entries in shipping records	Shipment Delivery
Preparing shipping documents and recording shipment	Shipment Unit of product shipped Weighted unit of product shipped
Transportation bills	Unit audited Shipment
Handling claims	Claim handled Shipment Entry

Function	Work Units
Planning and supervision	Sales dollar Route Customer served Ton-mile Unit shipped
Total transportation	Dollar of shipments as delivered Unit of product shipped as delivered Weighted unit of product Unit or class of product

Standard gasoline cost per mile should be carried to five decimal figures. The standard should be based on estimated miles per gallon and the average or anticipated cost of gasoline per gallon. The standards can be compared against the actual cost per mile, which is obtained by dividing the gasoline expense by miles run. The standard for lubrication can be based on past experience; a comparison of the standard with the actual cost will reveal any excessive oil consumption.

Some tire companies will agree to replace tires and tubes on a mileage basis and to furnish road service and regular inspections for an agreed fee. If an arrangement of this type is made, the standard can be determined from the agreement. If no special agreement is made, the standard cost per mile of tire and tube replacement can be estimated by determining the total life of a tire in mileage and dividing this into the expected cost for tires.

When conditions change from one cost unit to another—for example, transportation differs between territories—a different standard should be provided for each territory. It may also be necessary to group equipment units according to their use and according to the type of country—rolling, mountaineous, or flat—in which they operate. The technique of establishing different standards for each region is useful because a comparison of rates between regions may indicate to management where new warehousing and plant locations are required.

Credit and Collection

The credit and collection department has the general function of extending credit and subsequently collecting the money. Expenses are also incurred for credit and legal services pertaining to the collection of bad accounts. The nature of the functions and the work units applicable vary considerably with different types of business concerns.

Industrial engineering methods can be applied to establish standard times for these office operations. These are usually set in detailed, broad standards based largely on past experience, and are expressed as the number of man-hours required to process a large number of orders rather than the number of minutes per line on an order.

A company may employ a centralized typing unit to provide typing and transcribing services for all departments. Before setting the standards for this unit, a survey must be made to determine the work performed and the kind of typewriters (manual or electric) used. Because letters vary considerably in form and content, they should be divided into categories. If both electric and manual typewriters are used, a separate standard for each must be established for each type of letters.

The typing of each letter involves both uniform procedures, such as positioning the necessary paper and carbon in the machine, and variable factors, such as the length of the letter and the number of erasures made. A job audit listing all the activities and a corresponding standard time for each activity should be made. Observation can determine the standard variable rate per line in the body of the letter. Each standard should also contain allowances for rest and delay. Work sampling can be used to set standards for transcribing materials consumed.

For the credit and collection functions, the work units could be these:

Function	*Work Units*
Preparing invoices—handling	Invoice
Preparing invoices—line item	Order line
	Invoice line
Preparing customers' statements	Statement
	Account sold
Making street collections	Dollar collected
	Customer
Posting charges to accounts receivable	Number of postings per hour
	Invoice
	Shipment
Posting credits to accounts receivable	Number of postings per hour
	Remittances
	Account sold

Function	Work Units
Handling window collections	Collection
Credit investigation and approval	Sales order Account sold Credit sales transaction
Credit correspondence, records, and files	Letter Account sold Sales order Item
Total credit and collection	Sales order Credit sales transaction Account sold

Analysis of the information appearing on the invoices should be made before establishing standards for credit and collection. If the number of lines on individual invoices differs, standard costs based on the number of invoices prepared would be a poor measure of performance. Standard costs based on the number of invoice lines prepared would be a better measure of production.

General Distribution Activities

Certain general costs relating to distribution activities, such as accounting, office, and clerical costs, vary in importance in different concerns. Often these distribution costs are not of sufficient importance to be treated as separate functions. Distribution finance expenses are also included as a cost of general distribution activities. The financial expenses considered here include those costs incurred in securing capital and administering the financial program of the business.

Past experience and knowledge of the conditions within each sales territory should make possible the preparation of standards for many general distribution activities. Detailed studies of invoices and charges can often supply an adequate work unit for such joint costs as telephones, stationery, and supplies. Generally, if a standard is established for each type of office supply used by each territory, the most effective and economical use of the supplies will result.

Because many different kinds of jobs may be performed in an office (some of them at infrequent intervals), a common basis of measurement is essential. A simple procedure is to reduce the jobs to equivalent units. One job can be used as a standard in determining the relative weight of every other job. Then by applying these relative weights to the actual units produced, the equivalent units of work performed will be developed.

The following list shows the units of measurement that can be applied to general distribution activities:

Function	Work Units
General accounting including auditing fee, salaries of general bookkeepers, and accounting supplies	General ledger posting Customers' orders Invoice lines
Sales analyses and statistics	Order Invoice line
Financial expense	Ratio of total distribution cost to sales Ratio of average distribution investment to sales Ratio of inventory turnover
Personnel expense	Number of employees Number of persons employed, discharged, and reclassified
Filing and maintaining order and letter files	Order Letter Units filed
Mail handling	Number of pieces in and out
Vouchering	Number of vouchers
Sales auditing	Number of sales slips
Punching cards	Number of cards
Tabulating	Number of cards run
Cashiering	Number of transactions
Fixed Administration and market research	Time spent

Often home office employees are involved in more than one function; for example, a secretary may work for both the sales and advertising managers. Rather than classify such costs as general distribution, they may be separated according to the functions involved. Each home office employee would be asked to furnish a breakdown by function and territory on how his or her time is spent. The time sheets of these employees will indicate how many hours are devoted to each function. Executives salaries may be treated in a similar manner, depending upon the estimated time allocation.

STANDARDS FOR NONREPETITIVE OPERATIONS

Standards for order-getting activities cannot be based solely upon a sales forecast because some consideration must be given to market potential and the amount to be spent for getting business. Certain guides can be used by management in determining what standards to establish for order-getting costs. Management can vary the amount of order-getting costs in limited market areas to observe the returns obtained from increments in these costs, and the results from these tests can be used to provide measurements. Competitors' actions are also especially important, especially in the areas of advertising and sales.

Direct Selling

Direct selling includes all expenses of securing orders by direct contact. This function does not include advertising and sales promotion but only those distribution costs that pertain directly to securing orders. Since each sales territory is often a separate unit in the organization, direct selling expenses can usually be charged directly to territories. Generally there are two broad types of direct selling, repetitive and nonrepetitive. Repetitive selling is well adapted to the establishment of cost standards. On the other hand, nonrepetitive selling is difficult to standardize.

On the surface the setting of a standard time for each sales call may appear impossible because individual differences exist between salespeople and sales situations. However, much progress has been made in standardizing sales techniques in product presentation and in the showing of photographs and samples. The prevailing practice in industry of using well-developed sales training programs is evidence of this uniformity. Careful study and experimentation are necessary prerequisites for setting a standard time for each sales call.

Time measurements may be made by time-study observers accompanying each salesperson for a period of time. The problem with this approach is that the presence of an observer may cause atypical behavior or disturb or embarrass the salesperson and/or the customer during the sales visit. Often the most practical approach is to obtain the necessary information from supervisors and from sales reports and use it to write standard job descriptions and set standards for the number of accounts per salesperson and calls per day. A standard list of activities to be performed may also be compiled for salespersonnel to follow in the field. They would then be required to turn in daily reports showing the time spent with each customer and on each product sold.

Time analysis is concerned with increasing the efficiency of salespersonnel, while duty analysis has as its purpose the improvement of effectiveness of selling time. The procedures for both are essentially the same, but in duty analysis the results are used to measure the salesperson's activities. The content of the sales call is analyzed in more detail. For example, the number of products mentioned in relation to the number of products sold per sales call is investigated.

In determining the standard for selling salaries management should conduct a survey of the entire sales organization to examine the work performed by each salesperson in the different sales territories. This survey will provide the necessary data for setting a standard salary rate for each class of employee in each territory.

Business enterprises can set a standard per diem rate for meals and lodging; other traveling expenses can be established as a standard rate per mile. In preparing the standards for travel each territory will have to be studied for the purpose of estimating how many miles each salesperson and each supervisor must travel to accomplish his or her sales quota. The survey may be made in detail to show the number of calls to be made each day.

Since such conditions as the channels of distribution, terms of sales, and the product manufactured and sold vary between companies, the work units chosen will also vary. The type of assistance the salespersonnel are supposed to render to each customer and the number of products they are expected to sell must also be considered in establishing a standard for the number of calls each salesperson is to make. Consideration must also be given to the type of sales call to be made because if some calls can be performed by telephone rather than personal contact, the standard number of calls can usually be increased.

The cost accountant and the marketing manager should use the principles that are most logical under the circumstances. For example, a standard cost for sales salaries established on the basis of customer call is logical if the calls are relatively routine, and if on the average the salesperson spends the same amount of time with each customer regardless of the price bracket. But this approach would be unsatisfactory if the salesperson spends a different amount of time in his calls on customers in the different price brackets. In this case standard costs should be established according to the time spent with each customer.

Since selling expenses are influenced by many factors, different standards may be required for each territory. The type of geographical area covered and the means of covering it influence the expenditures required to keep a salesperson in the field. The size of the towns and cities in a given territory and the distances between them all directly modify the number of calls a salesperson can make and the cost of making these customer calls. Often companywide standard expense rates per call or day cannot be established because costs vary so greatly in different geographical areas.

A percentage of gross margin or of gross sales has been suggested as a basis for establishing standards for sales salaries and expenses. However, the position taken in this chapter is that a more direct and reliable relationship can be established by studying the behavior of direct selling costs compared to changes in the time spent on calls, distance traveled, number of customers, and number of calls. There are very few conditions where a percentage of gross margin or of gross sales can be used as the logical basis for establishing standards for direct selling expenses. All products must be equally easy to sell, all customers must be alike in their responsiveness, and markups must be uniform if these work units are to be used correctly. Standards can be established as a percentage of net sales when commissions and bonuses are given to salespersons in direct relationship to sales. Obviously the reason for incurring direct selling expenditures is to achieve sales goals; however, this achievement is subject to many factors over which salespersonnel have little control. Therefore, sales goals are not completely suitable units of measure.

Direct selling expenses may be controlled individually or totally by reducing them to unit costs on such bases as cost per work unit, as these examples show:

Function	*Work Units*
Salespeople's training and education	Number of salespeople Number of sales calls
Routing and scheduling of salespeople	Number of salespeople Number of sales calls
Making quotations	Quotations made
Salespeople's traveling expenses	Miles traveled Days traveled Sales call Customer Sales order

Function	Work Units
Telephone solicitation	Telephone call Order received
Salespeople's equipment	Sales call
Salespeople's salaries	Sales call Salesperson-hour
Commissions and bonuses	Net sales dollar Product units sold Sales call Sales order Sales transaction
Subsistence	Days subsisted
Payroll insurance and taxes and supplemental labor costs	Payroll dollars
Entertainment	Customer
Handling sales adjustments and returns	Adjustments and returns handled
General sales office expense and supervision salaries	Salespeople Sales transaction Sales order Salesperson-hour Customer account
Total direct selling	Cost per unit of product sold Cost per sales transaction Cost per sales order Cost per customer served

The sales representative who works the maximum number of workdays and makes the largest number of calls per day is usually the most valuable to the concern. Since these factors should be considered, standards for selling effort may also be set, using such bases as the minimum number of calls per day, ratio of orders obtained to calls made, and dollar value of average order. If a salesperson reported fewer calls than were made, the order-call ratio would be boosted and the number of calls per day would decrease. If a salesperson's calls per day were high but the order-call ratio dropped, this would likely indicate that he or she has been making many calls but not taking sufficient time to do a good selling job. The dollar value of average orders may reveal that a salesperson is calling frequently and successfully but is receiving only small orders.

Advertising and Sales Promotion

The major objectives of the advertising and sales promotion function are to create demand for the company's product and to establish and maintain consumer goodwill. Advertising and sales promotion activities range from the complex situation where all advertising is handled by the company to the simple situation where all advertising is handled by an outside firm. Direct media charges for companies that obtain advertising materials from outside sources would include agency commissions and advertising material charges. For companies that prepare their own copy, the direct media costs would consist primarily of charges for space in the different types of media and copy preparation. Individual standards could be established for the preparation of advertising copy on the basis of direct copy labor-hours or copy units prepared.

The advertising and sales promotion function is one of the most difficult distribution efforts to measure in terms of cost standards. Accurate and immediate cost standards can be applied to some advertising and sales promotion activities, but for such expenditures as institutional advertising the cost measurement must be very general in nature and applied to periods of considerable length. Some of the standards used for advertising and sales promotion are quantity measurements only and do not reflect the quality of the output. Past experience is used extensively as a guide in budgeting advertising and sales promotion because companies often feel a need for continuity over a period of years in these projects.

If all territories are served by an overall advertising manager and if each territory receives advertising assistance from the home office, these indirect expenses will have to be allocated to each territory. An analysis of the time and effort this executive devotes to each territory can be made to determine the standard cost for each territory.

Since many forms of advertising and sales promotion reach more than one territory, advertising expenditures may be considered a joint cost and allocated to the various geographical areas. A standard cost could be established on the basis of the number of families who listen on an average day or night to the radio or television station involved. This information can usually be obtained from the broadcast station itself. Advertising cost can then be allocated to the territories on the basis of the number of listening families in each geographical area. Magazine and newspaper advertising plans can be reduced to the amount of space used and the publication rate for each periodical. Publishers of periodicals can also supply data concerning the number of readers in each territory. Costs of advertising in periodicals then can be allocated on this basis.

The standards established for dealer aid, which includes window and store arrangement service, displays, and demonstrations, should be determined after a study has set the amount of service each territory is to receive and its cost has been estimated. Standard costs can then be determined for each unit or customer. Where catalogs are used as a form of advertising, a standard cost can be obtained for each catalog unit. The standard cost of catalogs for each territory can then be established by multiplying the number of catalogs distributed in each territory by the standard cost per catalog.

The work unit established for the advertising of a single product or several products on a national basis should be based on the utilization of the advertising activity by the territories, customers, or some other segment of sales. For example, information on the number of families who listen to the radio or television in each geographical area could be obtained and used as the work unit. Publishers of periodicals can also supply data concerning the number of readers in each territory. This data can be used to express the unit of measurement for advertising in periodicals.

A complete study of the advertising program for the budget period should result in setting a standard advertising and sales promotion appropriation for each advertising medium and for each sales territory. Here are some bases for developing standard costs per unit:

Function	Work Units
Demonstrations	Demonstration
Technical and professional publications	Inquiry received Unit of space
Samples distribution	Samples distributed
Direct media costs Newspapers	Sales transaction Newspaper inches Gross or net sales (where this is chief medium used)
Outdoor billboards and signs	Billboard and other outdoor sign units
Radio and television	Minute of radio or television time Number of set owners

Function	*Work Units*
Letters, circulars, calendars, and other direct mail	Gross or net direct mail sales Item mailed or distributed Inquiry received
Directories, house organs, and theater programs	Unit of space Inquiry received
Catalogs	Page or standard space unit Gross or net catalog sales when identifiable
Store and window displays	Day of window trimming and display
Entertainment of visitors at plants	Visitors
Advertising allowances to dealers	Unit of product cost Net sales
Dealers' help	Pieces or units Customers
Advertising administration (salaries, supplies, rent, miscellaneous administrative expenses)	Cost per dollar of net sales Cost per dollar of all direct advertising and sales promotional costs

Even though it is impossible to budget advertising on as factual a basis as production, experience has shown that careful planning of expenditures, and comparison of actual expenses with the budget, avoid wasteful spending without impairing effectiveness. Many people are under the impression that cost standards are always based on sound engineering studies and rigorous specifications. Although this approach is desirable, less scientific standards can provide a forceful way of presenting information for the purpose of stimulating corrective action.

Historical methods of analysis applied to advertising costs are not a safe test of efficiency, yet it is possible that problems of advertising costs can be solved without the use of standards. However, the use of cost standards allows management to examine advertising operations to a greater degree. They lead operating management to a better understanding of the cost and financial implications of its activities. Management decisions that result from employing advertising cost standards help improve the profit position of the company.

VARIANCE ANALYSIS

The analysis of cost variances is the first step in identifying the factors that caused the difference between the standard and actual costs so the inefficiencies can be eliminated. Variances may be either favorable or unfavorable. Favorable variances occur when the actual costs or hours are less than the standard costs or hours, unfavorable variances occur when actual costs or hours are more than the standard.

With variance analysis, management has an excellent opportunity to determine the source and cause of the difference between actual and standard costs. However, the interpretation of variances may be difficult. The standard cost variances associated with marketing costs must be analyzed carefully because it is easy to misinterpret the results. Suppose the average number of sales calls per day is six. If one salesperson is making ten calls per day and his salary is average, he will have a favorable variance even though he may be calling on customers of very small potential or may not be spending enough time with each customer to obtain results. Conversely, another salesperson who is averaging only three calls a day would have a high salary per call and an unfavorable variance, even though he or she may be obtaining very good results. In the process of evaluating marketing segments attention should not be focused solely on finding problem areas where goals have not been met. Instead favorable variances obtained because goals have been exceeded should be investigated. Management must establish criteria for determining if a variance is significant enough to be investigated because usually all variances cannot be investigated. In establishing the criteria such factors as the absolute size of the variance, the characteristic of the cost, and the size of the variance relative to the total cost incurred in that classification should be determined.

The discovery of the variance must be rapid if it is to be of real importance. The effectiveness of the control is often in direct proportion to the speed with which a change is recommended after an unsatisfactory operating condition is discovered. The quality and price of materials are best controlled prior to or at the time of purchase. Overhead costs should be analyzed as the decisions that create such costs are made.

Little has been accomplished in the development of marketing cost-variance analysis. Often companies do not attempt to break down the variance for a given cost item into causal factors. Only a net variance is developed for each cost item. (This approach is illustrated in Exhibit 5-6.) This practice is not to be encouraged because it

Exhibit 5-6.   XYZ Company territorial marketing expense analysis for the

Function	Work Unit	Total Actual Expense	Total No. of Units	Actual Unit Cost	Standard Unit Cost
Direct mail advertising	Pieces	$2,000	10,000	.20	.10
Sales salaries	Calls	900	500	1.80	2.00
Delivery	Cwt.	1,600	40,000	.04	.05
Loading	Cwt.	3,000	1,500	.02	.01
Billing	Lines billed	120	6,000	.02	.03
		$7,620			

allows inefficiencies to be easily concealed. To be meaningful, the variance must be further explained in terms of such causal factors as volume, price, and efficiency. A more detailed variance analysis can be computed as shown in Exhibit 5-7.

The salespeople are judged on their efforts, the results obtained, and the control of their expenses. In the analysis above there is a favorable net variance of $70. The favorable effort variance of $120 resulted from the salesperson's making 20 less calls than scheduled. It is favorable only in the sense that the lower number of sales calls resulted in a saving. This saving must be measured against the failure to make the standard number of calls, which limited coverage of this territory.

If the organization has access to electronic data processing equipment, a more elaborate variance analysis is feasible. Exhibit 5-8 illustrates a variance report for advertising and sales promotion. Each marketing function could be analyzed in identical fashion.

Disposal of Variances

Many marketing managers prefer to dispose of the variances for their operations on the income statement. They do not feel that goods manufactured in one period should be inventoried at different costs from those manufactured in other periods so long as the underlying operating conditions remain unchanged. These managers take the position that since standards are carefully determined and revised when necessary, the variance accounts reflect losses and gains resulting from factors related to efficiency. Also, the net variances are generally

year ending December 31, 19___.

	TERRITORY 1			TERRITORY 2		
	TOTAL ACTUAL COST	TOTAL STANDARD COST	VARIANCE*	TOTAL ACTUAL COST	TOTAL STANDARD COST	VARIANCE*
	$1,500	$ 800	$ (700)	$ 500	$ 200	$(300)
	540	600	60	360	400	40
	1,200	1,500	300	400	500	100
	1,600	800	(800)	1,400	700	(700)
	80	120	40	40	60	20
	$4,920	$3,820	$(1,100)	$2,700	$1,860	$(840)

*Unfavorable variances are in parentheses.

insignificant and do not materially affect the reported income of a period.

Independent Cost Analysis

After the preliminary work has been done, the accounts needed for the system may be set up in the general ledger. Distribution standards may be incorporated in the ledger accounts by debiting the accounts for each function with the actual cost and crediting them with standard costs for the number of service units performed.

Exhibit 5-7. XYZ Company detailed variance report.

STANDARD RATES	
Standard calls	200
Standard units	40,000
Standard cost per unit	$ .03
Standard cost per call	6.00
ACTUAL RESULTS	
Actual calls	180
Actual units	41,000
Actual cost	$1,160.00
ANALYSIS OF VARIANCE	
Effort (180–200) 20 calls at $6.00 standard rate	$+120
Results (41,000–40,000) 1,000 units at standard rate of $.03	+ 30
Cost control (180 actual calls × $6.00 = $1,080 standard cost—$1,160 actual cost)	− 80
Total variance	$+ 70

Exhibit 5-8.   XYZ Company expense variance report, advertising and

DETAILED FUNCTION	DESCRIPTION OF UNIT	(1) BUDGET @ STANDARD		
		QUANTITY	COST PER UNIT	AMOUNT
Demonstrations	Demonstration	20	$ 30	$ 600
Technical and professional				
publications	Unit of space	10	15	150
Samples distribution	Samples distributed	1,500	1	1,500
Direct media costs				
Newspapers	Newspaper inch	200	10	2,000
Outdoor billboards and				
signs	Outdoor sign unit per month	2	600	1,200
Radio	Minute of radio time	10	15	150
Television	Minute of			
	Local TV time	10	250	2,500
	National TV time	3	1,100	3,300
Letters, circulars, calendars,				
and other direct mail	Item mailed	3,000	1	3,000
Catalogs	Page	4	60	240
Store and window displays	Day of window trimming			
	and display	5	60	300
Entertainment of visitors at				
plants	Visitor	1,000	2	2,000
Totals				$16,940
Supervision				1,500
Rent				500
Total fixed				$ 2,000
Total function				18,940

*F = favorable variance; U = unfavorable variance.

Many organizations have not found this advisable because of the constantly fluctuating nature of marketing costs. Also, integration of marketing cost standards is not as important as it is for production cost standards because marketing costs are not usually charged to inventory.

Since marketing studies are often isolated measures with limited purposes, they may appear to be in conflict with one another and with existing accounting reports. They frequently fail to identify the significance of any variance and to determine whether the variance was due to random or causal errors. This leads management to doubt the credibility of both the studies and the existing accounting systems.

sales promotion, January, 19___.

	(2) ACTUAL @ STANDARD			(3) ACTUAL @ ACTUAL		VARIANCES*		
QUANTITY	COST PER UNIT	AMOUNT	QUANTITY	COST PER UNIT	AMOUNT	NET (3-1)	QUANTITY (2-1)	PRICE (3-2)
22	$ 30	$ 660	22	$ 29	$ 638	38U	60U	22F
8	15	120	8	16	128	22F	30F	8U
1,600	1	1,600	1,600	2	3,200	1,700U	100U	1,600U
210	10	2,100	210	11	2,310	310U	100U	210U
3	600	1,800	3	500	1,500	300U	600U	300F
12	15	180	12	14	168	18U	30U	12F
15	250	3,750	15	230	3,450	950U	1,250U	300F
5	1,100	5,500	5	1,200	6,000	2,700U	2,200U	500U
3,100	1	3,100	3,100	2	6,200	3,200U	100U	3,100U
6	60	360	6	62	372	132U	120U	12U
4	60	240	4	58	232	68F	60F	8F
1,500	2	3,000	1,500	3	4,500	2,500U	1,000U	1,500U
		$22,410			$28,698	11,758U	5,470U	6,288U
					1,500			
					500			
					$ 2,000			
					30,698			

When each marketing cost study is independent, the economies of an integrated information system are not present and the cost of the individual studies is often excessive in view of their potential value. Thus one of the major flaws in marketing cost systems has been the lack of a compatible data base. The segments used for demand studies are not compatible with the classification of customers used for accounting purposes. The external data base is different from the internal data base needed.

Some accountants feel that executives will take standard costs and variances more seriously and be more responsive to cost reduction efforts if the standard costs, and thus the variances, are entered in the ledger accounts. The incorporation of distribution cost standards in the accounting system does provide an orderly and somewhat compulsory plan of cost analysis.

Once the standards of performance have been established, performance must be measured against these objectives. A few companies still rely on personal observation. The marketing manager visits the division manager's office to observe performance, and sales managers make calls with salespeople to check their methods of presenting products. The advantages of personal observation are the time saved in communication and the firsthand appraisal of such intangibles as employee morale, customer reaction, and personnel development. The disadvantages are the lack cf consistency in measuring performance and the total time requirement. Oral reports of performance generally do not result in a permanent record, which is more usually achieved with interviews, committee meetings, and formal reports.

Increasingly organizations are using written reports to evaluate segments because they provide the advantage of a permanent record that can be reviewed at later dates. The evaluation can be made in many different forms, from statistical data to a chart. In requesting information from salespeople, the marketing manager must consider the tradeoff between time spent preparing reports and that spent in actual contact with the customers. If salespeople see that their reports are being used by management, and in a way that is beneficial to them, they will be less resentful of having to spend the time filling them out. In addition, salespeople must keep their own records to plan and direct their work. They must be aware of their daily accomplishments if they are to make their quotas.

The marketing manager must obtain accuracy and cooperation. For instance, a salesperson may increase sales calls or other work units so that he or she will have a favorable variance. There must be some internal check to see how these sales calls relate to orders obtained. But marketing managers should be more concerned with developing a positive management attitude and reasonable reporting demands to ensure accuracy.

SUMMARY

Control is a basic function of marketing management. Only sound control techniques that are effectively administered will protect the company's present and future operations. Marketing managers need to know when a segment is not meeting expectations. If short-term profit performance is to be meaningful, it must be accompanied by an understanding of the consequences of the costs being incurred.

While it must be admitted that it is difficult to establish standards for some marketing functions and that a greater tolerance must sometimes be allowed in the consideration of variances, much marketing activity is fully as measurable as production. Many of the same techniques used to establish production standards can be employed in selecting marketing cost standards. Those activities accomplished by human effort are usually amenable to reasonably accurate measurement employing less scientific techniques.

Standard costing cannot be the complete answer to evaluating market segments. Intelligent leadership is needed to use this tool. However, standard costing does hold the promise of being able to provide management with better understanding of marketing data.

6

Merchandising

THERE is some confusion over the exact meaning of the term *merchandising*. It is sometimes used synonymously with *marketing* to refer to all the movement from manufacturer to consumer. In retail and wholesale operations it is often used to mean the buyer's function of selecting the proper quantity, quality, and assortment of goods to carry in inventory. Merchandising is closely tied in with the organization's marketing strategy. An organization's strategy involves both the specific group of consumers it hopes will become the major buyers of the product to be distributed and the marketing mix. The marketing mix refers to the dollar allocation among the different elements—advertising, service, and personal selling—that make up the complete marketing plan.

TRENDS IN MERCHANDISING

Merchandising is said to fill any gap in the marketing plan that advertising and salespeople have not filled. Merchandising, then, is the sum total of all the activity required to move the finished product; it is accomplished only at the actual point of sale. Displaying the product is one form of merchandising; others are branding, packaging, and advertising.

126

Displays

Studies have shown that the majority of all sales decisions are made after the consumer arrives in the store. Effective displays are required to create this demand, and they should be changed frequently. There will, however, be additional costs every time displays are changed, and the accountant and the marketing executive should work closely together to determine the proper tradeoff between incurring new display costs and keeping the present displays.

Consumer goods manufacturers should be most concerned with having adequate retail distribution for all their products. This is especially crucial because if consumers do not see the product displayed, the chances are very slim that they will search for it. Research studies have shown that if the desired size of a brand is not displayed, consumers will switch to another brand in order to purchase the desired size.

Attention-Getting Devices

The merchandising aspect of consumer goods usually involves developing attention-getting devices or events. For example, detergent manufacturers may place a towel in each package and use this in their advertising to impress upon consumers that they are getting a free gift. Competition for fabulous vacation trips are also offered in consumer goods. Some suppliers use this technique and give the buying organization so many points for every item purchased. Once so many points are accumulated, the organization is entitled to dispense free gifts or trips to foreign countries.

Self-Service Retailing

Self-service retailing has also had a big impact on merchandising techniques. The growth of self-servicing has increased the importance of merchandising because businesspeople realize that there is increased selling power if the consumer is able to see and touch the product. Self-service retailing makes it easier for consumers to identify and select the product they wish to buy. It also permits a reduction in labor costs. Through display and promotion, the retailer is able to increase turnover.

With the advent of self-service, retailers began to realize that the traffic flow in a store is important. If items that are bought regularly, such as milk, bread, and eggs, are located strategically around the store, consumers are forced to walk through most of the store and hence see more products, which may induce them to buy more of these goods. A variation on this principle is to place high-profit items next to goods that are bought regularly. Goods that are likely to be bought on impulse, such as candy and chewing gum, are usually placed near the cash register so they are visible while the customer is waiting in line to be checked out.

Discount Stores

Discount stores grew out of the increasing wave of customer wants in the 1950s. Until then, mass merchandising had been used widely only in chain stores in the food, variety, and drug fields, though specialty stores and junior department stores had experimented with it.

There are so many combinations of discount stores that it is often difficult to distinguish them from "traditional" or "orthodox" stores. Nevertheless, discount stores will be defined in this chapter as stores that utilize many self-service techniques in their sale of a variety of soft and general merchandise. Their gross margin is very low and they must rely on high turnover and volume to stay in business. The term *discount store* carries the connotation of cheapness or the second-rate. This is because it was first applied to second-rate operations selling nationally branded merchandise at reduced prices. Gradually discount stores improved their appearance and expanded into suburban areas. Abundant parking space and bright neon lights were added to help improve their image. As the quality of the merchandise also improved, sales of seconds and distress merchandise were avoided.

Most discount stores utilize the self-service concept because it offers so many advantages. Shopping carts were added to facilitate the self-service operation. There is psychology behind the widespread use of shopping carts in that they imply abundantly filled shelves and ease of purchase. Though these techniques have helped to create a bargain atmosphere, many managers of these stores still avoid the use of the word "discount" in their sales promotions.

Customer acceptance of discount stores has been high; it is felt that much of this acceptance is due not only to the lower prices but also to the advantages of convenience in parking and shopping that these stores offer. Discount stores generally stay open longer, catering to those customers who prefer to shop at night. These longer hours allow the entire family to shop together after the working members of the family arrive home from their jobs. In addition, people feel they can shop in quite informal dress because of the informal atmosphere of the self-service store.

Discount food stores. Discount stores have now gone into food operations and have moved to the convenient locations in the suburbs, where there is plenty of parking space. The emphasis is still on price. Some discount stores succeed in their food departments because they are able to operate them with low overhead. Some of them, however, are subsidized by the store's other departments. The justification for this is that the low-priced foods attract customers into the store.

There is some question, though, whether discount food prices are lower than those in conventional food stores. Most marketing authorities who have studied the issue contend that indeed they are. One reason many discount food stores are able to sell at lower prices is because they have eliminated the expense of trading stamps. Other food discount stores have cut customer service departments and, in turn, their labor costs. However, the advertising expenses of most food discount stores are higher than they are for conventional food stores.

Discount store casualties. Several reasons are common to most discount store bankruptcies. Lack of management knowledge is one (but this is a common cause of failure in all store operations, whether of the mass-merchandising class or not). Still, discount stores are relatively easy to establish, and many people who went into the field did not have the necessary retailing expertise. This was particularly evident in the early days of discount stores when real estate developers set up stores on a leasing arrangement.

Lack of adequate working capital is another reason for failure among discount stores. Store owners often attempt to expand too rapidly without the necessary financing. Many of them feel that they are under pressure to "get big fast," and they operate on too large a scale.

An inadequate accounting and information system is another common error among mass merchandisers. Management does not get the feedback of data that it needs for decision making. Communication breakdowns are inevitable when the proper data flow is not provided for in advance. Lack of controls is still another reason for bankruptcies among discount stores. When internal control (policing) is inadequate to provide for the protection of the assets, shoplifting is often prevalent.

Scrambled Merchandising

During and after World War II strict separation of stores according to merchandise became much less evident. One reason for this trend was the environment. Stores were unable to get their regular merchandise line, so they purchased what they could since consumer demand was high. "One-stop" shopping became a way of life when many stores stocked both food and general merchandise and drugstores began carrying luggage, appliances, toys, and food.

Leased Departments

Many pioneer discount stores were able to carry a more complete line of merchandise because they relied on leases. Space was rented for a fee generally based on a percentage of sales. The lessee provided the inventory, working capital, personnel, and knowledge to operate the leased department. Today it is quite unusual for a relationship between the leased department and the store to continue indefinitely. If operations prove profitable, management may wish to assume full authority over all store activities. Once it has the necessary working capital to operate a more complete line, it will probably want to discontinue the leasing arrangement. This is why most successful lessees avoid associations with large chains.

Arguments between store management and the lessee arise easily. There must be some agreement regarding the prices charged; otherwise the leased department may ruin the "bargain image" of the store. Policies should be established in advance regarding advertising. If this function is assigned to store management, the amount of time and type of sales promotion to be used for the leased department should be specified in detail. Operators of leased departments are placed in a unique position. They are given little or no recognition and must blend in with the department store. Most department stores go to great lengths to prevent their customers from knowing which of their departments are leased.

Another hazard faced by lessees is the possibility that store management may have to discontinue operations. If management is incompetent, the leased department operations will suffer. There have been examples where a lessee, caught under a long-term lease, has suffered large losses because the store managers were inefficient.

STOCK TURNOVER

One measure of success for any retail store, whether it is of the discount variety or not, is high stock turnover. Stock turnover is an index often used by the retailer to measure the flow of goods in and out of a department store. It is expressed as the number of times that inventory has been turned over during the reporting period. A high stock turnover rate is reflective of efficient merchandising effort. Good sales promotion and selection of inventory, along with effective pricing strategy, work together to affect the turnover rate.

Calculation of a turnover rate for the overall retail store has little meaning. The real merit of stock turnover lies in breaking down the calculation to as limited a variation in the products as is feasible. Separate calculations should be prepared for each type of merchandise. Different products have stock turnovers that vary considerably. For example, furniture, quality jewelry, and luxury items normally have stock turnovers that are quite low. On the other hand, unless the turnover for food and other perishables is high, the firm cannot operate for very long.

Stock Turnover Rate

The stock turnover rate can be determined using either a unit or a dollar basis. The following equation should be employed if the figures are on a unit basis.

$$\text{Stock turnover rate} = \frac{\text{number of units sold}}{\text{average stock in units}}$$

The cost of calculating stock turnover rates on the basis of physical units should be matched against the benefit before preparation on a wide scale is undertaken.

Stock turnover rates can usually be more easily prepared using a dollar basis. This dollar basis can be expressed as either retail or cost. It is very important to use like measures and not mix cost and retail, which is like comparing apples and oranges. In both calculations an average inventory figure is needed; this is usually the period's beginning and ending inventory added together and divided by 2. Instead of adding beginning and ending inventory and dividing by 2, for greater accuracy some organizations add beginning monthly inventories and divide by 13.

If the cost dollar basis is used, the equation becomes:

$$\text{Cost turnover rate} = \frac{\text{cost of goods sold \$}}{\text{average inventory \$ at cost}}$$

If instead the inventory figures are maintained on a retail basis, the following equation is used:

$$\text{Retail turnover rate} = \frac{\text{net sales \$}}{\text{average inventory \$ at retail}}$$

MARKUP

The difference between the retail price and the cost of the inventory is referred to as the markup. This is what is left over from the sales price to cover other expenses such as administration and selling and to give the organization a profit. There are several types of markups. The initial markup is the one placed on the inventory when it is offered for sale. Markdowns may later be necessary to move the goods. Thus the markup finally realized on the sale is referred to as the maintained markup. The maintained markup is the difference between the net sales and the gross cost of goods sold.

Markup can be expressed as an absolute dollar amount or as a percentage. The markup has more meaning in assessing the effectiveness of a merchandiser's effort if it is expressed as a percentage. The markup percentage can be used as a guide in pricing merchandise so that expected expenses will be covered and a profit earned.

The basis for the markup may either be expressed on inventory cost or on retail selling price. Most department stores express their markup percentage on retail selling price. One argument for basing markups on retail is that no markup is earned until the product is sold. Merchandise cost does not change after the product reaches the retailer. Selling price, on the other hand, does change as the result of markdown, and this affects the final markup earned.

The same dollar markup will always be a smaller percentage if it is expressed on retail as opposed to cost. For example, assume a desired $20 markup with an $80 cost. Using the retail basis, sales price becomes the 100 percent figure. When the markup is expressed as a percentage, it becomes 20 percent:

Net Sales	100%	$100
Markup	20%	$ 20
Cost	80%	$ 80

If, instead, cost is the basis, the markup becomes 25 percent:

Sales	125%	$100
Markup	25%	$ 20
Cost	100%	$ 80

If cost is used as the basis for determining the markup percentage, the cost items included must be well defined. If the supplier's invoice price does not include transportation charges, this cost should be added to the invoice price. Additional problems may develop if a cash discount is available. Some authorities argue that a cash discount should not be deducted from the cost basis on which the markup is computed because there is no assurance that the discount will be taken. However, cost accounting principles argue that these are correct deductions from product cost. Purchase discounts lost represent a financing expense.

Industry Norms

Despite the problems associated with using cost as a basis, some smaller independent retailers continue to do so. It is more difficult to analyze markup based on cost because most of the industry norms provided by the different retail associations use sales price as their basis. For instance, members of the National Retail Merchants Association may submit their sales and cost figures to a division within the organization known as the Controllers' Congress. This division compiles the data and then expresses norms for different sales volume classifications as a percentage of net sales. The results are published in a pamphlet once a year.

Even though stores are not required to submit their cost percentages, so many stores participate in the survey that most retail store managers feel the figures are representative. Even so, there is a danger in establishing standards and budgets strictly on these industry figures; the peculiarities of each firm's operations should be given some consideration. In addition, common industry figures are not a sufficient basis in themselves because some organizations may employ account titles identical to the industry's but charge different cost items to the account.

There are several other organizations (such as the Retail Hardware Association) that prepare averaged results so their members can compare their own operating results against the industry norms. These usually express intermediate income and expenses as a percentage of net sales.

As can be seen, it is very important for the marketing executive to use the same basis as the norm when engaged in comparative analysis. This means that the manager should know how to convert a markup percentage based on retail to one based on the cost, or vice versa. Suppose he or she wants to compare the firm's operations, which use markup percentages based on retail, with those of another firm in the industry whose markups are based on cost. The following equation can be used:

$$\frac{\text{Retail-based markup \%}}{100\% - \text{retail-based markup \%}} \times 100\% = \text{cost-based markup \%}$$

If instead the manager wants to transfer from using cost as a base to calculating the markup percentage on a retail base, the following equation can be used:

$$\frac{\text{Cost-based markup}}{100\% + \text{cost-based markup }\%} \times 100\% = \text{retail-based markup }\%$$

ESTIMATING INVENTORY

Certainly a physical count of the inventory on hand must be made at year end. Frequently however, an estimate of inventory is needed when the taking of physical inventories is impractical either because of lack of time or because the cost would not be worth the effort involved. For interim statement purposes an inventory estimate is usually sufficient.

Gross Margin Method

There are several estimating procedures available; the two most common ones are the gross margin method and the retail inventory method. Exhibit 6-1 illustrates the gross margin method.

Exhibit 6-1. Gross margin method of estimating inventory.

Cost of goods available for sale:		
Beginning inventory		$ 65,000
Purchases during period	$140,600	
Transportation-in	9,900	
Total purchases	$150,500	
Less: Purchase returns and allowances	500	
Net purchases		150,000
Total merchandise handled—cost of goods available for sale		$215,000
Deduct estimated cost of goods sold:		
Sales	$219,000	
Less: Sales returns and allowances	2,000	
Net sales	$217,000	
Less: Estimated gross margin ($217,000 × 26%)	56,420	
Estimated cost of goods sold		160,580
Estimated cost of ending inventory		$ 54,420

The upper portion of the exhibit is identical to the portion of the cost of goods sold statement that relates to the cost of goods available for sale. This method assumes that the gross margin percentage will be approximately the same in the short run. The actual sales and gross margin for several past years should be used to find a gross margin that represents an average. The estimated cost of goods sold is calculated by applying the estimated gross margin percentage based on sales to net sales. The estimated gross margin is then deducted from net sales to arrive at an estimated cost of the goods sold. An estimate of the ending inventory is determined after the estimated cost of goods sold is substracted from the cost of the goods available for sale.

Many of the figures, such as beginning inventory, purchases, transportation, purchase returns and allowances, sales, and sales returns and allowances, are available from the accounting records. The gross margin percentage is based on recent past operations. Once the estimated cost of goods sold is determined, an estimate of the ending inventory can be computed. This is accomplished by subtracting the estimated cost of goods sold from the cost of goods available for sale.

In Exhibit 6-1 the gross margin percentage is based on sales. If instead gross margin is determined as a percentage of cost, a conversion of the rate on cost to a rate on sales is desirable.

Gross Margin Ratio

Gross margin is the difference between net sales and cost of the merchandise sold; it differs from the maintained markup realized on the sales if there are cash discounts or alteration expenses on the firm's markup. Gross profit or margin divided by net sales gives the gross margin ratio, which is quite helpful in evaluating operations. Analysis of the trend in gross margin percentage indicates how well the major expense item of cost of goods sold is being controlled. The gross margin ratio focuses on a very important aspect of performance.

Retail Inventory Method

Retail stores often find the retail method of inventory valuation appropriate because their inventory records are usually not on a perpetual basis, In addition, the retail inventory method can be used when a wide diversity of items is sold. Though initially introduced in department stores, the method has spread to many types of retail organizations.

The determination of gross margin and net profit under the retail method of inventory valuation differs from that under the gross margin method. Goods available for sale are computed at both cost and retail under the retail method. Ending inventory at retail is determined by subtracting sales from the retail value of the goods available for sale.

One feature of department store operation that makes it easy to apply the retail inventory method is that goods within a department usually have about the same markup. In addition, since articles are purchased and immediately priced for resale, markups, markdowns, gross margin, and analysis are usually related to sales price, not cost. The retail method has been actively sponsored by the National Retail Dry Goods Association as an approach in estimating inventory, if properly administered. Exhibit 6-2 illustrates the retail method.

Exhibit 6-2. Retail method of estimating inventory.

	AT COST	AT RETAIL
Goods available for sale:		
Beginning inventory (January 1)	$ 40,000	$ 60,000
Purchases during January	200,000	340,000
Total merchandise handled—net cost of goods available for sale	$240,000	$400,000
Cost ratio: $240,000/$400,000 = 60%		
Deduct January sales at retail		360,000
Ending Inventory (January 31):		
At retail		$ 40,000
At cost ($40,000 × 60%)	$ 24,000	

As can be seen, the beginning inventory and purchases must be valued at both cost and retail. Records must also be kept of any adjustment to the original marked retail price such as markdown, markdown cancellations, additional markups, markup cancellations, and employee discounts.

Both the gross margin and the retail methods are only estimates of inventory; they do not replace an actual physical count. At least annually a physical count should be made to check on the accuracy of the estimates. Errors in the records, loss through theft or breakage, incorrect use of the estimating procedures, and inaccurate physical count are just a few of the factors that can cause some discrepancy between the estimate and the actual quantity count.

The retail estimating procedure provides for interim control of inventory, markups, and markdowns, and many department stores use it for each department for interim control purposes. The retail method eliminates the marking of cost codes on the merchandise. The inventory sheets can be kept at retail; the retail value is then converted to cost by applying the retail inventory method without referring to the cost of individual items.

Store Systems

Regardless of the estimating procedure used, accurate records must be maintained for sales revenue. A multiple cash register may be adequate for gathering the source data for a single store, and even four or five stores. However, for more complex or larger operations a more sophisticated form of data processing is needed. Analysis by department and merchandise classification is necessary. Some stores accomplish this by placing a code number on the price tag; the cashier rings up the code number when the sales price is recorded.

DISCOUNTS

The merchandising policy must state what the organization's course of action will be with regard to discounts. Two types of discounts are commonly used. One is the trade discount, which is not recorded in the accounting records; the sales price is the amount after the trade discount is deducted. This is a device used by a vendor for quoting sales price. Trade discounts should not be confused with cash discounts, which are price concessions given to encourage early payment of an account.

Trade Discounts

A trade discount is a certain percentage deducted from the list price. The result is referred to as the net price for the buyer. Trade discounts are widely used; however, the actual percentage discount varies among different industries. Sometimes a series or chain of discounts is offered the retailer. These discount percentages cannot be added and applied against the list price to arrive at the correct net price. For example, suppose a retailer receives the following trade discounts: 5 percent, 10 percent, and 2 percent against a list price of $100. These should not be added to arrive at a total of 17 percent, giving an incorrect net price of $83. Instead the first discount of 5 percent is applied against the $100 list price to give a $5 discount or a $95 net price. Next the 10 percent discount is applied against $95 to give a $9.50 discount or a net price of $85.50. Finally the 2 percent discount is applied against $85.50 to give a $1.71 discount or a $83.79 net price.

Cash Discounts

A cash discount is offered as an inducement for payment in advance of the due date. A common cash discount uses the terms 2/10, n/30, which means the seller will allow 2 percent to be deducted from the invoice price if the merchandise is paid for within 10 days; otherwise the amount is due within 30 days. *Dating* is the term given to the process in which the buyer and seller agree as to the date on which the discount begins. Since several dates are involved for each purchase—such as the date of invoice, the date of the receipt of goods, and the date represented by the end of the month—it is important that the parties agree in advance when the discount period begins.

With a cash discount term of 2/10, n/30, the buyer is able to save 2 percent of the invoice price by paying the bill 20 days early. This represents an annual rate of interest that is higher than the going rate. For that reason organizations should consider borrowing funds to pay the invoice within the discount period. The following formula may be used for calculating the annual cost of not taking cash discounts:

$$\text{Cost} = \frac{\text{discount percent}}{(100 - \text{discount percent})}$$
$$\times \frac{360}{(\text{final due date} - \text{discount period})}$$

For illustration, assume the terms are 2/10, n/30. The annual cost, expressed as a percentage, would be:

$$\frac{2}{98} \times \frac{360}{20} = .0204 \times 18 = 36.73\%$$

Since the interest rate is so high, this is another reason why the organization should have adequate working capital.

BRANDING

The merchandising and distribution of a product is easier if the branded item has been advertised. If consumers are informed enough to ask the retailer for a specific product, the wholesaler's task of selling it to the retailer is made much easier. Therefore brands should be adopted and promoted to create strong demand.

The brand name is a copyrighted means of labeling an organization's product. A brand may be a circle, square, or some other geometrical form combined with lines or dots. The generic name of the product may not imply quality to a consumer as well as the labeled, branded, and advertised product does. But when a brand name becomes so well known that it is almost part of the language, it ceases to serve its original purpose. For example "Coke," a registered brand name of the Coca-Cola Company, is often used to refer to any carbonated soft drink. The registered brand name of Kimberly Clark Company, "Kleenex," is frequently used to describe any facial tissue.

Trademarks

Trademarks are different from brands in some sense because they have legal connotations. Trademarks are registered when the product is shipped in interstate or foreign commerce. They must have some distinctive characteristics such as a symbol or lettering that separates them from a common English word.

Purpose of Branding

Perfect competition is practically impossible today because once a product is branded, it assumes a quality all its own. Branding allows for product differentiation and mass communication that allows customers to identify it easily. Its basic purpose is its distinguishing ability that removes the product from pure competition. This differentiation allows the marketing executive to have some degree of control over the product—though the control may backfire because customers know whom to contact if the product does not meet their expectations.

Familiarity of brands is very important and is usually created by advertising. There would be no point to advertising if there were no brands because a company's advertising campaign would promote only the product, its competitors' as well as its own. If the brand label were removed from some products such as cigarettes, many consumers could not distinguish between brands. This is where the merchandiser's function becomes important—he or she must develop brand identification and preference.

Some products are not as appropriate for branding as others. The identity of the product is lost if it is assembled or placed inside another item and is not visible. For products of this nature, sales promotion can overcome anonymity to some extent by emphasizing the product that contains the branded product.

Brand Image

The act of branding by itself has little marketing significance unless the organization is willing to spend the necessary money in sales promotion to create the brand image and identity. In selecting a brand name, the marketing executive must be sure that it has not been used by another product. The brand chosen should fit the image that the organization is trying to create. Many people think that the brand should have a jingle or rhythm that makes it easy to memorize.

Organizations attempt to find some distinctive features in their products so these can be used to create a special image for themselves in the market. The personality surrounding a brand is referred to as the *brand image.* Composed of real or imaginary qualities, the brand image is the picture that arises in the consumer's mind when the product is mentioned. It includes both the product's physical features and what the public conceives the product to be. One consumer will perceive a brand in one way, while a second consumer will perceive it in another way. The picture that consumers have of a product is very important regardless if it has been formed objectively or subjectively.

Brand image is especially important for products that are consumed in the presence of others. These products take on a special meaning because of the social environment in which they are used. The high-status image of Cadillac and Lincoln automobiles has been developed perhaps as much through advertising as through high engineering standards and product quality.

Whenever a customer's reference group exerts strong pressure, there should be a trenchant emphasis on brands in advertising. This applies to products such as furniture, clothing, and magazines. Reference group influence is likely to be strongest when the product is conspicuous—for example, food or drink that is used in entertaining and home furnishings.

Since every brand has an image, good or bad, it is important for management to decide what attitudes it desires in its customers. Since the image is formed through mass communication as well as by exposure to the product itself, management should plan its advertising, sales promotion, and packaging to help create the image desired.

Family Names

Sometimes the same family brand is applied to several products for different purposes. One is to assemble a complete product line. Another is to create a good brand image that can be easily transferred to new products when they are introduced in order to reduce the amount of money that has to be spent in promoting a new product. Some companies permit individual brands to be identified with the overall organization only briefly in the introductory stage. Their ultimate purpose is to promote competition among their own product lines and make each brand independent.

Greater visibility is achieved if products carrying the family brand are placed side by side on store shelves. Family brands allow for greater repetition of the brand name because each time consumers see an item in the product line, they see the brand. If customers are satisfied with one product bearing the family brand, they will be more likely to try another product bearing the family brand.

Family names do have some weaknesses, however. Individual products lack distinctiveness, and a major failure for one product can hurt the image of other products. Consumers' attitudes toward the entire family of products can become negative simply because one product fails to live up to their expectations.

Private Brands

Many retailers buy unbranded merchandise and then attach their own private brand to it. The significance of private brands is that they are confined to a certain chain of stores. If the store's name is well advertised and trusted, there will be a carry-over to the brand, and it will not have to be advertised separately. However, private brands have the strong limitation of being expensive to develop. A single store that has a limited advertising budget could not support the expense of private brands.

It is interesting to study consumers' attitudes toward products bearing private labels and identical products with nationally advertised brands sitting beside each other on the store shelf. Both products may have been manufactured by the same firm; one has been marketed under its brand name and the other has been sold in bulk for private labeling. Even though the private-labeled product has a cheaper price, the branded item may outsell it for psychological reasons. People who do buy private or off-brands usually do so for the cost saving, so reduced prices can transcend brand preference. The buyer of off-brands often rationalizes his or her avoidance of well-known brands by citing an unwillingness to pay for the company's advertising.

Reseller Brands

A firm may find it profitable to produce for reseller branding if it has idle production capacity. Thus it is able to utilize whatever capacity is not being used to produce its own products and earn a contribution to the firm's profit.

There is some danger in producing for reseller brands because the manufacturer is often making goods for a competitor. This is especially true if products of the same quality are involved and if the geographical area serviced by the manufacturer and the reseller is the same. However, if the reseller does not obtain his products from the manufacturer, he may turn to alternative supplies. So if the manufacturer refuses the reseller's business, he will have lost this contribution to fixed costs and income. The marketing executive should rely upon the accountant to supply the contribution margin involved. Then management will have to determine what, if any, market the reseller is capturing from the firm. The market captured will usually be much smaller if the reseller is interested in a different-quality product.

Brand Loyalty

Experimental evidence shows that brand loyalty results from both effective marketing strategy and the consumer's own need to be loyal to a brand. Sometimes brand loyalty can develop even though there is no objective reason for it.

The cohesiveness of the reference group influences the brand loyalty of its members. The more cohesive the group, the higher the probability that its members will prefer the same brand as the group leader.

Many authorities question whether there is such a thing as true brand loyalty. Certainly there is brand preference, but many things can cause a customer to switch from one brand to another.

Probabilistic Brand-Choice Models

Probabilistic brand-choice models assume that consumer behavior can be predicted by mathematical formulas. Predictions are based on readily observable data rather than on attempts to understand buying behavior by tracing it to its ultimate causes. Many people feel that these models give more accurate results than behavioral science techniques, which focus attention on the causes of behavior. Through the use of these models, marketing executives obtain a better insight into the nature of brand loyalty and brand-choice behavior.

In the following brief discussion of stochastic models, no attention will be given to the mathematics of the model or to measurements problems, and little effort will be made to summarize the models of individual behavior into market models of group buying behavior. Only a few generalizations will be given.

Buyer behavior is seen as a probabilistic or random process in a stochastic model. The probabilities that a consumer will purchase a certain brand form the major elements of the model. Marketing strategy, price policies, and product characteristics each affect the probabilities. Brand loyalty and switching can be studied through three different stochastic models: the learning-theory models, the Markov models, and the zero-order models.

Learning-theory models. Learning-theory models were the earliest brand-choice models; they were devised by several mathematical psychologists who were researching the learning and forgetting of simple tasks. Even the most brand-loyal customer may switch to other brands because he or she wants a change or has been encouraged to try another brand because of price or some other marketing strategy.

The consumer who vows never to buy a certain brand may later actually buy that brand. Learning theory also says that once a customer buys a specific brand, there are identifiable probabilities that that customer will purchase the same brand again or switch to another brand. Learning-theory models are based on the premise that all previous brand choices do affect the consumer's next brand choice.

Markov models. Rather than depending on the premise that all brand choices in the past affect future brand choices, the Markov models consider only the buyer's last few brand purchases. The simplest model of this type, the first-order Markov model, considers only the next-to-last choice in relation to the last choice.

Zero-order models. Zero-order models consider the consumer's choice in a single time period without reference to his or her prior brand choices. The learning of brand choices is not considered; instead supporters of the zero-order model feel that the probabilities of brand buying remain unchanged despite the passage of time. They feel that in the short run the consumer displays considerable loyalty to certain brands and this inertia enables researchers to predict future behavior without investigating past behavior.

Expert statistical skill is needed to use stochastic models. The basic assumptions behind the model must be clearly defined. There is a mixed feeling among marketing scholars as to the benefit and validity of results gained from stochastic models. However, they are a useful tool for firms that want to test the influence of promotional activities on brand switching if these firms find it profitable to make the necessary expenditures for gathering marketing data and obtaining skilled analyses.

This is where the accountant and the marketing executive must work closely together to determine how much advertising is required to create enough brand loyalty to allow a price differential. For example, suppose they find that 10,000 units of their branded item can sell at a 5-cent price differential in a specific market, but that it requires $6,000 of advertising to create this much brand loyalty. They should question the benefit of this advertising expenditure. Before deciding that they have really lost $1,000 ($5,000 total price differential − $6,000 advertising), they should determine if there is any future to branding or any carry-over to other products of the organization.

FORECASTING

One of merchandising's functions is to establish plans and goals for each of the organization's segments. These goals can be expressed as desired markups or stock turnover rates. Sales volume must be estimated because it will become the basis of the sales planning function. In forecasting future sales, data is needed from both external and internal sources.

Sales Planning and Internal Factors

In forecasting the demand for an organization's products, reference should be made to historical demand. Unfilled orders, together with past sales data, would indicate a figure close to past demand. Unfortunately, most companies do not keep a record of orders that were not filled. When this record is unavailable, future demand estimates are based only on those past demands that were satisfied—which is reflected in historical sales.

A trend may be projected through studying actual sales for the corresponding period last year and for several previous years. There is a danger in using only historical sales data in the forecasting procedure. The internal environment may have changed, which will have an effect on future sales. For example, the organization may have changed its credit policy so that the new, more liberal credit terms act as a stimulator on sales. A certain department may have changed its location within the store, and this could affect sales. For instance, a move from an isolated location on the fourth floor to a more prominent one on the ground floor may make a marked change in the department's sales pattern.

The simplest way of using past data in forecasting is to average all available data for a specific number of past periods. The limitation of this approach is that the most recent historical data is given no more significance than data from accounting periods years before. This would be a drawback in the changing market environment that is typical for most organizations. This limitation would also apply if the company has changed any of its major features.

Moving averages overcome the weakness of the simple average since they employ only recent data. Data from periods a year or more in the past is not used in arriving at the average. In addition, the average is updated each month by dropping the oldest data and adding the most recent figures.

In forecasting sales, not only indicators of market potential but also estimates of the amount of marketing effort that will be made on behalf of the products involved must be used. If the organization is experiencing some labor problems or unrest, the possibility of a strike should be considered. Likewise, if an expected shortage of material might slow down production, the effect of this should be included in the forecast.

Sales Planning and External Factors

In addition to the many internal factors that affect sales, there is a host of external factors that have varying impacts on future sales. Obviously management has much less control over these external factors.

There are many different kinds of external information that can be used. If a causal relationship can be established, the forecaster may have better success in his or her estimates. For example, past results may show that there is a relationship between sales and disposable income or gross national product. A relationship may be established between the organization's product and other products.

The state of the economic and social environment plays a significant role in forecasting sales. If unemployment is high and everyone is pessimistic that conditions will turn around in the near future, a conservative sales forecast should be made. An increase in the number of the organization's competitors as well as more aggressive sales promotion by the present competitors will likely cut into future sales unless counteraction is taken. Likewise, the impact of expected changes in fashion or fad should be considered.

Closely related to market potential is the type of economic and social environment in which the products will be offered for sale. Anticipated changes in the federal government's monetary and fiscal policy should be studied to see what effect they will have upon the organization's business activities. Tax code revisions for both business and personal taxes are important considerations. Government policies on taxation, international trade, and the national economy are but a few of the environmental factors that affect the firm's sales. Even though the government's monetary and fiscal policy is designed to influence general economic conditions and not one particular firm, it can have a particular influence, and this should be foreseen.

Price Index

Accountants use present dollars to report their results, which means that the dollars are mixed as to the price index. In a period of galloping inflation, this becomes a crucial problem. Management may be delighted with increasing sales dollars. Yet, in reality, sales volume has not increased. The firm may be selling the same amount of merchandise at higher prices. If the cost of the merchandise has gone up by the same percentage, the organization is not in a better market position. In forecasting sales dollars the change in prices should be considered.

Forecasting with Prices Held Constant

If it is assumed that the sales price will remain constant, one of the complexities of forecasting is eliminated. Suppose that analysis of past sales data reveals the following:

	Last Year	*This Year*
January	$20,000	$30,000
February	24,000	33,000
March	28,000	

The trend experienced this year is 10 percent calculated as follows:

$$\frac{\$3,000}{\$30,000} \times 100\% = 10\%$$

February's increase over last year is 37.5 percent, as follows:

$$\frac{\$9,000}{\$24,000} \times 100\% = 37.5\%$$

This is somewhat less than the 50 percent increase experienced between January of this year and January of last year, which is calculated as follows:

$$\frac{\$10,000}{\$20,000} \times 100\% = 50\%$$

On the basis of these calculations and a consideration of other factors, management may forecast that the percentage increase of March sales will be less than 37.5 percent over March of the preceding year. If a 25 percent increase is used, March sales are forecasted as:

$$\text{Planned March sales} = \$28,000 + (25\% \times \$28,000)$$
$$= \$28,000 + \$7,000$$
$$= \$35,000$$

This is an increase over February sales of 6.06 percent, which is calculated as follows:

$$\frac{\$2,000}{\$33,000} \times 100\% = 6.06\%$$

Forecasting with Fluctuating Sales Price

A more realistic approach is to assume that there will be price increases along with changes in sales volume. For example,* assume that a price rise of 15 percent is expected next year. This price rise, together with other factors, will cause a decrease in sales volume of 6 percent. Last year's total sales were $100,000, with an average sales price of $20, giving 5,000 individual transactions, as follows:

$$\frac{\$100,000}{\$20} = 5,000$$

Reflecting the price increase, this year's sales price will be:

$$\$20 \times 115\% = \$23$$

The number of transactions will decrease by 6 percent, giving 4,700 individual sales transactions:

$$5,000 - 300 \, (6\% \times 5,000) = 4,700$$

Next year's forecast sales, on the basis of this formula only, will be:

$$\$23 \times 4,700 = \$108,100$$

*This example was adapted from Albert P. Kneider, *Mathematics of Merchandising* (Englewood Cliffs, N.J.: Prentice-Hall, Inc., 1974), p. 173.

This computation results in an $8,100, or an 8.1 percent, change in sales:

Next year's sales = $108,100
Last year's sales =   100,000

Forecasted changed in dollar
           sales = $ 8,100

$$\frac{\$8,100}{\$100,000} = 8.1\% \text{ forecasted increase in dollar sales}$$

Forecasting Techniques

Many forecasting techniques use macroeconomic models that are supposed to represent the business economy. These models allow the forecaster to combine his or her knowledge of economic data, seasoned judgment, and intelligence to predict future economic activity. The inputs are expressed in national income accounting terms and are gathered from a variety of government sources. The use of national income accounting enables the forecaster to measure total economic activity and then break it down into business segments.

Executive Input

The experienced judgment of key executives within the firm may be used in forecasting. These subjective estimates of future demand are based on intuition and evaluation of market conditions, and reflect many things that are often difficult to quantify, much less define. Though the manager's knowledge is built on experience, less tangible factors such as his or her philosophy of life (whether optimistic or pessimistic) will influence the estimates made.

The importance attached to executive input varies from firm to firm. In some organizations management's evaluations are used to refine sales forecasts developed through other sources. In others the sales forecasts of the key executives form the first step in the forecasting process; to their estimates scientific techniques are applied. In small, owner-managed organizations executive judgment is relied upon almost exclusively because there is little or no numerical information about the future available. Mathematical forecasting is most effective for products that have a stable market pattern. A firm that manufactures goods whose market fluctuates considerably, and whose sales require extensive promotion, must usually rely on subjective estimates.

New Product Forecasting

In forecasting the demand for new products there is no historical data to rely upon. Past experience must be used. The experienced forecaster may have made demand estimates for other new products. He or she must analyze how accurate these estimates were, and if there is any similarity between this new product and others that have been introduced.

Even though the factors involved in making subjective estimates cannot be quantitatively analyzed separately, they should not be discredited completely. In almost all circumstances, even when numerical data is available, objective estimates are further refined by executives expertise and intuition.

Sales Force Estimates

The organization's sales force, resellers or agents, should also provide an input in the forecasting process. Their input can be extremely useful, but only if certain inherent weaknesses are recognized at the outset. Salespeople often have quite limited views on the future plans of the overall organization because of their level within the firm. Obviously, then, their estimates will be made from a narrow viewpoint. On the other hand they are closer to the actual consumer and may be better able to assess the market potential and environment than the forecaster. Customers may reveal their future buying plans to a sales representative with whom they are in daily contact.

Just as expenditure budgets contain "fat" or "buffers" when they are prepared by the person who will be held accountable, so do salespeople's forecasts when they become quotas against which the individual will be evaluated. The "buffer" in this case takes the form of conservative estimates. The average salesperson will provide him or herself some leeway in case the market is not as successful as it is perceived to be. For this reason the estimates of the sales force should be reviewed before they are submitted to top management.

Customer Surveys

Questionnaires may be mailed to gain information from customers as to their buying intentions. Hired interviewers can also be used for this purpose. The positive features of such surveys overcome the many negative ones if there are only a few, large customers. However, regardless of their numbers, customers must be willing to provide information about their future buying behavior. Of course, if they are willing to cooperate in revealing this information but do not really know their future purchasing plans, they will be of little or no use.

Projection

Projection is the simple forecasting technique of extrapolating a series of historical data into the future. The organization's sales may be plotted on graph paper and an "eyeball" fit of a straight line to the data then made. The historical data may also be analyzed mathematically and percentage increases applied to historical sales.

The projection method assumes that the independent variable is time and the dependent variable sales volume. However, there is no causal relationship between these two because time does not cause anything. The factors that cause sales volume to change are not considered in the projection method. Projection simply looks at the past to determine what the future will be; the forecaster should also look at those conditions that will influence sales in the future.

Regression Analysis

Projection techniques assume that the future will be similar to the past. They can be replaced by more sophisticated methods such as the regression-fitting technique.

Regression analysis is a forecasting technique that estimates the extent of the relationship between two variables. It measures the tendency of the dependent variable to change as the independent variable changes. The dependent variable would be the sales volume and the independent variable could be various measures of marketing activity, such as sales promotion dollars and number of salespeople. Population, income, and other measures of market potential could also assume the role of the independent variable.

Time Series Analysis

Time series analysis breaks down historical sales volume data into four basic components: trend, seasonal, cyclical, and random elements. If the time series model is multiplicative, the trend would first be identified and then the other components would be treated as corrective factors. If the model is additive, each component would be added to give a sales prediction.

The trend factor in a time series analysis takes into effect the expected growth or decline in the product's sales. The seasonal component reflects recurring and regular patterns of time, such as the month-of-year and day-of-week factors, which influence demand. The cyclical component results from basic factors in the business cycle or other regularities in the demand variations that occur in time periods extending beyond the length of the forecasting period. Any change in demand that cannot be explained by the other three components is said to be caused by random factors.

Regression and time series analysis can be done efficiently with a computer. Even though the technical aspects of the statistical procedures involved are beyond the understanding of most marketing executives, they should know these techniques are available so that they can arrange for them to be performed by the people with the necessary skill. Forecasts of general business activity, reliable seasonal adjustments, and enough regularity in the basic demand pattern are necessary to make the time series analysis meaningful.

Documentation

The forecasts should be written. There are certain underlying assumptions for each forecast, and these should be stated at the outset and well documented. Major national catastrophes fortunately do not happen often enough to be included in most underlying forecast assumptions; however, if one should occur, it would destroy the accuracy of most forecasts. For this reason there should be a statement to the effect that it is being assumed that such a catastrophe will not occur.

Documentation of the assumptions allows the forecast user to evaluate the significance of each assumption. The documentation should also list the major sources of information and the techniques used to arrive at the final forecast. All this data provides a good basis for a review of the accuracy of the forecast, and enables the forecaster to refine his or her techniques and assumptions so that future estimates will be more accurate.

Summary

In forecasting future sales some of the factors mentioned in the chapter will have only a short-run impact, while the effect of other factors can be expected to continue for a long time. Several external and internal factors were mentioned. Management must evaluate its own case to see which of these factors apply to the industry as a whole and which apply only to a specific organization.

The mathematical computations given in this chapter should not be used blindly. Good judgment is required so that only the appropriate computation will be applied to a specific circumstance. None of the merchandising techniques discussed here can replace a sound marketing plan.

7

Planned Packaging

SINCE World War II packaging has grown from a mere way of covering and shipping a product into a market force all its own. The widespread use of self-service retailing has made the package an essential part of many products. Many companies find today that their packaging control and organization have not expanded rapidly enough to handle the many new complexities. Now this business embracing papers, metals, glass, and plastics is being broken down into specialties within specialties. Package designers are being forced to become specialists, for business is realizing the important role packaging plays in marketing.

IMPORTANCE OF PACKAGING

Before the advent of self-service retailing, the consumer had fewer choices to make in purchasing goods. He or she relied to a large extent on the judgment and recommendations of a salesperson. In most cases the goods bought were counted or measured out in view of the shopper. Now that self-service has eliminated much of this personal merchandising, the relationship is between the package and the buyer. The burden of communicating the product's features and why it is a better buy than competing products rests on the package.

The problems of packaging are the same whether the product is for personal or for manufacturing use.

The package serves not only as the container for the goods but also as a means of communication. With so much competition, firms have to rely on effective packaging to sell their products. Descriptive phrases such as "Good to the last drop" are designed to induce the consumer to buy a particular brand. The package strives to differentiate the product in the user's mind. Thus packaging is one of the components in the marketing mix that leads to a sale.

Functions

Since it serves so many functions, packaging is a problem for both the product manager and the sales manager. While some products require no packaging, most use both a retail and a wholesale package. The wholesale package's purpose is to protect the contents while in transit and in storage. If the product is not solid, some form of container is required. Liquids must be packaged so that they will be portable. Some products even have to be packaged in several containers; for example, soft drinks may be packaged in a bottle, these bottles are placed in a carton, and several dozens of these cartons are placed in a box for delivery to the wholesaler. Obviously the amount of packaging adds to the cost of the product.

Another obvious function of packaging is to protect the product and facilitate handling during distribution. Some products are delicate and break easily and thus would be most difficult and expensive to move if they were not packaged. Foods and other products require packages for protection. (Many foods would spoil if a package did not protect them from oxygen, moisture, and sunlight.) The package may continue to serve a function after it reaches the consumer or it may serve as a dispenser for the product. Sometimes the product is physically consumed directly from the package.

Packaging is an element of merchandising policy related primarily to product identification and consumer choice. Market research has shown that packages are not just protective containers; they have the ability to promote sales through the creative use of symbols, colors, and designs. Innovative packaging can change the total effect of the product as perceived by the buyer. The package must be sufficiently distinctive to be easily recognized by potential customers. It must help build consumer confidence in the product it contains. If the package does not persuade the consumer to buy the product, it is nothing but a container.

Packaging designs are used to encourage impulse buying in all stores, especially in self-service outlets. Good packaging can substantially stimulate sales of consumer and industrial products by improving display and utility and by facilitating handling and storage. The package must attract customers' attention. This is the reason so much emphasis is placed on correct design and use of color. Since everyone loves a mystery, an intriguing package may induce customers to buy the product just so that they can open the package. This stimulation of desire is especially evident in the dry cereal business. These packages offer deals, sets, and combinations that appeal to children. What the package says is more important to this group of prospective customers than the item itself.

Complex Business

It is essential for manufacturers to realize that packaging today calls for the employment of highly skilled designers with trained imaginations. Artists designing labels must creatively portray the objectives defined by marketing strategy. If they are to fully satisfy the manufacturer's needs, designers should understand production processes and know how to investigate the properties of materials. They should also know how to relate these properties to the needs of consumers. Some packaging designers work within the company, while others are brought in from outside. Often the producers of packaging materials and machinery can offer valuable advice. These outsiders have a specialized knowledge that can greatly aid in solving a firm's packaging problems.

Cost

For some products the packaging may be more expensive than the ingredients going into the product. Packaging cost is especially high for food products, accounting for up to 10 percent of the retail price. With so large a cost outlay, the firm should be getting something besides a container for its product. The package should noticeably increase the attractiveness and salability of the product.

Almost any conceivable package shape or color can be produced, but the cost of an unusual package may be prohibitive. The package production machinery must be considered. If highly specialized machinery is required to produce a certain shape, the accountant and marketing executive must determine whether this machinery can be used if this particular package shape is changed. Some individualized shapes can be inexpensively made from plastic or glass molds; in these cases the cost of the package will be small in relation to its power in generating sales. The purchase and use of packing and wrapping supplies is an area in which significant reductions in cost can be made. Because of the competitiveness of most businesses, all expense items should be constantly reevaluated for possible cost reductions. And since consumers' purchasing habits change, the packing and wrapping used must be periodically reviewed to accommodate these changes.

Regulatory Requirements

The product label may also serve as a means of informing and educating the consumer. This is especially true for drugs, products that must be used or served in a special way, and dangerous products such as poisons.

Before finalizing the packaging plans, government and industry regulatory requirements should be studied. Some carriers have regulations that are stricter than the legal requirements. Even if the Food and Drug Administration does not require the manufacturer to inform users of the nature of the product, the smart marketing executive will use the label to help the consumer receive maximum benefit from the product.

People are also entitled to know the product's ingredients simply because they feel more secure having this information. Those who are allergic to certain substances need to know a product's content to protect themselves. The package may also contain some information about the product and proven methods of preparation. Recipes are often used on food products for this purpose. Many marketing executives overlook an inexpensive form of direct advertising to prime prospects by failing to include inserts in the package.

Consumers' Behavior

Knowing the targeted customer's characteristics and what he or she wants is just as important in package design as it is in product development, advertising, and other aspects of marketing. A whole network of social and personal beliefs and attitudes underlies the purchase and use of a product, and an understanding of consumer behavior affects how the product will be packaged or labeled. Even more significant is the ability to forecast how this behavior will change.

PACKAGE CHARACTERISTICS

The manufacturer and designer must determine what appeal they wish the package to make. The package should first of all have a general overall appeal—a pleasant shape, appealing color, attractive surface design, and distinctive, legible lettering. Then market investigation will indicate which market or which part of a certain market should be concentrated on.

Family Resemblance

Manufacturers often use the package design to create a family resemblance among related items in the seller's line. This resemblance is particularly important when introducing a new product. Each product shares the goodwill created by the other products in its family group, and will, in turn, help promote the sales of these other products. Thus similarity in package forms may encourage the purchase of one product through a carry-over of recognition and possibly of goodwill from another product. A known trademark provides a linking agent between one product and another. This is why manufacturers want a trademark or brand name that will become embedded in the consumer's memory.

The desirability of close association depends very largely on whether the products are alike in form or are associated in use. A simple basic design for a whole range of products can be established, even though the individual products may have different colors.

Convenience

The growth of the aerosol industry has been nothing short of phenomenal, and new aerosol innovations appear regularly in a receptive market. In aerosol packaging the product results directly from the creation of a new packaging technique. Convenience of use and decorative features have caused the rapid growth in this industry. Established products like room deodorants and starch have enjoyed large annual sales increases after employing aerosol packaging.

The effective package is convenient not only to the consumer but also to all the distributors who handle the product. A consumer-attitude study should reveal how much difficulty the consumer had in finding the product in the store, in storing the product at home, and in using it. Consumer interviews will also reveal some pet peeves in the design of packages. Hard-to-open packages and packages that are difficult to close after first use annoy consumers. In addition to preferring a container that is easy to handle, consumers often indicate that they choose a package on which the label is easy to read more often than one with a label containing small print. Consumers often desire better directions on how to open the package and how to use the contents. The packaged product should also be well adapted to the retailers' and wholesalers' facilities for handling merchandise. Proper packaging design not only can save capital by cutting high or space-consuming inventories of packages but also may decrease shipping damage and returns from customers.

Size and Shape

The size and shape of the package is another important consideration in packaging design. There are some limiting factors; for example, the amount of the product packaged should be influenced by the amount the consumer wants. The package should be neither too small nor too large for the consumer's needs. Its ideal size and shape depends not only on the consumer's needs but also on the physical nature of the product. Liquids are often packaged quite differently than durables. Usually they are packaged in cylindrical form, while durable products are often packaged in rectangular shapes.

The package may conform to the product's shape if that is convenient. The size of the product depends in part on whether it is durable or nondurable. The size of durable products is determined by the size of the product itself, while the size of nondurable products can often be controlled. Liquids, fabrics, and other nondurables can be packaged in sizes geared to the consumer's needs.

The consumer's income also influences the size of the package he or she will buy. It may be convenient to carry and store a large amount of a product, but if most consumers cannot afford to purchase a large quantity at one time, the product should be packaged in a smaller size. Because income, family size, and consumption needs vary, manufacturers have had to develop more than one package size for their products.

For packages that do not have to conform to the shape of the product, there are any number of possibilities. Ease of handling is of prime consideration. Because storage space in the home is limited, the package should be compact and easy to store. This is why cylindrical bottles are often placed in a rectangular container.

Operators of self-service stores prefer a package that is easy to handle and display. If the consumer can see and hold the package, the chances are greater that it will be purchased. Since most forklift trucks, warehouse trailers, and hand equipment are designed on the basis of a 48-inch cube, if the package is a module of a fraction of this cube, the material handling system will be cheaper to operate. The size of the package is usually determined by the normal order size placed by the buyer. Some products are customarily sold at wholesale by the gross, thousand, dozen, or hundred. Packages of odd shapes and sizes should be avoided because they may prove very difficult for the retailer to stock and display.

Another limiting factor on the size and shape of the product is government control. The Packaging and Labeling Act, which gave the Commerce Department the responsibility for determining if package sizes are too numerous to allow the consumer to make value judgments and comparisons, is an example of government control.* Still, the size and shape can often be adjusted to make the product appear dainty or the quantity generous. Esthetics are very important in packaging; an external wrapper must have a shape that will not offend the eye and that will psychologically reflect the value or appearance of the contents.

Visibility of Products

With the advent of such new packaging materials as polyethylene, polypropylene, rubber-base film, and vinyls, the possibilities for greater visibility have increased. An almost infinite variety of film types, thicknesses, and coatings is available; many of them have been tailored for specific packaging application in the food industry. Several years ago films were developed before the markets were found for them; today the markets and products are determined and then the films are designed to meet the needs of these products and markets.†

The value of the product will often be enhanced if the package permits the product to be visible to consumers, for consumers like to see what they are buying. For example, glass has proved to be an excellent medium for the sales promotion of certain kinds of merchandise. Baby food could be packed in cans, mothers prefer glass.

The development of film reduces waste and decreases the cost of bringing meats, fresh fruits, and vegetables to the consumer. In addition, this type of package offers convenience in handling. Toys, hardware items, and soft-goods lines also depend heavily on visible packaging for fast turnover.

Dual-Use Containers

Homemakers prefer to buy products in dual-use containers. Such reusable packages as plastic cartons, plastic bags, wooden bowls, and

*Marsh H. Blackburn, "Increased Sales Through Packaging Innovation," *Trends in Packaging Technology and Marketing* (New York: AMACOM, 1968), p. 8.
†Nelson Allen, "Designing Films to Meet Product Needs in the 1970's," *Planning for Tomorrow's Packaging Realities* (New York: AMACOM, 1969), pp. 65–66.

pottery crocks say "You don't have to throw me away," and this pleases most consumers by making them feel thrifty and wise. A promotional advantage is obtained if the cost of the product is not substantially more than it would be if packaged in a single-use container. If the cost is considerably more, it may be a handicap. Containers of this type are frequently used for gifts and novelty items. A classic example of this advertising technique is placing hard candy in apothecary-type jars as opposed to plain-Jane boxes in order to increase sales price.

Color

Thoro is a right color for cach packagc and person; thus color is one of the most flexible and psychologically effective marketing tools. A change in color on a package has been shown to cause an increase in sales of from 15 to 20 percent. The designer must be careful in choosing colors, for using color to please and using it to create action are two entirely different things. The designer's aim should be to choose a color scheme that attracts the eye, is quickly recognizable, and is easy to read. Strong colors or shades that clash with one another should be avoided because they are unpleasant and offend the natural taste of the prospective buyer.

There are two trends in the use of colors. One is the classic presentation of packaged goods with natural colors and conservative labeling. The other uses shades that do not reproduce natural colors but rather combine drawings and letterings with coloring in a modernistic design. Modernistic colors and design do not blend with classical lettering any more than natural colors and traditional design blend with modern lettering.

Violent shades of purple, red, and black suit certain consumer goods. In fact, it has been discovered that personal items move rapidly in red containers since red symbolizes warmth and friendliness. Since red is the hottest color and motivates the fastest action, it is used very much in packaged goods, especially in the impulse-buying area. Red also is appropriate for certain male products since it appeals strongly to men. Black is widely used to suggest a costly product, often in combination with other colors, notably gold. Since white symbolizes purity and cleanliness, it is effective for nearly all products consumed by or applied to the user.*

The use of natural colors is certainly logical for foods and products used daily. Consumers are attracted by packages that remind them

*Walter P. Margulies, *Packaging Power* (New York: The World Publishing Company, 1970), pp. 112–115.

of nature and of the origin of the goods when they are selecting this type of product. Brown is often used for coffee packages so that the consumer can "smell and taste" that brand. Brown is also good for tobacco and baked-bean labels. Even though it is not necessary to use colors that suggest the character of the product, it is very important to avoid those that would violate expectations. There are certain psychological traits in human nature that must be respected. Nearly everyone would resist blue mashed potatoes or purple bread regardless of the product's quality.

Studies have shown that different shades of a given color have different effects. Clearly people do judge the aroma and taste of a product by the color of its package. The color of a food package sets up expectations regarding the flavor of the contents, and these expectations will influence the actual taste of the food.

The recent development of fluorescent inks adds to the drive for gaudier packaging. Packages with this ink have greater color purity and visibility, which attracts customers. Recently violent eye appeal is being sought by using clashing colors on packages. These packages do attract the eye; however, the desired effect may be lost because the eye gets tired and a sensitive customer is often repelled rather than attracted by the violence.

Research has indicated that different colors produce different reactions in different people. Generalizations about color appeals are therefore largely meaningless. Colors in packaging design have to be chosen in light of the nature of the product, the people to whom it is being sold, and the personality that is to be built for it. It has been scientifically determined that people generally react to color according to their national and racial origins. Yet almost everyone favors the same combination of colors; it is the order of preference that varies.*

IMPULSE-BUYING APPEALS

Part of the large sum of money manufacturers spend annually for packaging is for the functional purposes of the packages: to protect the product, to make it easy for the consumer to carry it, and to facilitate display. However, the proportion allocated to the seduction of unwary shoppers is substantial. Designers working closely with customers have found that modern theories of psychology apply to

*Ibid., p. 111.

their field because packaging can be an effective means of increasing sales through impulse buying. Often shoppers are not conscious of the effect a package has on them and do not realize what color or design caused them to take a particular package.

Appetite Appeal

When designing food packages, the technique of appetite appeal can be employed. It is one of the most powerful techniques because the supermarket customer is shopping between meals. Many cake mix packages contain illustrations of luscious cakes with dripping icing that whet the consumer's appetite. It is not sufficient merely to illustrate the product on the package; it must be shown in its complete and most delicious form with all the supporting details. Butter labels often illustrate pats of butter served with waffles or steak and potatoes. Ice cream manufacturers have begun using illustrations of pie à la mode and homemade sundaes on their packages. Highly realistic pictures of the product in actual use, spread over a large area of the package, help create appetite appeal.

Glamour Appeal

Since consumers are not attracted by pure functionality, effective packaging creates hope, promises, and images. Glamour appeal is always useful in the cosmetic and female adornment markets. Usually aimed at the younger woman in the mass market, it uses glamorous illustrations on the package. Cosmetics and beauty aids are often sold in exclusively designed containers. Though the package cost can be quite high, the products carry a very comfortable profit margin.

Snob appeal is used to attract both men and women; packages using this appeal are designed to have a rare and expensive look. Gold and silver metallic wrappers on everything from soap to margarine often raise the price of these items, but experience has proved that fancy wrappings are a powerful selling influence. Package designers have also found that a crest and a coat of arms suggest a superior product. The consumer feels he or she is one of the privileged few to buy these goods.

Economy Appeal

The economy appeal is probably the most popular because housewives have been led to believe that bigger sizes are better buys. Usually this is true; however, many buyers can be misled on this point. Manufacturers use several different packaging techniques in the economy appeal. Labels are often designed to make the container appear larger than it really is, and the use of white space on the label gives the package a larger appearance. Very flat packages appear to be much larger than rounded or square ones that weigh exactly the same. Packages also often contain the words "free" on the outside. Immediately the consumer is led to believe that the product is a bargain, even though the premium has actually increased its price.

Child Appeal

Manufacturers have found that children are an important factor in selling many products for the home. The food industry has adopted a wide variety of containers and wrappers made of plastics. These versatile materials can be designed for many special purposes, including child appeal. Cellophane bags showing their edible contents and free toys have a strong eye appeal to children. Children are also intrigued by backs of packages that are used as puzzles, cut-out toys, and cartoon characters. In embarking upon a policy of child appeal, the manufacturer must not neglect other basic selling factors. Since the purchase is usually made by the parent, the child appeal should be reserved for the back of the package. Manufacturers should not overlook the fact that children will ask for items by brand name if exposed to television advertising of the product or the package.

PACKAGING FOR NEW PRODUCTS

As soon as the new product's specifications are determined, the organization's packaging department should begin planning the package. If the organization does not have a packaging department or the available expertise, a professional designer should be consulted. If the package will be made by another firm, producers should be asked to submit designs. The package may not be firmly decided on until after the product has had a trial test in the market. At that time more information will be available regarding consumers' reactions to the colors, shapes, and sizes of alternative designs.

Repackaging

The package for an established product may have to be redesigned for any of several reasons. Regardless of the reason, the first step in redesign is a complete analysis of the old package. If the package is well known, the change should be subtle so that a new impression is made but the average consumer is barely aware of the change.

The organization may feel that a new more up-to-date package will create new interest and awareness. It may perceive that consumers have grown tired of the existing package and desire a change. Salespeople may also be inspired to promote the product because of its new package. The organization may feel that a new package size or method of opening or closing the package will be more convenient. Consumer's habits may also have changed and a different package may better meet their needs.

The influence of cost may require an appraisal of the packaging materials. A new type of material or closure may be less expensive to produce. In turn, this savings may allow the organization to reduce the selling price of the product and consequently increase sales volume.

Testing the New Package Design

Once the new package is designed, both physical and market tests must be conducted. The physical tests can be done in the laboratory as well as in the field. They should determine how the package withstands moisture, cold, heat, leakage, and rough handling. Since laboratory tests often simulate treatment more severe than what the package would receive from the user or in transit, they enable the firm to see what package failures can be expected in relation to the probabilities of occurrence. If the probability is high that these events will occur, the package must be redesigned.

Market tests can be conducted in both the laboratory and the field. The opinions of qualified management personnel in regard to various package designs are obtained in the laboratory. This approach has some merit, but it must be remembered that executives are not typical package users and they can only estimate what the user's reaction will be.

The package can better be observed in the field where it is handled and displayed. In the retail store the effectiveness of the design can be tested. It is difficult to tell if a new package design has caused any sales increase or decrease because so many other variables such as competition, seasonal change in demand, and advertising affect sales volume. Motivational research, which is concerned with the question of why people behave as they do, is a more effective method of testing design. It examines the likely effects on consumer choice of different shapes, colors, designs, and other packaging variables. By conducting tests under controlled conditions and by eliciting people's reactions before launching a new packaging program, market researchers have been able to give management valuable guidance. Consumer attitude studies are also helpful in pinpointing the disadvantages of the firm's present package or of a competitor's package.

These studies are safer than a purely deductive approach to determine consumers' attitudes. Most consumers are particularly qualified to give significant information on the desirable size and shape of the package. They are also the best source to indicate whether a package gets to them in good condition and if the contents have deteriorated in quality during the distribution process.

If both the product and the package are new or substantially changed, samples may be given or sold to a limited number of actual consumers. The samples should be used in the normal environment of consumption in order to determine consumers' reactions. After analyzing these reactions and making any necessary adjustments, the product can be sold under normal competitive conditions. Care should be taken to see that the test markets are as nearly representative of the national market as possible.

SOCIETY AND PACKAGING

Increasingly society is questioning what is referred to as the "deceit and trickery" in packaging. One complaint is that odd-shaped bottles only confuse the consumer since he or she is not able to compare the size with that of competing products. Another is that narrow necks on bottles are used only to make the bottle appear taller. Even though price and quantity are marked on a package, many shoppers do not calculate the cost per quantity purchased. Some consumer advocates contend that the reason shoppers do not make this comparison is that they have difficulties with arithmetic. These advocates feel that the weight should be stated clearly so that price/quantity comparisons can be readily made.

Throwaway packages are increasingly being viewed as a mixed blessing. Nonreturnable containers appeal to both the retailer and the consumer because neither has to bother with handling and returning the empties. With the rising concern about pollution, however, the throwaway package is coming under fire. Each year the packaging consumption per person rises, which adds to the solid-waste disposal problem. Public interest groups may influence the population to buy only returnable containers. We need better technology for the recovery and reuse of packaging materials.

Many advocates of consumers' rights do not believe that government advertising regulations and the Food and Drug Act are adequate protection. They stress that marketing executives must behave more responsibly. With so much attention being given to consumerism, firms should hesitate to introduce a new package that could be considered deceptive and therefore harm the organization's goodwill.

SUMMARY

As the amount of disposable income per capita in the United States continues to rise, shopping will be more discriminating and diversified. The consumers of the future will expect value, and before they put down their cash for a product, they will want to be assured of getting it. The practical and emotional needs of consumers are resulting in very demanding standards for packaging. The intensifying competition for the shopper's attention and dollars is putting more responsibility on the package than ever before. The consumer cannot actually examine the contents of many packaged products at the point of purchase, so the package alone has to convince him or her that the product is worth the money. Manufacturers who are misinformed about or who resist packaging changes may find their products selling less successfully than those of their competitors. A poorly designed package tells the consumer that the maker of the product does not care. Market-wise manufacturers are willing to make an extra effort to prove they really do care about both their consumers and their products. They are endeavoring to keep abreast of changing consumer buying habits and preferences and improve their packaging accordingly.

Product planning must determine product-package-price combination that will best meet customers' needs. The marketing executive should review all existing packages. There have been cases where a failing product became successful because the package was changed. Studies of the product's package may prove just as profitable in generating extra sales as analysis of the product itself.

8

Distribution
and
Logistics

LOGISTICS is concerned with the flow of goods from the source to the user. It is an interdisciplinary science because it involves several fields of study. In military terminology logistics refers to the movement of men, machines, and supplies. In business it refers to the logical arrangement of the functional areas required to achieve a specified goal. Logistics and physical distribution are concerned with the creation of time and place utility. However, some people argue with this definition because they feel that it implies some movement and handling of materials. This is not true because handling of material should be eliminated to the extent possible; the ideal amount of handling is no handling at all.

LOGISTIC SYSTEMS

Various terms and interpretations are used in connection with physical distribution and logistic systems. Most people feel that logistics is broader than physical distribution, which is only the outward movement of products from the seller to the consumer or customer. A logistic system has several components: transportation, handling of materials, location, inventory management, packaging, warehousing, and communications between the people in each functional area of the system.

Material handling is often defined as that portion of the business system that involves the moving, packaging, and storing of materials, supplies, and products. It does not include the manufacture or modification of material, or any operation that changes the appearance of the product. Most distribution activities can be categorized as material handling activities.

The management of the logistic system overlaps several managerial functions such as accounting and finance, purchasing and marketing. The segments of the system are usually scattered among several of these functions. For instance, the management of the warehouse may be assigned to the marketing organization, while control over raw materials inventory may be the responsibility of the purchasing department. Since the purchasing function is so closely related to production, raw materials control may be divided between production and purchasing.

System Design

Before beginning an analysis of the logistic system, the objectives should be stated. In almost all circumstances one of the objectives will be improved service and reduced costs. Other tangible measures of improvement may be stated, such as better production stability or greater utilization of the investment already committed. Obviously some of these objectives are inconsistent with each other.

The scope of the logistic system project should also be stated. At the outset management should have indications as to where the problem lies—whether it is in production planning, purchasing, or in the control of inventory. The investigation may reveal that the actual problem is of a different type, but it is important to decide at the beginning of the project what areas will be investigated first.

Work teams. In designing the physical distribution system it may be helpful to divide the workers into two groups. One group would have responsibility for the day-to-day work of designing, testing, and installing the system. This team should estimate the operating costs of the system and then select the necessary equipment and transportation techniques. The leader of this operations team should have the background and experience to know whom to ask for opinions and comments. He or she should be objective enough to accept criticism of the project design. Since the success of the system design often depends upon how effective this person is, great care should be taken in his or her selection.

The project leader of this analysis team does not have to be able to apply all the accounting and technical methods used to evaluate the physical distribution system. The leader should, however, insist that technical assistants explain the methods they are using so that he or she can better evaluate their significance. It is often helpful for the analysis team to include a person from each of the areas represented in the logistic system and allow everyone to use his or her experience in the appropriate areas. This way the people who will operate the system will know they have influenced the system's design.

The other team working on the project is the management supervisory committee, which will have representatives from sales, production, finance, and management. One of this committee's purposes is to provide available data on policy matters to the analysis team. Though the supervisors' duties involve counsel and review, they should not stifle the analysis committee's inquiry process. Too often the management supervisory group kills new ideas in the early stages because it does not want to make any changes.

Once a study of the logistic system is initiated, management cannot assume that the project team will carry it out. If it does, the system study will probably become bogged down in technical details because those assigned to work on it may find more interesting tasks, which they will claim are pressing. To prevent this, management must continue to give attention to the study. Those working on the project team should be convinced that their accomplishments are being noted by management. Continuing management involvement may best be facilitated through the supervisory committee.

External consultants. Outside consultants may be employed to work with the organization's employees on the logistic project. An outside consultant offers the experience and technical ability that the firm may need temporarily. An outside consultant also tends to be objective because his or her association with the system will end as soon as the project is finished. A consultant is less likely to be influenced by the personalities of the internal staff, and therefore will usually find it easier to make recommendations for changes. The organization should make sure that the consultant knows what his or her objectives are and in what area he or she is to work.

Timetables. Timetables should be set out for each phase of the study. Budgets should also be established in advance for each task or group of tasks. Plans should be made to allow for periodic review sessions. The comparison between actual results and predetermined objectives may require some modification of the overall plan.

Customers' viewpoint. The analysis of a logistic system must be continuing. There is no one correct way to establish this type of analysis.

The initial approach may be either from the customers' viewpoint, that is, considering their needs and interests, or from the firm's vantage point, that is, considering the demands placed upon the organization. Most industrial logistic studies in the past have concentrated on the physical distribution system from the customers' viewpoint.

Since the characteristics of the customers are of such great importance in designing a physical distribution system, a profile of customer groups can be made to show their size, space, and geographical location. Their pattern of buying should be studied in order to determine if different geographical location buy in different patterns. The characteristics of the customers who buy high-volume items should be compared to those of the customers who buy low-volume goods. The volume that customers buy will influence the geographical distribution of markets.

The product demand and order characteristics should be subjected to statistical analysis. Some products are expected to show seasonal demand; it may surprise management to find that other products have fairly predictable fluctuations. Once a study is made of demand variations, some of the previously unpredictable fluctuations may show a pattern that can be forecasted with some degree of accuracy.

Firm's vantage point. If the approach chosen is from the firm's vantage point, information should be gathered concerning the products and channels of distribution. A detailed list of each product's features should be made that includes such characteristics as the following: its weight and size, any special handling requirements, perishability or shelf life time, and packaging features. Additional data is needed on what channels of distribution will be used. The number of agencies and middlemen as well as the functions they perform should be detailed. A flow chart of the product as it passes through each point in the distribution channel until it is received by the customer can be used. The plant and warehouse facilities should be evaluated so that maximum use will be made of the capabilities available. Once a broad type of analysis is made, whether from the customers' viewpoint or the firm's, areas in which additional detailed studies are needed will become evident. Opportunities for reducing lead time may be indicated. Changes may be needed in the data processing system so that more accurate costs can be determined for feasibility studies. Inventory management covers so many areas that very likely better methods can be applied in this area.

Before implementing a new or revised distribution plan, marketing management should test the results on paper. The effect of changed locations or of different modes of transportation could be studied.

The analysis should not be restricted solely to marketing functions because there may be changes in manufacturing facilities that will improve the effectiveness of the logistic system. By testing on paper such factors as lead time and changes in warehouse locations or in the manufacturing plant site, marketing executives can determine where the largest cost savings will be.

System Costs

In determining the costs associated with a logistic system, reference must be made to economic concepts. Many of the costs determined by accounting principles have little or no relevance to a decision concerning the expansion or abandonment of a distribution system. This is especially true for allocated indirect costs and sunk costs. If the facilities exist and cannot be used elsewhere, the organization has lost the opportunity to recover this investment. Sunk costs result from irrevocable decisions made in the past. However, a portion of the administrative costs may be direct costs of the logistic system that will vary when changes are made in elements of the system.

Out-of-pocket costs that require the payment of cash and opportunity costs are often relevant to this type of analysis. Opportunity costs result when an organization chooses one alternative over another and loses the return that could have been earned from the rejected alternative.

Some costs associated with the logistic system may be difficult to determine. However, this should not be used as an excuse for omitting any consideration of these cost; instead an estimate should be used. Almost always in cost determination there is a tradeoff between the cost of arriving at very exact figures and the benefit this exactness will have.

Cost reduction. Since the investment many firms have in their logistic system is significant, they should be anxious to search for cost reduction opportunities in this area. Economies in the logistic system can be achieved through planning as large a volume per move as is practical. Transportation rates are lower for volumes in hundred-weight than for less-than-volume shipments. Since the unit cost will be lower for volume shipments, management should look for ways to take advantage of these savings. Of course, there are physical limitations to the size of the load that can be handled at one time.

In designing a logistic system there are several basic principles that can be applied with professional judgement, common sense, and experience. One is that all unnecessary handling should be eliminated because no value is added to the product through such action. The best material handling function involves the least handling effort. The handling of material should also be integrated. Much attention should be given to the movement flow. Continuous movement is more economical than intermittent starts and stops. Economies will be achieved if the system provides for a steady flow of goods from production to consumption. Cost savings will also be achieved if the number of transfer points is kept to a minimum. Material that is being moved should not be stopped until it is as close as possible to the next point of use.

As far as possible, the handling should be performed by mechanical means rather than by hand labor because automatic handling reduces costs. Mechanized techniques may decrease the physical distribution cost per unit by eliminating some warehousing labor. Certainly the selection of distribution equipment is of great importance because of its impact on cost. The equipment cost should be compared against the use that will be made of the equipment. Equipment built for motion should be used for that purpose; if the need does not exist, the feature is superfluous and unnecessarily adds to the cost of the machinery.

Most marketing executives prefer to use standard equipment and operations because they generally result in cost savings. The more variety there is in the type of equipment used, the more expensive operations will be. Standardized equipment also allows for a more comprehensive study of work patterns so that routine procedures can be planned in advance. Standardization should be extended to the product's container or package in order to eliminate expensive repackaging and handling of products. There is a point where standardization ceases to be economical; that point is where inflexibility enters the scene. Flexibility is also important for the equipment used to handle the goods. There is always a tradeoff between the advantage of standardization and the advantage of flexibility.

Plant Location

In designing a logistic system, a number of choices must be made among the variables involved. One of the important variables is the number of manufacturing facilities and their locations. Organizations will want to select a plant site that minimizes all costs associated with the product. This means that the manufacturing plant site must meet the production requirements for such available resources as water, power, and labor, and their costs must be kept low. The cost of bringing raw materials into the manufacturing facilities, as well as delivery costs to customers, must be considered.

Multiplant systems. There are numerous ways that a logistic system employing several plants may be used. If there is more than one manufacturing site, management must decide which product lines will be produced at each plant. If all product lines are not produced at each plant, the firm must establish a policy concerning the shipment of product lines. The policy must state whether products that are not produced in plants located near the customer will be shipped directly or be sent to one location and the order filled as one unit. The firm may decide that each production facility should serve a specific market region.

In deciding upon the number of producing plants, economies of scale should be studied. If the volume of sales warrants large-scale operations, it may be feasible to build several plants scattered within the territories they serve. Under these circumstances each individual plant should be large enough to achieve the scale of plant where unit product cost is lowest. By establishing the plants at various geographical locations, transportation costs will be reduced.

Product Design

The design of the product influences the transportation rate to be charged as well as the manner in which the product is handled and stored. If the product is designed so that it can be stacked with other products or folded, transportation charges will be lower. In choosing the shipping container, the possibility of damage to the product should be considered. The Uniform Freight Classification sets forth rules regarding package description.

Pricing

The pricing system that the firm chooses affects its ability to design a physical distribution system. There are two pricing systems; f.o.b. and delivered. Under f.o.b., the seller gives the buyer title to and responsibility for the goods at some designated point, which may be the seller's warehouse or the carrier's dock, and the buyer assumes responsibility for the transportation charges. For example, let's assume that the purchase contract specifies which party is responsible and the exact location where the responsibility changes by indicating "f.o.b. Memphis." This means that title is held by the seller until a common carrier in Memphis receives the goods. The common carrier will act as an agent for the buyer. While the f.o.b. pricing system is simple to state, it threatens the seller's authority over the distribution system.

If a delivered pricing system is used, the transportation and handling costs are paid by the seller, and the price includes these costs. Quantity discounts for specified volumes of orders will then be applied to the delivered price. In order to protect the legality of the pricing system, the seller will either set the delivered price the same for all customers in the seller's marketing area or establish zones in which separate uniform pricing schedules will apply.

Features of both pricing systems may be combined into a basing point system. Under a basing point system, a price is quoted, with additional freight to be paid from the basing point. However, the freight charges added to the price will not necessarily be the actual transportation charges because the system does not imply that the goods must be shipped from the base point. A seller's plant site may be set as the base point for pricing purposes. To the price that he has chosen he will add transportation charges to the buyer's plant, based on the common carrier rates available. The goods, however, may be shipped from a warehouse located nearer to the customer than the manufacturing plant. The savings between actual transportation costs and the charges passed on to the buyer would then be the seller's.

Delivered price systems and basing point pricing systems are easier to administer and therefore more popular. They permit prices to be quoted with more accuracy. Generally customers do not wish to have a voice in the transportation decision; their only concern is that the correct goods arrive on time. If the seller must arrange for the transportation, he can exercise more control over his logistic system. He has the freedom to choose a more costly but faster mode of transportation where he believes this would result in a competitive advantage.

The buyer may choose as part of his marketing strategy to absorb part of the transportation charges. The base point chosen might be a warehouse located near the buyer. When items move from the plant or from a more remote warehouse, the extra freight would be the buyer's expense.

Legal Considerations

When there is legislation limiting price discrimination, as there is in the United States, the firm must be prepared to defend its position if it charges different prices to each customer. The Robinson-Patman Act prohibits discounts or price differences that exceed differences in cost that can be determined; however, the discounts given do not have to be as large as the cost difference. An analysis of a firm's logistic system is a basic defense against charges of price discrimination.

The use of quantity discounts is often questioned as some people believe that they are given solely because large buyers use their power to obtain them. In order to defend these volume differentials, a firm must be able to show that it has achieved a cost savings because the product was sold in this specific quantity.

WAREHOUSES

A decision must be made about the production facilities, and the number and location of the warehouses must also be determined. Warehouses may be either maintained at each plant or established at central points for the receipt of the products made at each plant. The warehousing function becomes the center of the logistic system because of its role in inventory control.

Location

In choosing the site for its warehouses, the organization should consider the availability of its products and the increased costs of additional warehouses. If customers are willing to wait several days for their orders to be filled, the number of warehouse establishments can be reduced. Since the investment in mechanical delivery equipment is usually quite large, warehouse facilities should be consolidated as much as feasible. This will usually reduce the storage cost per unit.

There must be a tradeoff between establishing enough warehouses to ensure good service to customers and keeping costs at a reasonable level. The geographical market should be estimated so that the warehousing sites chosen will allow for rapid delivery, both into the facility and out. If the geographical location of purchasers is known, the best site will be in the market area. For seasonal products and products for which the buyer is unknown, the best location of storage facilities will be near the production plant. Seasonal demand and production are other factors that influence how many warehouses will be used. The scope of the market is another influencing factor.

Within the warehouse extreme care should be used in planning the layout so that an effective work flow that does not require wasteful motions will evolve. Goods that are commonly ordered together should be stored near each other. Not only will this eliminate time in filling the order, but it will also reduce the errors made by warehouse employees since it will enable them to become more familiar with the merchandise lines they are handling. Products that have a high turnover should be stored close to a terminal so their delivery is facilitated. The remote areas of the warehouse should be used for seasonal products and slow-moving goods.

Facilities
The storage of the goods must be adapted to the needs of the organization. There are many different forms of warehouses varying in degrees of specialization. Some are designed to hold such special products as drugs, precious minerals, and stones under tight security. Others are built to maintain the correct temperature for handling such products as food and plants. These types of warehouses would not be adequate for bulk products or products in a fluid state.

Not only do warehouses vary in their physical characteristics but they also differ in their legal status and in the legal ownership of the goods stored. A warehouse may be publicly or privately owned, or privately operated as a leased facility. Often a leased warehouse has been designed by the operator but sold to an agency under a financing arrangement and leased back.

Public Warehouses
A public warehouse offers its space to anyone, usually for short-term commitments. Generally it provides custodial and handling services. The organization may find that it is profitable to ship in large quantities to public warehouses and save on freight costs. The public warehouse owner becomes a consignee for the goods and distributes them in smaller quantities. In addition to breaking down a large shipment for reshipment, the owner may provide facilities where the goods can be displayed to prospective customers.

The public warehouse may also play a role in the financial aspects of the firm because it can issue warehouse receipts. Because so much working capital is needed when the goods are produced, the firm that must manufacture well in advance of sales often faces a financial crisis. By using the warehouse receipts as evidence that the goods have been produced, the organization may be able to secure a loan when it otherwise could not.

Public warehouses also regulate the flow of goods because an organization may not want to make a large shipment to a retailer without the assurance that it will be paid. However, management knows that freight charges will be lower if bulk shipments are made. The best alternative is to ship in bulk to the public warehouse. If necessary and desirable, warehouse receipts may be used as collateral for a loan. When the retailer needs some of the shipment, he may get the receipts from the bank and then give them to the warehouse owner in exchange for the goods.

Public warehouses also offer the advantage of flexibility. Rather than invest a large sum of money in warehouse personnel and equipment that may not be needed permanently, the organization may find that the best solution is to use public facilities. All too often an organization faced with a temporary demand for storage rushes out and buys a warehouse, committing itself to significant fixed costs that will recur whether or not the warehouse is used again. Very few of these costs can be dropped in the short run. Obviously there are such warehousing variable costs as the wages paid to the staff, but even these are often quite difficult to stop immediately when the warehouse becomes empty. Almost all the costs associated with a public warehouse are variable and can be controlled in the short run. Usually only the space used is paid for, and this is a variable cost. (There may, however, be an agreement on a minimum fee to be paid regardless of usage, and this is a fixed charge.) Public warehouses also permit flexibility of location since general merchandise warehouses are scattered across the country.

It can be assumed that a public warehouse's staff is well trained and offers the expertise in management and operations that most organizations do not have. If, however, the storage of goods is a large part of the firm's activities, the firm may find it can do its own warehousing cheaper. And if special warehousing facilities are required (as for food products), the firm may have no other choice but to provide for its own storage if there are no available warehouses designed for its purpose.

Field Warehouses

Field warehouses operate differently from other warehouses. The warehouse owner goes to the product's location and takes possession of the goods on the manufacturer's site. A field warehouse may be owned by a private organization or a public warehouse operator. Under this kind of arrangement, the products are stored in the custody of a public warehouse operator who is legally responsible for them. Field warehouse receipts can be issued on these goods and used as collateral for a loan. The advantages of field warehouses are that they improve the speed of delivery and usually reduce transportation costs.

Bonded Warehouses

Products on which there are heavy domestic excise taxes, such as liquor and tobacco, are often stored in bonded warehouses. The taxes and duties on these goods have to be paid before they can be removed from the bonded warehouse for distribution. Producers can avoid the prepayment of taxes by keeping their goods in bonded warehouses; this cuts down on the amount of working capital needed.

Warehousing Decision

In deciding which form of warehouse best meets its needs, the organization should look at the funds that it has available or can be made available for the investment. The type of commitment that it is making should be thoroughly understood. The sale and lease-back arrangement is commonly used because organizations want to conserve their own funds and use other individuals' money for warehouse construction. Most sale and lease-back arrangements carry heavy penalties if the contract is canceled. This has the effect of transferring the economic risk of ownership to the lessee even though he does not have title to the warehouse.

Public warehouse facilities may not be convenient to use in a highly integrated logistic system. It may be too difficult and costly to keep the organization's accountants, salespeople, and customers informed as to the makeup of the inventory currently stored at each location. However, most public warehouses employ competent managers and render efficient service. In addition, they offer the firm the advantage of flexibility since short-term commitments can be made. However, this flexibility may be expensive; generally it costs more for storage space in a public warehouse than in a private one that is as efficiently managed. But in evaluating this cost difference, the owner of a private warehouse must include the imputed interest lost by tying up funds in the warehouse.

Before deciding to eliminate a private warehouse and use a public facility, management should carefully consider what cost savings will result. Any indirect cost (such as administrative overhead) that is allocated to the private warehouse will not be eliminated if the facility is sold. For example, suppose that management is considering closing its private warehouse and using a public warehouse. A review of the annual costs charged to the warehouse and transportation functions discloses the figures shown in Exhibit 8-1. A public warehouse will charge $7,000 per month or $84,000 a year to handle the volume of inventory the firm is now carrying. Before management concludes that the transfer to a public warehouse will save $11,300 (the cost of private warehousing—$95,300—less $84,000), it must analyze the components of the costs charged to the private warehouse and determine what effect this move will have on other organizational functions.

Exhibit 8-1.   Annual costs for warehousing and transportation.

EXPENSES	FUNCTIONS	
	PRIVATE WAREHOUSING	TRANSPORTATION
Salaries	$60,000	$27,000
Telephone and telegraph	5,000	4,000
Packing supplies	15,000	1,000
Utilities	1,500	200
Taxes and insurance	7,000	12,000
Administration	2,800	3,500
Gasoline and oil	—	13,000
Depreciation	4,000	28,000
	$95,300	$88,700

For example, suppose that the marketing executive and the accountant estimate the following will occur if the organization changes to a public warehouse:

1. All salaries of employees warehouse will be eliminated except for one clerk who earns $8,000. (Termination pay will be ignored in this simple illustration.) There will be a $7,000 increase in transportation salaries because the finished goods must be transferred from the manufacturing plant to the off-site public warehouse.
2. Long-distance and telegraph charges are allocated directly to the functions. All of the warehouse's long-distance and telegraph charges will be eliminated; the transportation function's charges for this cost will not be affected. The remainder of the telephone and telegraph cost represents an allocation of the organization's basic service charge; the warehousing share of this amounts to $3,000. Since some other function will have to absorb this basic service expense, the warehouse's telephone and telegraph charges will be reduced only by $2,000.
3. Packing supplies for the warehouse will be reduced by $13,500. For the transportation function, this cost will increase to $2,700.
4. Part of the utilities expense represents a basic service charge; this amounts to $800 for the warehouse, and it will not be eliminated if a transfer is made to the public warehouse.
5. The firm will be able to sublease part of the warehouse for an annual rent of $10,000. Taxes and insurance will not be affected significantly.

6. Administrative costs will be allocated to each function on a ratio determined in advance. The transfer to a public warehouse will not significantly affect the organization's total administrative costs.
7. Gasoline and oil expenses will increase $2,000 because of extra transportation necessary to carry the finished goods to the public warehouse.
8. The warehouse machinery and equipment can be sold for their book value and no gain or loss will be realized on the sale. These funds of $100,000 can be invested in marketable securities paying 8 percent.

Exhibit 8-2 shows that the organization will not decrease its total cost by changing to a public warehouse. This is the type of analysis that should be the starting point from which other alternatives are

Exhibit 8-2. Cost comparisons.

	WAREHOUSING			TRANSPORTATION		
EXPENSES	PRIVATE WAREHOUSE	DIFFERENCE*	PUBLIC WAREHOUSE	PRIVATE WAREHOUSE	DIFFERENCE*	PUBLIC WAREHOUSE
Salaries	$60,000	−$52,000	$ 8,000	$27,000	+$7,000	$34,000
Telephone and telegraph	5,000	− 2,000	3,000	4,000	—	4,000
Packing supplies	15,000	− 13,500	1,500	1,000	+ 1,700	2,700
Utilities	1,500	700	800	200		200
Taxes and insurance	7,000	—	7,000	12,000	—	12,000
Administration	2,800	—	2,800	3,500	—	3,500
Gasoline and oil	—	—	—	13,000	+ 2,000	15,000
Depreciation	4,000	− 4,000	—	28,000	—	28,000
	$95,300	$72,200	$23,100	$88,700	$10,700	$99,400

Decrease in cost of warehouse	$72,200
Sublease rental income	10,000
Opportunity of earning interest at 8% on $100,000 from sale of warehouse equipment	8,000
	90,200
Less increase in transportation costs	−10,700
Net advantage of discontinuing private warehouse	$79,500
Cost of public warehouse	84,000
Net annual advantage of keeping private warehouse	$ 4,500

*Difference in cost between keeping private warehouse facilities and using a public warehouse.

investigated. For instance, the firm may be able to sublease a larger portion of the warehouse and thus increase rental income. Conversely, it may find it profitable to sell the warehouse and eliminate some of the taxes and insurance costs. Sometimes inventory is stored in idle buildings that have been discarded from manufacturing operations; these often have no economic cost because they cannot be disposed of.

TRANSPORTATION

The mode of transportation plays a significant role in the operation of the logistic system. There are many more transportation alternatives available today than several years ago, when the choices were limited to barge or railroad. The principal modes of transportation from which the organization can choose are highway, motor, air, water pipeline, and railroad. Any of these modes may be combined in a variety of ways to form the organization's complete transportation system. Each mode has its own specifications for packaging and handling. Schedules vary between different modes; and the firm may eliminate certain modes because of this factor alone.

Air Transportation

Quite obviously air transportation offers the advantage of speed. Air freight reduces the distance between the production facilities and many markets to just a few hours. It opens up many market areas that were previously considered inaccessible. For example, fresh fruits grown in Florida can be sold throughout the world. By using air transportation, the marketing executive faces less risk in entering a new market because there is no initial need for a large investment in facilities located in the new market served. If the new market does not prove profitable, the firm can pull out of it fairly easily without worrying about costs sunk in warehouses and inventory.

Improvements are being made in the handling of air freight at the points of origin and delivery. It made little sense to incur the cost of jet service when the goods remained for hours at the airport because loading and unloading techniques were inadequate. Surface carrier pickup and delivery service is also being improved so that the ultimate customer will receive the product on a timely basis.

Common and Contract Carriers

There are a number of legal transportation forms. The firm may choose to own and operate its own transportation facilities as opposed to using either common carriers or contract carriage. A common carrier operates under close supervision; it provides services under a published schedule with corresponding rates, and the geographical area in which it operates is well defined. A contract carrier provides transportation services under regulatory authority to customers at individually negotiated rates. Private carriers transport the goods they own; the transportation function is incidental to the business operations.

Rates

Transportation rates are very complicated because there are numerous types of origin-destination routes. The cost of service and the value of service provided are two bases for rate systems that have been used in transportation. The choice of one over the other depends upon the strength of the carrier's competition as well as on the economic position of the carrier. The size and volume of the shipment and the distance involved also are influencing factors. Under the cost-of-service concept, the charge includes the cost of providing the service and a return on the investment. There are strong limitations to this method as it is difficult to determine the cost of a specific service.

The value-of-service concept is grounded in the premise that some products can bear greater transportation cost than others. The assumption is usually made that those products with a high value-bulk ratio can bear high transportation costs. By assigning more costs to certain products, relief is gained for the other products. But consideration must be given to the maximum transportation charge that a unit can absorb without being priced out of the market.

Optimum Routing

As an organization's transportation systems become more complex, determining a good route will require more of management's attention. There are several different types of routing problems. One involves determining the shortest route between two points; the example would be a manufacturing firm that has to transport raw materials from its supply source to its production facilities. If instead several sites must be visited, the problem is to establish the shortest total route. For more complex situations, the marketing executive may find it necessary to refer to mathematical models involving a matrix or network. A firm cannot simply adopt one transportation mode or another without first studying the various systems. Since different transportation systems charge different prices, the marketing executive must evaluate all of these characteristics before deciding which mode or combination of modes to adopt. Management often justifies uneconomic routing by saying that the extra expense provides necessary customer service, and fails to investigate what real service different carriers offer for the bids they submit. Many times the transportation service affects other distribution costs; for example, handling costs can be reduced if unit-load techniques are employed. In a unit-load system, the movement of definable packages or items is based upon the use of lift trucks, cranes, tractor-trailer trains, and other flexible handling equipment.

Company Image

The transportation function has the responsibility of portraying the company's image because everything from the vehicle to the package used will be visible to the public, many of whom are prospective customers. A clean, neat driver delivering company products in a new car or truck creates a good impression. People who see this driver are more inclined to believe that the company is well managed and efficient. The driving habits of the deliverymen are also important. Prospective customers who see the organization's drivers run stoplights or engage in other traffic violations are often lost to the firm. The packaging material is also a carrier of the organization's message.

COMMUNICATIONS

The communications system links the facilities of the logistic system. The organization generally uses a variety of communications services such as telephone and telegraph, mails, and teletype circuits. There is almost always a tradeoff between speed and cost. While mailing usually costs less, the user is generally sacrificing speed for this dollar saving. Since material handling is such an integral part of the logistic system, much attention should be devoted to performing analysis of the costs associated with this function. Possible improvements should be studied. There are several alternatives available for this analysis. If a standard-cost system is in operation, the analysis will be easier to adopt, because time-study data and more detailed costs will be available. The following example compares a manual and a mechanical method; the same type of analysis could be used for two manual or two mechanical methods.*

*Source: E. Ralph Sims, Jr., *Planning and Managing Materials Flow* (Boston: Industrial Education Institute, 1968), pp. 129–131.

Manual Handling Costs

Direct labor
Payroll taxes
Supervision and other indirect labor costs
Depreciation on handling equipment used
Packaging costs
Other direct costs
Total cost for specified time period
Tons or other measurement handled for specified time period
Cost per ton or other measurement

Mechanical Handling Costs

Direct labor
Payroll taxes
Supervision, training, and other indirect labor costs
Depreciation on handling equipment used
Taxes and insurance on handling equipment used
Fuel energy costs
Repairs and maintenance costs for handling equipment
Packaging costs
Interest expense on funds used to purchase handling equipment
Other direct costs
Total cost for specified time period
Tons or other measurement handled for specified time period
Cost per ton or other measurement

Costs for any time period can be used, from daily costs to monthly, quarterly, or annual. The important thing is to keep the time frame the same for all costs and tons handled or other measurement. In the example given there was no allocation of administrative and plant overhead. It is not likely that the choice of one method over the other would change the cost allocated. Other costs were not included because the purpose was not to obtain a full cost. If the handling equipment is rented rather than bought, the rent expense will become a direct cost replacing depreciation and interest expense.

INVENTORY MANAGEMENT

Inventories play an important role in the logistic system. The effectiveness of inventory management determines what level of stock must be maintained. While management desires to keep the inventory investment as low as possible, it must balance the cost of ordering and storing inventory with the cost of lost sales. Few firms find it feasible to place an order every time they receive an individual customer order. Instead orders for material must be placed at intervals for batches of stock.

Management often has conflicting objectives for inventory management. A high inventory turnover rate is a desirable objective in itself, but it can result in stockouts. Maintaining a steady supply of goods does not have to be incompatible with a high inventory turnover rate. Adequate attention has to be directed to both of these issues to make certain that they are in line.

There may be a strong incentive for management to buy in large volumes to take advantage of quantity discounts. However, for this to be profitable, the organization must have a large enough sales volume. Otherwise part of the inventory will be lost through deterioration and pilferage, and there will be high storage and handling costs.

Reliability of Service

When an organization is out of stock, this results in intangible costs to the firm because customer relations are hurt and the firm's reputation as a dependable source of supply is damaged. Customers like to have items available for their use without having to carry a large inventory themselves. In addition, there are often tangible costs that can be measured. Stockouts interfere with production and delivery schedules. They cause the organization's facilities to remain idle or to be utilized at an inefficient capacity level; then later, when a large inventory is received, these same facilities may be overtaxed.

To avoid the problems associated with stockouts, many managers overreact by investing excessively in inventory. This results in unnecessarily high storage and insurance costs, as well as a large capital investment. An excessive inventory level also subjects the organization to risks from deterioration, theft, and obsolescence.

Management must establish a policy governing the inventory levels it feels it should maintain. On the one hand, it has the cost of carrying inventory to consider. Included in this cost are such factors as storage and insurance and the risk of loss through fire, theft, and obsolescence. It must balance the cost of carrying inventory against the loss of contribution margin from the sales it could not make because certain products were not in inventory. Not only will the organization lose contribution margin on these products, but it may also lose consumer goodwill. The cost of lost customers depends upon the characteristics of the business and is difficult to quantify. The seller must decide what, if any, delay is permissible between the time a request for material is made and when the material is delivered. If management adopts a policy to assure its customers a high degree of service reliability, it must recognize that a larger investment in inventory is required. Some products have a long sales life and are not subject to rapid market changes or deterioration. Others such as novelties or high-fashion products, have such short and intense sales periods that a large inventory investment is not advisable. Management should try to match its purchases with sales and avoid excessive inventory buildups. Even if such seasonal products as Christmas greeting cards can be carried over to the next season, management often finds that the cost of storage and its associated risks do not make carry-over feasible.

The type of product the organization offers for sale should also affect its policy on service reliability. Products are often grouped into convenience, shopping, and specialty items, depending upon the care and time that the customer spends in purchasing them. If the product is determined to be a specialty item, customers generally will tolerate a delayed delivery they would be unwilling to accept for a shopping or convenience item. Executives of firms that manufacture and market shopping and convenience products should devote much time to ensuring a high standard of service reliability.

The degree to which customers are willing to substitute one brand for another will also affect an organization's policy regarding service reliability. If a convenience item is not in stock, the consumer will usually buy a substitute or go to another supplier rather than wait for the product to be delivered. The standard of reliability offered by the firm's competitors must also be considered in establishing service policy.

Safety Stock

It is unrealistic to assume that the inventory flow will always be such that a new shipment arrives just as the last unit is sold. Since such perfection in timing rarely occurs, an allowance should be made for safety stock. In setting a basis for safety stock levels, the reliability of the suppliers in delivering the merchandise on time must be estimated. If this reliability is uncertain, management must plan to carry a larger safety stock to meet contingencies. Sophisticated buyers keep records showing vendor delivery performance and use them in choosing suppliers. Buyers of industrial goods often require a guarantee of delivery before they will place an order with a firm.

There is almost certain to be some variation in lead time (the time span between placing an order and its receipt into inventory), in the transportation system or in some other step of the cycle. Management must plan for these unexpected delays. In forecasting its usage of inventory or for sales purposes, it must rely on educated estimates. If usage exceeds these estimates, management must have some extra inventory on hand to meet this contingency. Safety stock provides a buffer against a stock shortage due to a demand level higher than anticipated or a lead time longer than forecasted.

A system study may reveal ways that new communications techniques can cut lead time. Feasibility studies may show that more rapid transportation can be used. It may even be less costly in the long run to use more expensive but faster means of transportation.

Economic Order Quantity

The optimum size of a purchase of raw material or a shop order for a production run that will result in the lowest annual costs is referred to as the economic order quantity. The following is a variation of the formula for computing this:

$$EOQ = \sqrt{\frac{2QO}{C}}$$

where Q is the annual quantity used in units; O is the cost of placing one order; and C is the annual cost of carrying one unit in stock for one year. For example, suppose it is estimated that 1,250 units will be used annually; the cost of placing an order is $20 and it costs 25 cents per year to carry one unit in inventory. On the basis of this data, the approximate economic order quantity would be:

$$EOQ = \sqrt{\frac{2(1,250)(\$20)}{.25}} = 200,000$$

$$= 448$$

This basic EOQ formula does not consider the impact of quantity discounts. Generally the larger the size of the order, the lower the unit price will be.

Carrying costs. The cost of placing an order and the cost of storing inventory must be estimated in order to use the EOQ formula. Both physical storage and capital costs should be used in determining the carrying cost per inventory unit. The base for estimating handling costs should be the warehouse actually used. For instance, if the primary warehouse is full, and additional, more costly facilities must be used, the carrying costs will be increased. The funds that are tied up in inventory earn no return until they are sold. These funds could be invested elsewhere and earn a return. An allowance should be made for imputed interest, dividends, or some other earnings in determining the carrying cost.

The product's characteristics and its susceptibility to obsolescence and spoilage affect carrying costs. The physical storage cost of food and other products that are highly susceptible to spoilage and cannot be stored indefinitely should include a cost for this risk. The cost of carrying technical products should also include a cost factor for the risks from obsolescence. Products such as toys and clothing are subject to style and fashion changes. The cost of carrying seasonal products is often high because management may find that in order to dispose of these at the end of the season, the price must be reduced sharply.

EOQ limitations. Many managers do not know either the cost of placing an order or the cost of carrying inventory, and display little interest in trying to find out. Often distribution cost accounts are not detailed enough to provide for an exact cost determination of these factors. Obviously the more exact the data used in the formula, the more accurate the answer will be. However, estimates can be used to arrive at reasonably accurate costs. EOQ can be predicted with good success for an "ivory tower situation" in which demand or usage is regular. Unfortunately this is not the case for most real-life situations. The actions of customers, suppliers, employees, and other people all directly affect the regularity of events.

Reordering Inventory

Because there are so many facets of inventory management, problems can arrive in many different ways. One facet is concerned with knowing when to order inventory. There are several mathematical computations available to estimate average demand and the deviations from it. However, the overriding factor is the organization's attitude toward customer service. If its policy is to maintain enough inventory to meet customers' demand 90 percent of the time, it cannot expect its costs of maintaining inventory to be minimized. There will always be a tradeoff between maximizing customer service and minimizing inventory maintenance cost. Inventory management is less complicated if reordering is possible.

The marketing executive faces a more complex dilemma when

he or she must decide on the quantity of goods to order when reordering is not possible. Some of the uncertainty may be removed by computing conditional losses. Suppose the marketing executive must place an order for Christmas cards several months before the holiday season begins. He or she knows that if the firm should run out of cards before the Christmas season is over, it cannot place another order in time for it to arrive because the supplier is running his manufacturing process early. The marketing executive feels that anything not sold at the end of the season represents a loss since it will have to be sold below cost. Since designs change each year, the firm has found that it is not wise to carry Christmas cards over to the next year. Besides, the cards are costly to store and sometimes become soiled and faded. Analysis of sales in past years and forecasts for the current year reveal that the probabilities of events are as given in Exhibit 8-3.

Exhibit 8-3.   **Probabilities of events.**

DEMAND LEVEL	PROBABILITY OF SELLING
1,050	.20
1,100	.30
1,150	.40
1,200	.10

Source: James A. Constantin, *Principles of Logistics Management* (New York: Appleton-Century-Crofts, 1966), p. 337.

For ease of computation, suppose each box costs $10 and can be sold for $15 during the holiday season. At the end of the season, extra promotion costs are incurred to advertise whatever cards are left. Since the cards can be sold only at a small percentage of their original price, the revenue from the end-of-season sale counterbalances the extra costs of sales promotion. No consideration is given in Exhibit 8-4 to the revenue and extra advertising costs in connection with the cards sold at the end of the season.

As can be seen from the first event in Exhibit 8-4, the firm cannot sell more than it stocks. If only 1,050 boxes are purchased, profit will remain at $5,250. (No consideration is given here to the costs from the loss of customer goodwill when stockouts occur.) In Event 2, when 1,100 boxes are stocked, the maximum revenue will be $16,500, resulting in an income of $5,500. Event 3 has a maximum income of $5,750, since 1,150 boxes are stocked. The maximum income for all events is when demand is greatest at 1,200 boxes and that quantity is available for sale.

Exhibit 8-4. **Detailed costs and revenue for events.**

	Boxes Stocked	Demand Level	Total Cost	Total Revenue	Conditional Income
Event 1	1,050	1,050	$10,500	$15,750	$5,250
	1,050	1,100	10,500	15,750	5,250
	1,050	1,150	10,500	15,750	5,250
	1,050	1,200	10,500	15,750	5,250
Event 2	1,100	1,050	$11,000	$15,750	$4,750
	1,100	1,100	11,000	16,500	5,500
	1,100	1,150	11,000	16,500	5,500
	1,100	1,200	11,000	16,500	5,500
Event 3	1,150	1,050	$11,500	$15,750	$4,250
	1,150	1,100	11,500	16,500	5,000
	1,150	1,150	11,500	17,250	5,750
	1,150	1,200	11,500	17,250	5,750
Event 4	1,200	1,150	$12,000	$15,750	$3,750
	1,200	1,100	12,000	16,500	4,500
	1,200	1,150	12,000	17,250	5,250
	1,200	1,200	12,000	18,000	6,000

Adapted from a similar table in James A. Constantin, *Principles of Logistics Management* (New York: Appleton-Century-Crofts, 1966), p. 338.

Exhibit 8-5 summarizes the conditional income for the four events described in detail in Exhibit 8-4. While Exhibit 8-5 does not contain figures other than those listed in Exhibit 8-4, it displays them in a form that is easy to refer to.

Expected value. The data in Exhibits 8-3 and 8-5 are combined in Exhibit 8-6, which shows the expected monetary value for each level of demand. The expected value for each stock level is computed by multiplying the probability of the occurrence of the demand level by the conditional profit for each level of event. The products for

Exhibit 8-5. **Conditional income for events.**

	Units Stocked			
Demand Level	1,050	1,100	1,150	1,200
1,050	$5,250	$4,750	$4,250	$3,750
1,100	5,250	5,500	5,000	4,500
1,150	5,250	5,500	5,750	5,250
1,200	5,250	5,500	5,750	6,000

Adapted from a similar table in James A. Constantin, *Principles of Logistics Management* (New York: Appleton-Century-Crofts, 1966), p. 338.

Exhibit 8-6.   Expected monetary value for events.

Demand Level	Probability of Demand	1,050 Stocked		1,100 Stocked		1,150 Stocked		1,200 Stocked	
		Conditional Income	Expected Value	Conditional Income	Expected Value	Conditional Income	Expected Value	Conditional Income	Expected Value
1,050	.20	$5,250	$1,050	$4,750	$ 950	$4,250	$ 850	$3,750	$ 750
1,100	.30	5,250	1,575	5,500	1,650	5,000	1,500	4,500	1,350
1,150	.40	5,250	2,100	5,500	2,200	5,750	2,300	5,250	2,100
1,200	.10	5,250	525	5,500	550	5,750	575	6,000	600
			$5,250		$5,350		$5,225		$4,800

Source: James A. Constantin, *Principles of Logistics Management* (New York: Appleton-Century-Crofts, 1966).

Exhibit 8-7.   Conditional opportunity losses.

Demand Level	Income from Stocking Exact Demand Level	Income from Stocking				Income Difference Between Stocking Exact Demand Level			
		1,050	1,100	1,150	1,200	1,050	1,100	1,150	1,200
1,050	$5,250	$5,250	$4,750	$4,250	$3,750	—	$500	$1,000	$1,500
1,100	5,500	5,250	5,500	5,000	4,500	$250	—	500	1,000
1,150	5,750	5,250	5,500	5,750	5,250	500	250	—	500
1,200	6,000	5,250	5,500	5,750	6,000	750	500	250	—

Exhibit 8-8.   Expected losses for events.

Demand Level	Probability of Demand	1,050 Stocked		1,100 Stocked		1,150 Stocked		1,200 Stocked	
		Conditional Loss	Expected Loss	Conditional Loss	Expected Loss	Conditional Loss	Expected Loss	Conditional Loss	Expected Loss
1,050	.20	—	—	$500	$100	$1,000	$200	$1,500	$300
1,100	.30	$250	$ 75	—	—	500	150	1,000	300
1,150	.40	500	200	250	100	—	—	500	200
1,200	.10	750	75	500	50	250	25	—	—
			$350		$250		$375		$800

Adapted from a table in James A. Constantin, *Principles of Logistics Management* (New York: Appleton-Century-Crofts, 1966).

each alternative stock level are added together to give the expected monetary value. In all events except for the demand level of 1,200, it must be reemphasized that the firm cannot sell more than it stocks. Expected monetary values show the optimum order to make, which is 1,100 units for the data in Exhibit 8-6, because that is the order for which the total expected value is highest.

Expected opportunity loss. A slightly different approach using the expected opportunity loss is illustrated for the same data in Exhibits 8-7 and 8-8. In Exhibit 8-7 the profit of stocking the same number of units as the demand level is given in the second column. Obviously the ideal situation is to match exactly the inventory level with the demand level. The conditional incomes for each inventory level are obtained from Exhibit 8-5. These income figures are compared against the income earned from stocking the same inventory as the demand level. They represent the conditional income that is lost from not stocking the correct inventory level. Part of the income difference results from overstocking inventory and being unable to sell it at the seasonal price. Opportunity loss accounts for the other income differences. For example, if the demand level is 1,200 and only 1,050 items are stocked, the firm has lost the opportunity to earn $5 income on these 150 units demanded that were not supplied and sold.

In Exhibit 8-8 conditional losses from each inventory level are multiplied by the probability that the event will happen. The products for each inventory level stocked are added together to give the expected loss. The inventory stock level that has the lowest expected loss represents the optimum order quantity. This is the same answer obtained by using an expected monetary value analysis.

Both the expected monetary value and the expected loss methods give marketing executives only guidelines. As mentioned earlier, no cost consideration is given to the current or future loss of customer goodwill from stockouts. Management might decide that since this is such a complex issue, the firm should increase its inventory level above the optimum one indicated by either the expected monetary value or the expected loss method. This would especially be true when the results from the next higher stock level are only slightly less favorable than those from the optimum one.

Despite the fact that the question of what customer service level to maintain is strongly affected by subjective factors, management needs at least some objective guidelines on the cost of maintaining certain service levels. A payoff table similar to Exhibits 8-3, 8-4, 8-5, and 8-6 can be prepared to arrive at conditional values and expected monetary values.

Exhibit 8-9. Conditional income for alternative inventory levels.

STOCKED	DEMANDED	LOST SALES	PRODUCT COST OF SALES @ $5	WAREHOUSING COSTS @ $1	CONTRIBUTION OF LOST SALES @ $4	TOTAL COSTS	SALES REVENUE @ $10	CONDITIONAL INCOME
Alternative 1.			Stock 100 units to meet demand 60% of the time					
100	100	—	$ 500	$100	—	$ 600	$1,000	$ 400
100	200	100	500	100	$ 400	1,000	1,000	—
100	300	200	500	100	800	1,400	1,000	−400
100	400	300	500	100	1,200	1,800	1,000	−800
Alternative 2.			Stock 200 units to meet demand 70% of the time					
200	100	—	$ 500	$200	—	$ 700	$1,000	$ 300
200	200	—	1,000	200	—	1,200	2,000	800
200	300	100	1,000	200	$ 400	1,600	2,000	400
200	400	200	1,000	200	800	2,000	2,000	—
Alternative 3.			Stock 300 units to meet demand 85% of the time					
300	100	—	$ 500	$300	—	$ 800	$1,000	$ 200
300	200	—	1,000	300	—	1,300	2,000	700
300	300	—	1,500	300	—	1,800	3,000	1,200
300	400	100	1,500	300	$ 400	2,200	3,000	800
Alternative 4.			Stock 400 units to meet demand 100% of the time					
400	100	—	$ 500	$400	—	$ 900	$1,000	$ 100
400	200	—	1,000	400	—	1,400	2,000	600
400	300	—	1,500	400	—	1,900	3,000	1,100
400	400	—	2,000	400	—	2,400	4,000	1,600

Adapted from a table in James A. Constantin, *Principles of Logistics Management* (New York: Appleton-Century-Crofts, 1966), p. 358.

In addition to product cost, there are two other costs directly associated with inventory. One is the cost of storage; the other is the opportunity cost of income that the organization was not able to earn because it did not maintain a large enough inventory to meet customer demand. Product cost and warehousing costs are objectively measurable, and are recognized by accountants on their income statements.

Accountants do not recognize the contribution from lost sales as costs on their financial statements. Opportunity cost is used only for internal analysis. Assume in Exhibit 8-9 that the sales price is $10, the inventory costs $5, and storage costs amount to 20 percent of cost or $1 per unit. Different levels of stock that can be practically stored are estimated. These levels are in the range of demand that has been forecasted for the specific lead time involved. Adjustments will have to be made if the demand time period and the lead time period are not the same. It is assumed in Exhibits 8-9 and 8-10 that there is a one-week lead time, and the demand levels illustrated are also for a weekly time period. The probabilities of meeting customer demand would have to be developed over a long enough time period to represent accurate percentages. Again, the organization cannot sell more than it has stocked regardless of demand.

The conditional income value from Exhibit 8-9 is multiplied by the probability of demand to give the expected monetary value for each additional inventory level. The inventory level whose total expected monetary value is the highest becomes the most profitable level to maintain. In Exhibit 8-10 setting the reorder point at 300 units is the most profitable for the dollars invested. During the one-week lead time, stockouts will be prevented 85 percent of the time. This becomes an objective quantitative base to which subjective factors involving inventory levels can be applied.

Selective Inventory Control

ABC system. The ABC system of inventory management is a very practical approach. Inventory items are grouped into different classes, and varying degrees of control are applied to each class. The inventory class in which management has most of its cost receives the greatest amount of managerial attention. In order to categorize the individual inventory items, the following analysis must be made.

In Exhibit 8-11 only a few inventory items are used, with their respective unit prices.These items are listed in descending order of total consumption cost in Exhibit 8-12. The items are next divided into three classes: Class A contains items X4 and X5; Class B, items

Exhibit 8-10.   Expected monetary value of alternative inventory levels.

		STOCK 100		STOCK 200	
DEMAND	PROBABILITY	CI*	EMV†	CI*	EMV†
100	.60	$400	$240	$300	$180
200	.10	—	—	800	80
300	.15	−400	− 60	400	60
400	.15	−800	−120	—	—
	1.00		$ 60		$320

		STOCK 300		STOCK 400	
DEMAND	PROBABILITY	CI*	EMV†	CI*	EMV†
100	.60	$ 200	$120	$ 100	60
200	.10	700	70	600	60
300	.15	1,200	180	1,100	165
400	.15	800	120	1,600	240
	1.00		$490		525

Adapted from James A. Constantin, *Principles of Logistics Management* (New York: Appleton-Century-Crofts, 1966) p. 360.
*Conditional income.
†Expected monetary value.

Exhibit 8-11.   ABC analysis of inventory according to unit price.

ITEM	UNIT USAGE	UNIT PRICE	TOTAL COST
X1	3,000	$ 5.00	$15,000
X2	12,560	.50	6,280
X3	16,000	.25	4,000
X4	3,300	12.00	39,600
X5	1,000	24.00	24,000
X6	10,000	1.00	10,000
	45,860		$98,880

Exhibit 8-12.   ABC analysis of inventory according to consumption cost.

ITEM	UNIT USAGE	TOTAL COST
X4	3,300	$39,600
X5	1,000	24,000
X1	3,000	15,000
X6	10,000	10,000
X2	12,560	6,280
X3	16,000	4,000
	45,860	$98,880

X1 and X6; and Class C, X2 and X3. Exhibit 8-13 shows that only 9.4 percent of the total units account for 64.3 percent of the cost. Since so much cost is tied up in these units, the greatest degree of control should be applied here. The organization should decide to maintain a very low safety stock for items in Class A because they represent a substantial investment. Orders will be placed much more frequently for these items. Less control will be applied against Class B and even less control will be used for items in Class C. A perpetual inventory should be maintained for items in Class A, and possibly for those in Class B. The periodic inventory method will usually be satisfactory for Class C items.

Exhibit 8-13.   ABC analysis of inventory according to class.

CLASS	UNIT USAGE	PERCENT OF TOTAL	TOTAL COST	PERCENT OF TOTAL
A	4,300	9.4%	$63,600	64.3%
B	13,000	28.3	25,000	25.3
C	28,560	62.3	10,280	10.4
	45,860	100.0%	$98,880	100.0%

Operations Research

Operations research techniques have been developed to study the costs and potential savings of alternative physical distribution techniques. The application of operations research is generally most efficient in large organizations. There are a number of linear programming methods that can be used in materials handling. One of these is the assignment problem. This can be applied when there are a number of delivery vehicles ready for unloading, with several different locations and varying costs. Use of this type of problem will enable optimal assignments to be made so that total cost will be reduced.

Linear programming techniques may also be useful for analyzing which territory to assign to each warehouse, and for choosing the warehouse site. These techniques are more easily adaptable when the markets for the product are fairly well defined. This is often the case for industrial products and consumer products that are sold to warehouses.

Another method that is mathematically similar to the assignment problem is the transportation problem. The transportation method is a simple form of linear programming that can be used in choosing the territory each warehouse is to serve. It can be used when items are stored at several points throughout a plant, and must be delivered to various organizational segments. The cost of moving the goods from each segment varies. The transportation problem will show how all segments can be supplied in the least expensive way.

Scheduling problems can be better understood through the study of the *queuing theory* (sometimes called the waiting time theory). This theory is primarily concerned with processes that arrive at random time intervals; the servicing of the customer is also a random problem. Assuming that there are costs associated with waiting in line, and also that there are costs associated with adding more service channels, management will wish to minimize the sum of the cost of waiting and the costs of providing service facilities. The queuing theory will produce measures of the expected number of people in line or the expected waiting time of the arrivals, and these measures can help management determine the most desirable number of service facilities.

Limitations of Management Tools

Certainly management should realize that it cannot use one formula or analysis to solve all its inventory management problems. The limitations of each management tool should be understood. The results obtained should merely provide guidelines for action. Any number of intangible as well as tangible factors can make even the most careful computations invalid. This does not imply that managers are wasting their time in performing the computations or analyses because these do provide guidelines for action that would otherwise be unavailable.

SUMMARY

It is quite difficult to make improvements in the logistic system. Often certain people in the system have developed their own "empires" encompassing each independent function, and they will tend to resist any change that coordinates all functions into one system of technical developments. Hesitancy on the part of all executives is to be expected; any number of excuses will be given for leaving the physical distribution system as it is. Some executives may feel that there are so many individual factors involved that it is not feasible to make changes. However, as the study of the logistic system proceeds, potential cost-saving modifications in the organization's physical distribution will become evident.

The conditions under which the logistic system will operate gradually change. As markets grow and new products are developed, the logistic requirements will vary. The physical distribution system must be sensitive to these factors. A rigid plan may be economical under expected conditions; unfortunately market conditions vary so much that a rigid plan is often not feasible. The plan must be flexible enough to meet changing demands. There is even greater uncertainty in planning long-range developments in the logistic system.

Cost analysis is indispensable to good management of the logistic system. It may not be feasible to use a complete analysis for all projects or alternatives proposed; cost approximations may be acceptable. It can certainly be argued that accurate costing of physical distribution accomplishes almost nothing if management does nothing after receiving the results from the cost analysis.

9

Effective Pricing

THIS chapter considers the effect of pricing in an economy in which both public and private institutions exercise economic control. Price is only one element among many in determining whether a product is a success or a failure, and its relationship to other elements in the marketing mix, such as persuasive sales promotion, product quality, and delivery terms, makes it difficult to discuss pricing out of context.

Business people are continually making pricing decisions. In so doing, they have to deal with an immense variety of conditions. In industries in which products are different, the individual firm has some control over the price it will charge. However, in industries in which the products are homogeneous, firms do not possess any control. A change in price in these industries can cause a drastic change in the volume of sales.

While pricing is a very complicated function, it is not generally regarded as one that requires a specialist. The majority of prices are set by people who have no special training or experience in this area. It is often difficult to analyze the effects of certain information on a particular pricing decision. Since management often relies heavily on intuitive judgment in arriving at a final decision, pricing is considered an area where management becomes an art.

PRICE DETERMINANTS

Many factors must be considered in arriving at a selling price for a given product. These can be broadly classified as internal and external. Internal factors include cost, inventory supply, and management objectives. External factors may include such things as trends, fads, market supply and demand, and competition.

Since proper pricing is so crucial to a firm's profitability, it is imperative that the executives who have the responsibility for setting prices be aware of the relationship between the organization's objectives and pricing theory. Both long-run and short-run profitability, as well as survival, are firm objectives whose very nature requires that effective prices be established. In order for any organization to continue in the long run, it must be able to obtain for its products a price that covers all costs; if it is a profit-making organization, it must also be able to return a reasonable rate to its investors.

It must be admitted that many organizations have limited freedom in determining prices for their products. This is one reason why the information needed for pricing decisions varies among organizations. The number of competitors and the market structure are major influencing factors. The characteristics of the product lines must also be studied so that the demand for an item can be estimated. A successful organization also analyzes its customers so that it can better understand how much significance price has in their decision to buy. There must always be a tradeoff between the information that the marketing executive would like to have and the cost of gathering this data. This means that marketing executives must determine what information is specifically relevant to their decisions. Unfortunately, very few firms have explicitly examined their costs and the likely effects of price changes on demand. This does not necessarily imply that most firms charge the wrong price.

"You cannot argue with success" is a favorite expression in the business world. However, one could challenge this conventional wisdom by asking how much *more* successful a firm could be if it studied the impact of changes in the marketing mix. Often an organization's prices have been arrived at by a trial-and-error process in which some thought has been given to additional revenue and cost. Sometimes the only basis management has for raising its prices is the recognition that its salespeople are not having much difficulty selling its product. Sophisticated analyses of marginal cost, marginal revenue, and elasticity of supply and demand are missing.

The pricing policy an organization adopts has many ramifications.

For example, marketing executives not only must set prices for each of their firm's products and services, but they must also decide if they want to offer quantity discounts, and if so, at what volume of orders. If they choose to go through distributors, they must decide if they want to charge different distributors the same price. They must also investigate the possibility of offering cash discounts and determine what terms to offer if they adopt them.

Also associated with the establishment of a pricing policy is the question of varying prices in order to push an item at certain times in the business cycle. Price revision is almost a continuous process because marketing executives must constantly study the changing environment in which their product is offered for sale. The effect on price of complementary and substitute products must be considered. For instance, if there is a strong demand for tennis rackets, the price of tennis balls, which are a complementary good, could go higher. The marketing executive may lower the price of tennis rackets in order to create a market for the firm's complementary product—tennis balls.

PARTIES INVOLVED IN PRICING

The pricing policy established affects persons within the organization as well as those outside. Because of this impact, organizations often establish a pricing committee whose purpose is to analyze the data obtained to arrive at a decision. In almost all situations there will be some conflict of interest in establishing a product's price.

The salespeople generally prefer to set the price as low as possible in the hope of selling more units and possibly increasing their bonuses. But this price may not be the optimal one for the organization as a whole. In order to avoid suboptimization, company-wide objectives must be determined and distributed so that the organization is working toward goal congruence. Some of these objectives may not be in harmony and therefore cannot be sought at the same time. For example, in the short run it may not be feasible to try to obtain a large share of the market and profit maximization at the same time. Obviously since market share has a great impact on profit maximization, an organization may strive to obtain maximum market share in the short run so as to increase its chance of profit maximization in the long run. There are several definitions of profit maximization, ranging from a specific net income to a rate of return on capital. While many organizations interpret profit maximization as a rate of return on capital, there is no complete agreement on what the capital is comprised of.

Cost Accountant

The cost accountant is likely to be involved with the pricing decision because he or she wants to make sure that costs are covered. The accountant may apply the payback method to the data to see if capital outlays are covered within a desired time period.

However, the cost of any one product may not be a satisfactory price determinate, both because there are various ways of calculating costs and because the effect on sales volume is not considered.

It should also be pointed out that while costs have a very important influence on pricing decisions, customers and competitors are major influences, too, and should not be disregarded. Organizations should consider cost, prices, and demand simultaneously.

Sales Personnel

Since the price quoted can serve as a major form of sales promotion, top advertising management must be involved in the pricing procedure. The salespeople are the ones who must explain to prospective customers why their organization's price quotation is higher than that of a rival firm; therefore they must understand why these differences exist. If a price is lowered, it is an inducement for consumers to buy (they will have money left over to spend elsewhere). Quoted prices can have a psychological value. A $.98 price appears to be much cheaper than a price of $1.00, and an illusion is created whereby people think they are paying less than they actually are.

Consumers

In establishing the pricing policy of an organization, executives must be certain they know what type of customer they are trying to reach. Rarely can an organization expect its products or services to appeal to everyone. Smart executives also understand their customers' needs.

Customers are motivated by different factors, which vary over time and between products. Often they are not the "bargain hunters" trying to get the best value at the lowest price that they are perceived to be. Customers satisfy many needs when they make a purchase. If they are asked why they bought a specific item, they might be at a loss to explain the reason.

While buying behavior is almost impossible to explain in general terms, it can be said that most customers feel obliged to justify their purchases at least partially on a price basis. It is the relative price, or how the customers perceive that price, that is of greatest importance in analyzing buying behavior. For example, some customers will view a price cut as signifying a reduction in quality, or become suspicious that the seller is afraid of being stuck with excessive inventories because the demand for this product has decreased. Other customers may conclude that the product is outdated and is being replaced.

Surprisingly, a price increase may actually stimulate sales because customers may feel that the quality of the product has improved. Consumers in the most highly developed countries tend to accept a higher price as an indication of higher quality. This is the reason why pricing a product higher than competitive brands does not necessarily deter consumers from buying it. They may have, in addition, some notion of the law of supply and demand and think that the price increase indicates a limited supply. This leads to the rationalization that they had better purchase the item before the supply runs out.

Competitors

While marketing executives can establish almost any price they desire, their competitors do influence the upper limits. The executive in charge of pricing should have a good understanding of the structures of competition, whether perfect or imperfect. Through a study of the competitive situation, this executive can get a better feel for the characteristics of the product that are applicable to pricing strategy. Rarely is it considered good pricing policy to set a price materially above the competitors', unless a higher-quality product or service is being offered. Competitors' prices, then, are considered to be a flexible limit. Such market structures as perfect competition, oligopoly, and monopoly will be discussed in detail when supply and demand are introduced later in this chapter.

Middlemen

There are many areas of conflict between the producer and his middleman. The lower the price the middleman pays the manufacturer for the product, the higher will be his return. On the other hand, both parties must consider what price the customer is willing to pay. It is in the manufacturer's interest to keep the retail price low because then more customers will buy the product.

Another area of conflict centers around the question of whether more than one middleman will be allowed to carry the product. The middleman may prefer to sell the product on an exclusive basis, while the manufacturer will generally prefer a wider distribution through several middlemen. A wider distribution does add complexities to the pricing policy because each distributor may have varying cost structures and require different returns.

In establishing the pricing policy, the marketing executive must be fair and allow each middleman to make a normal return on the product. It *is* difficult to agree on an adequate return; many factors, such as supply and demand, will affect this agreement. Certainly the price that the final customer will pay for the item is a strong limiting factor. Once the price range is generally agreed upon, each party can work backward to the different distribution stages.

Government

The local, state, and federal governments each have an impact on pricing policies, with the state and federal governments having the greatest effect. There are designated unfair competitive practices, one of which is entering into a price agreement with competitors. Certain industries such as oil and agriculture operate under additional restrictions. While there are a number of laws that affect pricing, the average business is affected in only a minor way by legislation in its pricing decisions.

Robinson-Patman Act

The Robinson-Patman Act is the federal pricing law that affects most businesses. Any firm that wants to give quantity discounts, lower prices in order to meet local price-cutting situations, or grant special advertising concessions must be aware of this act. The Robinson-Patman Act is a part of the antitrust legislation of the nation because it amended Section 2 of the Clayton Act. It is not a law against the raising or lowering of prices; it is solely directed at the relationship between prices that different customers pay in a single market. The act is not concerned with sales to ultimate consumers.

One objective of this act is to ensure that all businesses are charged the same price by their suppliers if the cost of serving them is the same. Another is to suppress the pseudoadvertising allowance and the payment of brokerage or commissions under dummy brokerage firms. Discrimination in pricing or in terms of sale between purchasers of commodities of like grade and quality is prohibited.

The act was motivated by a desire to protect small organizations from misuse of the advantages that large size and buying power may give to some of their competitors. It was thought that large buyers going into a market could persuade some sellers to give them extraordinary concessions in the form of lower costs for materials and merchandise merely because they made large purchases.

The Robinson-Patman Act places the burden of cost justification of price differences on the seller. Each organization should first classify its products or commodities into groups; costs of production and distribution must then be analyzed on a product and on a market or area basis. Products that are perfect substitutes for each other may be considered different if their brand labels differ because of their imputed value. If an organization does charge different prices to its customers for a similar product, it has several possible defenses. One is to state that it is not in interstate commerce; however, this is the most difficult defense to prove. Another is to state that its pricing practices do not have a substantially undesirable effect on its competitors or its competitors' customers; the Federal Trade Commission's interpretation of undesirable effect on competition makes this defense also difficult to prove. The disposal of obsolescent and seasonal goods or other nonrepetitive sales of distress merchandise is an exception where price differentials are accepted. The defense used most often by organizations is cost differences. However, to properly use this defense, many businesses would be required to prepare, calculate, and submit accounting information that may not be easily obtainable from existing records.

The use of distribution cost accounting makes it legally feasible to charge different prices to different types of consumers. This practice passes on to consumers the advantages of buying in those quantities or by those methods that result in a saving for the seller. The Accounting Division of the Federal Trade Commission studies pricing policies and cost data on Robinson-Patman cases. A respondent may elect to justify price differences on the basis of the cost of doing business with different classes of customers. Price variations are allowed for differences arising in the cost of manufacturing different quantities, the cost of sales, or the cost of delivering certain quantities. Price differentials granted must not exceed differences in the cost of serving different customers.

The cost justification can be applied only if the price differential is offered to all customers who meet the conditions on which the differential is based. Price differentials based on differences in the functions performed by the different classes of customers may be granted without any requirement for cost justification. This is because customers in different functional groups are normally not in competition with each other.

Under the Robinson-Patman Act, manufacturers may at any time be called upon to justify, on the basis of cost, quantity discounts given to large-quantity purchasers. The act permits quantity discounts if the same discount is given to all customers purchasing the same quantity. If a company grants quantity discounts, the discount rates should not be established on quantities so high that only a few favored customers can take advantage of them. The quantity ranges in each discount class must be established so that substantial proportions of the company's customers will fall in each range.

Regardless of type or form, discounts are extremely difficult to justify. They are generally available to larger purchasers, thus creating unfair competitive market conditions for smaller purchasers. Costs that would have to be considered in justifying the various discounts are distribution, manufacturing, and buried costs. The justification of each of these would be necessary to prove that the discounts were given in good faith and not in restraint of trade and competition.

Savings in distribution costs is the most often advanced justification for price differences. The wording of the statute has frequently been interpreted as ruling out the possibility of cost justification on the basis of differences in production costs. Rarely are savings in manufacturing costs used as a justification because the greater portion of the products manufactured are not produced on special order. The majority of production activities are performed to meet the needs of all consumers.

No standard type of distribution cost analysis is required by either the Robinson-Patman Act or the regulations of the Federal Trade Commission. To determine cost differences satisfactorily, however, cost statistics regarding all distribution functions must be obtained. Joint costs must be apportioned on bases that appear reasonable and equitable under the individual circumstances. The method used for purposes of price setting under the Robinson-Patman Act will largely depend upon the manner in which the distribution activity is organized.

To determine distribution costs applicable to products and classes of customers, analysis of the formal books of account is required. The information obtained in the accounts is often not sufficient to justify pricing policies. Analyses are also required of such statistical records as those that record the functions of credit and collection and the activities of sales personnel.

The vague wording of the Robinson-Patman Act leaves ample room for interpretation. Price discrimination implies competition between purchasers within a given market area; therefore the producer must define his competitive markets (the area of competition is not defined in the act). Since the regulations refer only to commodities, there are many borderline cases between services and commodities. The answers to many of the questions concerning the act's effect on business operations depend upon the attitude and policy of the Federal Trade Commission.

COST-BASED PRICING METHODS

Not only is cost needed to justify price differentials under the Robinson-Patman Act, but it is also needed in the actual establishment of the price. It is very difficult to determine what relationship between costs and prices is most practicable and profitable. The final determination of the cost-price relationship can have social and political implications. The selling price established gives companies some control over the final prices charged for their products. They have an even greater control over the costs they incur.

Cost-Plus Pricing

Under cost-plus pricing methods, or backward-cost pricing methods as they are sometimes referred to, cost does play a vital part in pricing because product development and its costs are related to the price range determined applicable. A desired percentage is added to the product cost either on a variable-costing or a full absorption-costing basis. There are several methods of cost pricing, and the method used by a firm depends on top management's general goal for future business. Management may desire to cover all costs, as well as render a profit figure, with its selling price.

Determining what profit figure to add is difficult. Profit can be calculated as a return on estimated fixed investment in the product, or as a return on costs associated with the product. Some managers argue that current assets vary directly with sales; therefore as prices and expenses increase, current assets should increase. Thus they feel that the ratio of capital employed should consider the ratio of sales to current assets and of sales to fixed assets. Others argue that profit consists of two parts. One is the return on invested capital, which is called interest; the other is the return for the risk of the enterprise.

Regardless of the cost concepts used as a basis for price setting, one of the first steps is to group an organization's costs into various types. Manufacturing costs should be separated from marketing and administrative costs, and then detailed into material, labor, and overhead costs. A further breakdown should be made of all costs according to their fixed and variable elements.

Full-Cost Pricing

The full-cost pricing method involves determining the product's direct costs, which are those costs that can be traced or attached to the product. To this figure a charge is made for indirect costs that are incurred by the overall organization and cannot be traced to one cost center. These costs are allocated as a rate per direct labor-dollar, direct labor-hour, machine-hour, or on some other acceptable basis. The preferred approach is to determine in advance of operations what this allocation rate will be so that products can be carried into finished goods inventory with an estimate for overhead. Once full cost is determined, a profit figure can be added.

Though the process appears simple, there is a problem in determining what level of activity indirect costs should be allocated to. However, this difficulty can be overcome. A normal volume can be estimated or determined and used to allocate costs. In determining normal capacity, both plant capacity and sales potential must be considered. Sales expectancy should be used for a long enough time period to level out cyclical variations. Normal capacity should first be determined for the organization as a whole, and then for its various departments.

The cost-plus method of pricing is not without drawbacks. Determining the full cost of any product involves cost allocations based on judgment, opinion, and custom. Calculation of normal capacity is not a simple matter because many judgment factors must be considered. In addition, direct and indirect costs are often difficult to separate; this is especially true in distinguishing costs for various jobs using the same resources. The accountant's full costs fail to consider the opportunity costs of a product; instead only those costs of a specific alternative or job are considered, and possible other uses of the firm's resources are ignored.

Full costing includes allocation of such indirect costs as depreciation, and some people feel that sunk costs should not enter into the pricing decision because these costs are irrevocable. For example, if an organization purchases a special machine designed to improve its product, the price should not be raised just to cover the extra-period cost from the depreciation on the machine. This machine represents a sunk cost.

Variable Costs

Because of the difficulties encountered in using full or absorption costing, many managers have turned to the variable-costing concept for use in the pricing decision. Only variable costs are treated as product costs under this concept. Since this method is more sensitive to cost-volume-profit relationships, it is generally considered better. It allows management to determine prices for either the short run or the long run, because the effect of different prices can be related to total fixed costs. Variable costs can be compared with the selling price to determine what will be left over to cover fixed costs and profits.

The variable-costing or contribution approach, like the full-costing approach, is not immune to criticism. One of the main objections to this method is that prices may be lower than under the full or absorption method. Probably the most common answer to this argument is that the full-costing method does not take into account all costs either. It often makes no provision for marketing and administrative expenses in the calculation of cost per unit, so these must be covered by a "plus" to the cost figure.

Differential, Incremental, and Marginal Costs

Some authorities define differential, incremental, and marginal costs as all the same. However the approach followed in this chapter is to refer to marginal cost as the per unit change in cost from one alternative to another, and to use differential and incremental costs interchangeably as applying to the total cost change from one situation to another. This assumes there is no additional fixed cost in the production of additional units, so that any price higher than variable cost will yield a profit.

In a competitive situation, the lower the bid, the higher the probability of getting the contract. However, if the bid isn't high enough to cover incremental costs, the organization would be better off not receiving the contract. In arriving at a decision, competitors' actions must be estimated. Both the capacity at which an executive's own organization is working and the estimated workload of competitors are influential. If an organization is already working near full capacity, costs will be higher.

Incremental costs, which for the most part are variable, generally offer a minimum below which the product should not be sold. However, in some situations management will have to sell below variable cost just to have some revenue to apply to existing costs. These situations are rare and generally involve skilled workers whom management wants to retain on its payroll during temporarily bad conditions in order to avoid having to train new workers when the situation improves.

Conversion Cost

The conversion-cost pricing method attempts to direct manufacturing and sales efforts to those products that require less labor and factory overhead, or conversion costs. The theory behind this method is that if two products have the same profit per unit but one requires less labor and overhead, then if efforts are directed toward that product, more units can be produced and sold and therefore greater profits can be realized. This method allows no profit for materials used in the conversion process. It does not consider the effect of an increase in supply on price, though in a competitive situation this might have to be considered.

Standard Cost

Standard cost for pricing can be used with either the variable-costing or full-costing approach. Standard costs are considered especially valuable for pricing because they are based upon a careful study of what can be done with the production facilities available. Standard cost for pricing assumes that the well-organized plant can and does meet standard production cost at normal operating volume. This approach suggests that a more logical method of competitive pricing is to spread the fixed cost on the basis of optimum utilization of equipment. Direct labor and material costs included in the selling price are based on an efficient operation exclusive of excessive rework, scrap, and down time. Use of this approach in developing cost-selling price comparisons results in consistency among the various products.

Standard costs can be readily adjusted to reflect anticipated changes in the prices of material and labor. Care should be taken to make adjustments in standard cost whenever significant changes in raw material prices, labor rates, or even overhead derived from rates based on normal volume occur. Standard costs used in conjunction with other information can be of considerable aid in determining the profitability of each type of product manufactured.

The advantages of using standard cost for prices are the reduction in detailed work, which aids the accountant, and the availability of cost estimates, which aids the manager in charge of the pricing decision. With the use of standard cost in pricing, the various variances may be calculated quickly and accurately.

Cost-based pricing methods really don't offer a good basis for pricing; however, to ignore costs in setting prices is nonsense, as a profit-making organization must cover its costs in the long run if it is to survive. Costs offer limitations below which the product should not generally be sold.

One of the main objections to any cost-based pricing method is that it does not take into account the effect of price on the quantity sold. Customers and competition are given little or no consideration. However, those who use this method do not allow the "plus" to be rigid; they vary the profit percentage by product in order to achieve a mix that will allow a maximum return. Probably the best argument for cost-based pricing is that management uses costs just to estimate a competitive price for its product, and will adjust this price to take into consideration the normal profit returns in the particular industry.

In spite of the seemingly minor role of cost in pricing, there is a useful and important relationship between cost and price. This relationship is vividly displayed through examination of the familiar supply and demand model. Economists believe that supply and demand determine price; in turn, business costs help determine supply. The matching of supply and demand and price and costs determines what things will be produced by whom and for which customers. Broadly speaking, the supply side, when expressed in dollars, is the cost of production and distribution, and the demand side is the revenue obtained for that production and distribution.

For every purchase there must be a sale, and price takes into account the interests of both buyers and sellers. In time, if reductions in costs do not keep pace with reductions in selling price, the supply of a given product will be reduced. Cost then offers a resistance to the lowering of selling price both in the short run and in the long run, though this resistance is subject to considerable variation. Cost also influences price to the point that organizations try to keep cost to a minimum by adopting the most efficient methods of production. The method that gives the lowest product costs will replace a more costly method.

PRICING THEORY—SUPPLY AND DEMAND

At any point in time there exists a relationship between the market price of an economic good and the quantity demanded of that good. This relationship between price and quantity demanded can be expressed in a demand curve.

Demand Curve

In deriving a demand curve, it can be concluded that *ceteris paribus* (holding all other variables constant), the quantity demanded of an economic good by the individual consumer will vary inversely with the price of that good. Thus almost all products have a downward-sloping demand curve—the higher the price, the lower will be the quantity demanded.

Obviously the price established must meet the acceptance of some customers; otherwise no units would be sold. In turn, these customers must be large enough in number to justify continued production. This is the reason for deriving the demand curve: the characteristics of the individual consumer must be analyzed. It is recognized that changes in tastes, income, and the price of other goods also affect the quantity demanded; however, these are treated as constants in the concept of the consumer's demand curve. A movement along a given single demand curve is referred to as a *change in quantity demanded*, while a shift in a demand curve is referred to as a *change in demand*. This distinction is important for the pricing executive because a change in quantity demanded refers to the effect of changes on that good. A change in demand refers to the effect of changes in variables other than the price of the good upon the quantity demanded.

The marketing executive also needs to understand the effect of the principle of diminishing marginal utility on his or her products. Marginal utility is the change in total utility a consumer receives from acquiring one more unit of the product. The rate of change is assumed to decrease as quantity increases; this assumption is referred to as the *principle of diminishing marginal utility*.

Rational Consumer Expenditure

Assuming that consumers are rational, given the principle of diminishing marginal utility, they would allocate their expenditures so that total utility is highest. Since economic goods differ in prices, they must choose a pattern that ensures that a dollar spent on any economic good will give the same marginal utility. The principle of rational consumer expenditure says purchases will be made so that the marginal utility of goods (such as a, b, and c) is proportional to their prices. That is;

$$\frac{MUa}{Pa} = \frac{MUb}{Pb} = \frac{MUc}{Pc} = \ldots$$

Superior and inferior goods. In studying consumer demand for a specific product, management should determine if it is a superior or inferior good. Inferior goods are defined as those the consumer would purchase less of at higher income levels. Superior goods are those that would be purchased in greater quantity at higher income levels.

Elasticity of Demand

Not only does the law of demand apply to price theory, but also the relationship between customer behavior and price changes must be understood. Elasticity refers to the ratio of relative change in variables that are thought to be related. If the quantity demanded is very responsive to price changes, a given relative change in price will cause a more than proportionate change in quantity demanded. This can be expressed in the following form:

$$- \frac{(\Delta Q)/Q}{(\Delta P)/P}$$

The negative sign in front of the formula is used to avoid ambiguity. Because price changes are associated with opposite changes in quantity, the ratio $\Delta P/\Delta Q$ will be negative for all downward-sloping demand curves. If no negative sign preceded the formula, the expression would be negative and possibly confusing. The greater responsiveness of quantity demanded to relative changes in price results in a larger numerical value. The price elasticity of demand is high if a small change in price results in a material change in quantity sold. If this expression is less than 1, or unity, the demand curve is referred to as being inelastic. If elasticity is less than unity, total revenue will increase when the price is raised.

Elasticity of demand indicates to marketing executives whether a price can be successfully raised or lowered. For example, if a slight increase in price does not decrease sales enough to decrease total revenue, the price rise would be considered successful.

A price is too high if a small decrease would increase the units sold so that total revenue would be increased. It must be remembered, however, that this price reduction would apply to all units sold, even those purchased by customers who were willing to pay the higher price. Marketing executives may find it quite difficult to determine the price elasticity for each product because the change in sales caused by a price variation is not consistent between time periods or markets.

Availability of substitutes is one of a number of factors that affect elasticity. This is readily apparent, for when the price of a product increases, consumers will likely consider changing to substitutes. The greater the number of accessible substitutes, the greater the elasticity of the product. Consumers will also be more likely to switch to another product if a sizable portion of their total income is spent on this product. The larger this proportion of total income, the more elastic the product demand will be. In addition, the more durable the product, the greater the elasticity of demand, because consumers can postpone replacement. If, on the other hand, the product is but a small part of the total cost of a single demand, it will tend to have low price elasticity. For example, in sewing a dress, the thread is an insignificant cost of the total garment and would therefore tend to have low price elasticity. Habit also plays an important role in price inelasticity. Products that consumers habitually buy are less likely to be affected by price changes because their price elasticity of demand is low.

The price of complementary goods also affects a product's demand. If the price of tennis rackets increases, the quantity of tennis balls demanded tends to fall. The concept of cross-elasticity of demand measures the responsiveness of the quantity demanded of one good to relative changes in the price of another. Cross-elasticity of demand is involved in both complementary goods and goods that are substitutes for each other. The cross-elasticity of demand for complementary goods is negative; it is positive for goods that can be substituted for each other when the price rises. The relationship of a good to other products is another factor to consider when price changes are anticipated.

Supply Curve

Sellers will react to higher prices by increasing the quantity of goods they supply; thus the supply curve (S) in Exhibit 9-1 is upward sloping. (Earlier in this chapter it was explained why the demand curve (D) is downward sloping.) Given a purely competitive market and the assumptions made earlier about buyers, the price will be determined in the market as shown in Exhibit 9-1. Given an initial price of P_1, the quantity demanded is only Q_2, though sellers are quite willing to offer Q_3 at this higher price. If these sellers refuse to lower the price, they will have excess inventory. Normally they will bid the price down to dispose of these excess goods; however, product costs will provide a floor under which they usually should not lower the price. (Earlier in the chapter some rare instances were noted when it might be better to sell a product below even its variable costs.) In a purely competitive market, price will change until it reaches P_e, the equilibrium price at which the quantity demanded equals the quantity supplied. Market equilibrium occurs at the price for which quantities supplied and demanded are equal.

If instead the initial price was P_2, the quantity sellers were willing

Exhibit 9-1.   Supply curve.

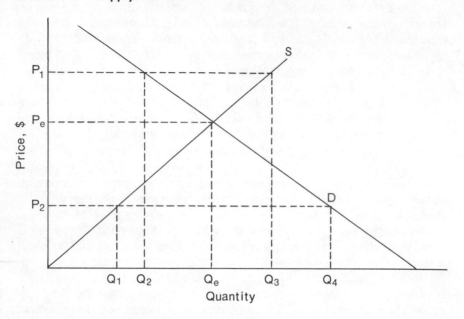

to supply would be Q_1, while consumers wanted to buy Q_4. This excess demand would bid up the price to P_e.

Price Elasticity of Supply

Price elasticity of supply measures the relative responsiveness of the quantity supplied to relative changes in the price of the good. The formula for elasticity of supply (which is the same as for the price elasticity of demand, except that no negative sign is needed since the supply curve's slope is positive) is as follows:

$$\frac{(\Delta Q)/Q}{(\Delta P)/P}$$

COMPETITIVE STRUCTURES

An individual firm's demand differs from the total market demand, depending upon the sellers' relationship to one another. If there is only one seller (a monopolist), the firm's demand and elasticity of demand will be the same as the industry's. Conversely, if there are a number of firms, each will sell only a portion of the industry's output. With so many competing firms, no one firm's output affects the market price, and the price elasticities of the industry are independent of any individual firm's demand curve. The degree of the difference between the two elasticities depends upon the competitive structure of the industry. In pure or perfect competition the difference is infinite, while, at the other extreme, in a monopoly, the difference is zero.

Pure or Perfect Competition

Pure or perfect competition exists where there are many producers and no individual producer (or worker) is a large enough segment of the market to have any influence on the market price. There is freedom of entry into the market. Since the products sold are homogeneous and there is no consumer preference for a specific product brand, there is usually no need for nonprice competition such as advertising.

Not many perfect competitive situations exist in the current economy. Some agricultural stock exchanges and metal products that are sold in markets more closely resemble perfect competition than any other pricing situation. However, most products are sold in competitive situations in which the pricing decision is complex. Most of the products sold are not homogeneous; their quality differs, even if the difference is only in the customer's mind, and prices can vary between individual products that are perceived as differing in quality.

A perfect market denotes a random relationship between buyer and seller—neither cares with whom he closes a transaction. A perfect market establishes the price for the seller, and he becomes a price taker. The extreme flexibility of prices does not ensure that the market will be cleared, for sellers will hoard if prices are too low, and buyers will not buy if prices are too high. The average price taker may not receive the actual price set in a perfect market. A farmer may receive the price less cost of transportation to market, and a seller of stocks gets the current price less brokerage fees.

As shown in Exhibit 9-2, the pure competitor cannot influence the market price by changes in output; the firm's demand is a horizontal line of infinite elasticity at the equilibrium. The pure competitor takes the market price for each product sold. The firm's average revenue (AR) equals the market price. Since all units are sold at the same price, marginal revenue (MR) equals the equilibrium market price.

Management operating under pure or perfect competition does not have a complex task in establishing the price of its product because

Exhibit 9-2.   Pure or perfect competition.

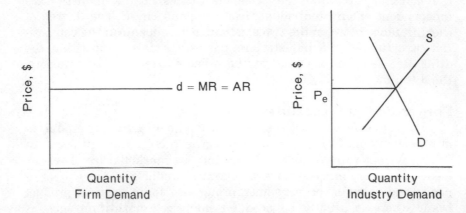

Firm Demand   Industry Demand

it merely accepts the price that competitors are offering. The reason
for this is that a perfect competitor is selling a homogeneous product
and does not command a large enough share of the market to affect
price. His competitors are not affected by his actions. Under these
circumstances, the smart marketing executive will not change the
prevailing price above or below this level.

Profit maximization. In perfect competition the firm is assumed
to be able to sell as much as it wants at a market price over which
it has no control. Profit maximization is easy because all the firm
has to do is find the specific output quantity that yields maximum
profit and sell at that output with the given market price. In choosing
its best Q supply, the firm refers to its marginal-cost curve (MC),
as given in Exhibit 9-3. Its point of profit maximization is where

Exhibit 9-3.   Profit maximization under perfect competition.

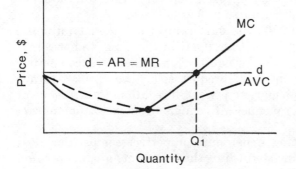

P = MC = MR, or point 1 above selling Q^1. If average revenue (AR) should lie below average variable costs (AVC), the firm would not operate, since the average revenue would not cover the incremental cost per unit. This explains why the supply curve of the competitive firm is that portion of its marginal cost curve above the lowest point of the firm's average variable cost curve. The industry supply curve is derived by adding horizontally all the firm's supply curves.

Monopoly

At the opposite end of the continuum from pure competition lies a monopoly. A monopoly in its purest sense is a market in which there is only one seller. This means the firm's demand is identical to market demand for the products; however, in order for this to have validity for the period being considered, the monopolist must not be afraid that other firms will enter the market, regardless of what market price he selects. For practical purposes, a monopoly also exists when the product of one firm has no close substitutes.

The market demand curve for a monopolist is downward sloping, so the price received varies inversely with the quantity sold. The monopolist's price is not independent of the output of the firm, as it is in perfect competition. Marginal revenue is not constant because there is a change in price for every change in quantity. Marginal revenue is the change in total revenue received when the quantity sold differs by one unit.

Exhibit 9-4. Marginal cost and marginal revenue.

Quantity*	Average Revenue or Price	Total Revenue	Total Cost	Total Profit	Marginal Revenue (MR)		Marginal Cost (MC)
1	200	200	120	80			
					160	>	110
2	180	360	230	130			
					60	>	55
3	140	420	285	135			
					20	=	20
4	110	440	300	140			
					−40	<	80
5	80	400	380	20			
					−100	<	120
6	50	300	500	−200			

*Output and sales are assumed always to be equal.

As can be seen in Exhibit 9-4, the marginal revenue for any given quantity will be less than the price or the average revenue. When an additional unit is sold, the firm's total revenue increases by an amount less than the price. Total revenue rises at first with quantity, because the reduction in price needed to sell the extra units is moderate in the first elastic range of the demand curve. Increasing quantity beyond the point where total revenue reaches its maximum puts the firm into inelastic demand regions. This point is four units in Exhibit 9-4.

Average total cost offers little aid to the marketing executive in pricing theory. While it is true that a business must cover its total costs to stay in operation in the long run, average costs have little relevance to the maximization of profit. In addition, a smart monopolist does not charge the highest possible price in order to maximize profits, as is sometimes believed, because then he might sell no quantity or only a small amount. Instead the maximum profit equilibrium for a monopolist is where marginal revenue (MR) equals marginal cost (MC). Marginal cost is the additional cost of producing one more unit. The maximum profit monopoly equilibrium in Exhibit 9-4 is at a total profit of $140, where marginal revenue and marginal cost are both equal at $20.

With a downward-sloping demand curve, as illustrated in Exhibit 9-5, MR is less than AR at any specific point. The maximum equilibrium

Exhibit 9-5.   Profit maximization under monopoly.

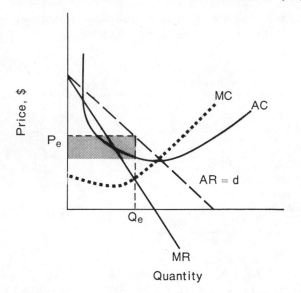

position is found where MC intersects MR. The price is found by going up to the demand curve to arrive at price P_e selling quantity Q_e. The shaded rectangle measures total profit.

Monopolistic or Imperfect Competition

Under monopolistic competition, it is assumed that there are so many sellers, each so small in relation to the market, that they have little or no control over the market price. This type of market structure is sometimes referred to as imperfect competition with many differentiated sellers. The service or product sold under this structure is assumed to be differentiated in the minds of buyers; sellers use advertising trade names, packaging, and other marketing methods for distinctiveness. It is further assumed that firms can easily enter the industry since there are no significant barriers.

Monopolistic competition postulates that each firm is so small that it need not fear retaliation from other firms in the industry if it changes its output or price. Even though there is some product differentiation, the goods are close substitutes and the cross-elasticities of demand are high. As a result, the firm does not have much freedom to vary price. A change in price will cause a relatively large change in quantity demanded because consumers will often switch their loyalty to another product. If the marketing executive of a monopolistic competition firm raises price above that existing in the market, he or she can expect to lose a large number of customers to competitors. However, for any one of these competitors, the increase in quantity sold is small because there are so many firms in the industry.

The demand curve shown in Exhibit 9-6 is more elastic at a

Exhibit 9-6. Profit maximization under monopolistic competition.

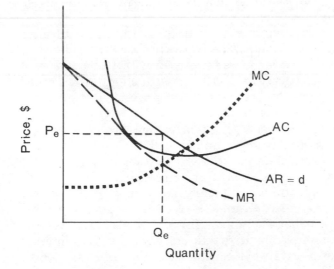

given price than that of the whole industry. Profit maximization under monopolistic competition occurs at a price where marginal revenue (MR) equals marginal cost (MC). If, as in Exhibit 9-6, there are pure profits in the short run, new firms will be attracted to the industry. In general, the demand for an individual firm's output would fall with this entry and become more elastic.

Each individual firm tries to keep its share of the market by building customer allegiance. It does this by increasing its advertising or other marketing methods, which would cause its total costs to also increase. As a result, the long-run equilibrium would contain no pure profit since the average cost (AC) curve would be tangent to the demand curve.

Oligopoly

The number of firms in an oligopoly is small, and there is little or no differentiation among the products they sell. Hence each producer is keenly aware of any competitor's pricing policies. There is mutual interdependence because each firm knows that if it cuts its price, its competitors will match the price reduction, and all firms in the oligopoly will be worse off. If it raises its price, its rivals will not follow and it will lose its share of the market. Where there are only a few sellers of homogeneous products, there is a strong incentive for all firms to charge only the prevailing price (similar to the situation under perfect competition). An oligopolist firm selling a homogeneous product would reduce its sales price only if it thought it could sell more units, knowing all the time that its competitors would likely follow its price reduction.

This is what leads oligopolistic firms to tacitly agree to price their products at a given figure. The prices are then considered to be administered. Antitrust laws are concerned with this problem of collusion. Before the antitrust laws were passed, oligopolists formed mergers, trusts, or cartels and collusively set prices. When all firms experience the same problems in the economy, it is easy for them to follow a policy that avoids fierce price competition. Each oligopolistic firm will establish a similar price, and it will be higher than the price that would prevail under perfect competition. Usually it will also be significantly above the level of marginal cost.

Because it is so risky to change prices, most firms in an oligopoly market structure use other techniques in competition. However, oligopolists also know that any successful action they take will be short-lived because their competitors will quickly move to counteract it. Therefore a firm must always consider the probable reaction of other, competing firms before it attempts to take any action itself.

Because there is a wide range of possible interactions between oligopolists, it is difficult to generalize what the demand curve will be. With tacit agreement between firms, the demand curve might appear as in Exhibit 9-7. The DD line represents the demand curve

Exhibit 9-7. Profit maximization under oligopoly.

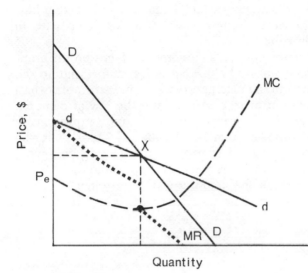

for all sellers when they move prices together and share a total market. The dd line represents one firm's demand curve when it acts alone in changing its price, and in turn loses sales to its competitors. Obviously the dd demand curve is more elastic. Below point X, any price cut is matched by the firm's rivals and the DD demand curve prevails. Above point X, dd prevails since its competitors do not match the firm's price cuts. These two demand curves generate different MR curves. Because of the discontinuity in the dotted MR curve, considerable shifts in the marginal cost (MC) curve would not change the price charged. Oligopolists' prices are sometimes described as sticky because prices remain stable despite significant cost changes.

In imperfect competition, whether under an oligopoly or a monopoly, firms must compete for their share of the market. A firm cannot sell as much as it wants to, and its share of the market is always uncertain. It never knows what its competitors will do if it raises or lowers prices. A firm operating in imperfect competition will try to sell as much as it can and push to the output where profits would be maximized.

Limitations of Supply and Demand

While it is easy to sketch a supply and demand curve on paper, in the real world the executive in charge of pricing must operate without ever fully knowing what the exact demand will be for each price offered. Many factors—business conditions, the political environment, and competitors' actions—affect demand. Not knowing how consumers will react to these changing factors makes it difficult to arrive at a good pricing policy.

The economist's demand curve also ignores the fact that different classes of consumers have varying characteristics; unfortunately the relationship of customers to the pricing process is more complex than that indicated by theories of price elasticity and the law of demand. In reality, each product has several demand curves representing different classes of potential customers. Because of this factor, the organization should offer different grades of each product to appeal to the special needs of customers. The pricing policy would then reflect the product's class as well as the demand of the customer group at which it is aimed.

PRICING STRATEGY

Negotiated Prices

While negotiated prices are most often found in the industrial world, they are also used by builders and other tradespeople in consumer markets. The pricing strategy is to charge the maximum price, but still get the job. Unfortunately many accounting systems are so weak that firms are unable to tell if the price they are offering will cover their costs, fixed or variable. Often tradespeople rely too heavily on past experience and think they are covering their costs when in reality they are not.

New Product Pricing

Establishing the sale prices of new products is extremely difficult; cost records may not be complete because of the lack of production experience or because sales are unproven at various prices. All demand schedules are estimates, but those forecasted for new products are more difficult to prepare because there is no past data to draw on in regard to price changes and quantities sold. An additional complexity is that while the cost accountant is keenly interested in recovering the capital outlay for the product as quickly as possible, the price designed to pay off capital investments in the shortest time may not be the one that will attract the largest possible market.

When introducing a new product, it is helpful to know if it is different, and how it is different, from existing products. Often a product with many new features can be introduced at a high enough price to cover manufacturing costs. Once it is favorably received, the price can be reduced because large-scale manufacturing has become feasible. With larger operations, the unit manufacturing costs should be lowered, and there should be some contribution to development and marketing costs, which are normally high for a new product. This policy of high prices during the introductory period, and lower prices after acceptance has been gained, is referred to as skimming pricing. In order to skim the price, the product must have a high demand and no substitute. When the price is lowered, care must be taken not to violate antitrust or competition laws.

Among the other pricing techniques that are used with new products is penetration pricing, which means a low sales price for the initial market, and then price increases with market acceptance. (Demand must be high enough to support the increases.) A good approach in pricing a new industrial product is to estimate the cost saving it will bring its users and use this as a basis for price setting.

If the new product does not have unique characteristics, its price must be adapted to that of its competitors. How rapidly competitors will enter the market will also affect the pricing decision. The firm may set the price high in the beginning, when it can capitalize upon its monopoly position, realizing that it may be forced to cut the price once competing products have been developed. Since it knows that success will attract competitors, the firm may want to conceal the profitability of the product if possible. It may use the strategy of charging a low price to discourage other firms from entering the market.

In distributing a new product, the marketing executive must determine which type of middleman can best handle it. The executive may decide to limit distribution to one channel so that the item can become established. In choosing distribution channels, he or she may find some middlemen who are unwilling to assume the risk of handling a new product line. Some middlemen require a higher margin on new products to justify the extra effort involved in promoting them.

Pricing in a Declining Market

When faced with a declining market, before deciding on corrective action management should determine the nature of the decline. If the overall economy is experiencing an economic depression, it is unlikely the correct answer will be in pricing. Declines that are of a seasonal or cyclical nature are also unlikely to be greatly affected by price changes. The decline may reflect a past enlarged sale pattern. Customers may be temporarily overstocked and will not buy more even if the product's price is lowered. If the demand for the product is derived from that for a complementary product, the decline may be corrected only by action taken on the complementary product.

Once the marketing executive has investigated the reasons for the decline and believes that a change in price would improve the situation, he or she should analyze the effect of alternative price strategies. Changing prices just to do something to combat the situation should be avoided. The short-run objective should include such goals as survival, having enough cash available to meet creditors' demands, and protecting the existing market by discouraging customers from producing the item themselves.

The marketing executive should make sure that price cutting actually exists and is not just a rumor. One strategy some executives follow is to let competitors know that they will match all price cuts. While some temporary loss in market position may be unavoidable under these circumstances, the implications for the long run are favorable.

SUMMARY

Pricing policy is a very important task in the business enterprise because of its relationship to firm profitability. Pricing decisions are not easy to make because separating and studying the individual elements that determine price is a complicated task. The environment of the firm will determine not only the type of pricing decision it will make but also how it will go about making that decision.

Many factors contribute to the success of a pricing program. Marketing executives cannot ignore their competitors' actions; however, neither should they follow a pricing policy that merely copies them. Each organization has its own unique characteristics, which it should capitalize on.

Cost plays a part in the pricing decision because the firm cannot operate in the long run without covering its full costs. The marginal-cost concept does have implications in the short-run pricing decision. The role of costs in pricing varies with the type of industry and the particular set of conditions surrounding a pricing decision at any given time. Any firm that can accurately determine cost and properly consider this factor in its pricing decision will surely gain in both the short and long run.

Though an awareness of the cost aspects of the product line is helpful, it is not the complete answer because any pricing method that relies solely on costs without a consideration of demand is definitely inadequate. Basic economic theory states that supply and demand establish selling price, and the production cost affects the selling price only through supply. Certainly the demand schedule for the product line is an important factor, but it is a difficult one to estimate.

While it must be admitted that in the final analysis executives often resort to an educated guess, this is no reason to assume that it is a waste of time and money to gather as much relevant information as is feasible. To set prices blindly is sheer folly and could lead to bankruptcy. Those executives responsible for pricing should have access to an information system that will supply them with needed data promptly. There is no single best method of setting price; the pricing executive must use creativity in combining different approaches.

10

Short-Term Planning

THOUGH the marketing manager must spend considerable time analyzing historical cost, he or she must also develop data for future planning purposes. If market planning is properly performed, spur-of-the-moment decisions that often prove incorrect will be reduced and wasted effort will be minimized. Planning permits the efforts of specialized groups to be coordinated so that the actions of one group will not damage another group's plans.

MARKET PLANS

One of the first steps in preparing market plans is to establish the goals that the plan is to achieve. These goals should reflect the company's judgment of its present market position and the market's future conditions. Marketing management should evaluate the means for achieving these goals before finally deciding on objectives. During this process management may realize that many of these goals are unattainable and that more realistic goals should be established. Then, alternative courses of action should be evaluated. This is the phase of planning that demands creative imagination.

Forecasts assist the manager in detecting a weakening territory or a competitor's new strategy. The sales forecast provides a basis for short-range operating decisions, as production can be scheduled more efficiently. Purchasing requirements can be made more economically if needs are specified in advance. The chances of overstocking inventory or running out of stock are reduced if management has forecasted sales in advance.

The marketing plan includes detailed objectives and the steps the marketing organization must take to achieve these objectives. These may be either long-run or short-run plans. Long-term plans are based on a forecast of what conditions will exist in the markets in five to ten years. They reflect management's program for obtaining a desired position in that market. While long-term goals cannot be planned in great detail, they can serve as a guide to management.

In most industrial organizations the factor that limits the magnitude of operating activity for a period is sales demand. Expected sales usually define the scope and size of an organization's operations. Before an organization can plan its sales by product line, it must understand and evaluate the markets. An organization must identify and measure its potential market so that it can properly plan its strategy. The market potential represents the amount of units or dollars of a product the entire market could be persuaded to buy from all sellers for a given time period, usually a calendar year. The market forecast, which is based on the market potential, is an estimate of what the entire market will purchase from all sellers for this time period.

Some industries have developed index numbers for calculating sales potential. This potential is then used to develop sales forecasts. For instance, suppose it is found that retail clothing sales multiplied by .40 equals the maximum potential that a wholesaler can expect. The wholesale potential in this territory would be:

$$\$54,570,000 \times .40 = \$21,828,000$$

SALES FORECAST

Once the market forecast is estimated, management can then determine what share of the market it can expect to obtain. An organization's future market share is the ratio of its sales forecast to the entire industry's market forecast. The sales forecast should be expressed as an estimate of dollar or unit sales of a product or product line. It may be that the firm's sales goals are unrealistic in relation to the market potential. If so, it can either expand its market or readjust its plans. The sales forecast serves as a goal to be accomplished, and becomes the initial stage of the budgetary process. Final marketing plans cannot be firmly decided until after the sales forecast is established.

Factors Affecting Sales Forecast

All organizations have their own distinctive characteristics, which is why they foresee the future differently. The organization's policy concerning product distribution affects the forecasting process. If that policy is to produce only high-quality, high-priced items, the organization has closed itself off to certain channels of distribution. It must then budget expenses that correlate with the distribution channels chosen. A family-owned corporation may not wish to expand into profitable national markets for fear of losing control.

Plant facilities and personnel must be considered in forecasting. The demand for the organization's product may be higher than the company's ability to manufacture because of scarcity of labor skill, material, or facilities. An organization might be able to sell a large number of products, but lack the plant facilities to manufacture or store the goods. In other situations the cost of buying or making the product may be so high that the company will be forced to increase its sales price. At this higher sales price the demand may be much lower. The marketing mix chosen, the channels of distribution selected, and the pricing policies adopted should be reflected in the sales forecast.

There are many other variables that complicate the forecasting approach. The type of product the organization sells may be either directly or indirectly related to consumer demand. Food and clothing are sold directly to the consumer, while products such as glass and steel are raw materials for finished goods. In forecasting the sales for an organization, the demand for the finished product is a major consideration.

Marketing personnel also must consider the effect on their product lines of changes in living patterns of consumers. If there is a large population movement to apartment living, there will be less demand for lawn and garden tools; if there is a population increase in the teenage group, the demand for fad clothing will likely increase. Management must be aware of these social changes and develop plans to meet them with appropriate market action. Advertising may be able to affect some behavioral patterns, but generally they are beyond the control of the organization.

Sales for previous periods are usually analyzed for possible fluctuations caused by labor strikes, wars, economic cycles, and seasonal variations. Seasonal patterns of demand for certain products have a large impact on organizations. For example, a firm manufacturing Christmas toys may produce at a normal volume all year long, but its peak sales will occur during a short time period. It must plan its cash flow so it will be able to meet obligations throughout the year. Instead of producing all year long, the firm may produce these products just prior to the peak sales session. During the rest of the year the idle facilities may be used to produce other seasonal products. Past sales trends are of limited use in forecasting if economic and market conditions are rapidly changing. In addition, if the organization has just introduced a new product or service, it can be assumed that its market share will grow until a competitor offers a product or service that cuts into sales. In analyzing the sales trends of some durable products, a correct forecast may be for reduced sales if there has been an increase in past sales. For example, if there has been a large increase in the sale of kitchen appliances, the market may be saturated and therefore future demand will be light.

Fluctuations in business cycles, which occur in somewhat regular patterns, affect individual organizations differently. Some experience increased sales during periods of recession. These are typically organizations that receive government contracts. Often the federal government, in an attempt to effect a change in the business cycle, will increase purchases. Sellers of luxury items generally experience a decline in sales with a downturn in the cycle.

The effect of price-level changes must also be considered in converting from past sales dollars. Obviously this price-level conversion is not necessary for units of sales.

Competitive forces, which are hard to predict, must be considered in preparing sales forecasts. Each firm's share of the market is determined by competition within the industry in price, product, and promotion. Regardless of its form, competition involves shifts in market shares among competing companies. The organization's proposed advertising expenditures should be used in evaluating the impact of these market shifts.

There are several means of gathering information for computing sales potential. Commercial credit reports like Dun and Bradstreet may report sales volumes of competitors. Numerous government agencies supply statistical data that can be of use in forecasting sales. This data is often broken down into small geographical areas. Some executives may start with predicting gross national product, which they then break down into an industry forecast, and finally, an organization forecast. A sales forecast is but one part of the marketing plan. The effort and facilities needed to generate these sales must be estimated. The physical units of these efforts must be decided on before they can be expressed in budgeted dollars. For example, the channels of distribution must be determined so that the labor time involved in the desired advertising campaign can include the amount of promotional material to be prepared and the media chosen.

Methods of Developing Sales Forecasts

There are two basic approaches to developing a sales forecast. In one, the marketing research department gathers and analyzes the data centrally. In the other, people who are familiar with operations and whose intuition has proved correct in the past originate the sales forecast. The sales manager of each segment and his or her staff may estimate future sales to their customers by product line. The salespeople have the responsibility for meeting such forecasts, and their interest in budgeting is usually stimulated if they are asked to participate by providing estimates. Top management must inform sales managers of any market information that applies to their segments. The company's research staff may be able to obtain additional data that is helpful. The drawback to this approach is that while salespeople are familiar with customer potential and current conditions, they are not well informed about broad economic developments. In addition, they may resent this time-consuming task.

The forecasts prepared by each salesperson should be reviewed by the sales manager because they are likely to be biased in one direction or another. Before changing the original estimates, however, the manager should discuss with each salesperson the need for revisions. Top management, in turn, should follow the same procedure in evaluating sales managers' forecasts—that is, these forecasts should not be changed without an explanation.

Many organizations use both statistical analysis and intuitive judgment in developing forecasts. The greatest benefit is derived from sales trend analysis when it is used with such other forecasting tools as an analysis of economic indicators, correlation analysis, and management's opinions on such influencing factors as competitors' actions, advertising, and new products. The prediction of these statisticians and economists must be compared with the intuitive forecasts of managers familiar with operations. If the two approaches result in materially different figures, the budget committee is charged with the responsibility of resolving differences.

The market research department may measure consumer motivation through a technique called *motivation research.* The subconscious motives of buyers are studied through "word association," depth interviews, and other behavioral science techniques. A buyer group may be asked what it plans to buy during some short period of time. Such surveys may be of greater use in determining market forecasts than establishing the sales forecast for a single organization.

Trend analysis. Expert statisticians and economists may be able to assist top management in forecasting long-range trends. Secular or long-term trends may be determined by plotting sales for previous periods on a moving-average basis. Cyclic trend analysis is also helpful in making long-term predictions. Cyclic trends are plotted by computing the percent of deviation between the long-term trend and the actual annual sales. Seasonal trends can be determined by plotting sales by months for several years, and then determining how they vary from the monthly average for each year. Statistical forecasts based on an analysis of general economic and market conditions assume that the future is likely to resemble the past.

Correlation analysis. Correlation analysis may also be used in the forecasting procedure. An economic indicator is an independent variable that is closely aligned with a dependent variable. The economic indicator is used to predict sales for the dependent variable. For example, in forecasting sales for baby equipment and clothing, the birth rate would be the independent variable. The industry would study the birth rate to see if it was ahead or behind the dependent variable, and this relationship between the independent and dependent variable would be measured by correlation analysis. A straight-line or linear relationship exists if the rate of change in the independent and dependent variables is constant. If the rate of change varies by different amounts, a curvilinear relationship exists. These relationships are often plotted graphically so that a regression line that provides the best fit for these variables can be determined. The regression line can then be used as the basis for forecasting sales for the dependent variable.

The closeness of this correlation between the independent and dependent variables can be expressed mathematically by the coefficient of determination. The affinity between two sets of data is measured by the coefficient of determination by studying the extent to which the regression line accounts for the total random variation, which would prevail if there were no regression line.

Often there are several independent variables that affect the dependent variable. In the example of the baby equipment and clothing industry, both the birth rate and the introduction of new, safer baby equipment would cause an increase in future sales. If family income increased, parents would be less inclined to use a second-hand baby bed and more likely to purchase a new, more modern one. Advertising and the price of the product can also be considered variables that affect future sales. Multiple correlation can be used when variations in the dependent variable can be explained by more than one independent variable.

BUDGETING

Many managers feel that they face so many uncertainties in marketing that budgets are impracticable. While it may be true that planning is difficult because of all the intangibles affecting success, marketing managers will have to deal with these uncertainties with or without a budget. In preparing budgets, they are forced to estimate market and sales potential, and then plan the organization's course of action to meet these inherent uncertainties. The budgeting process forces them to state future plans in financial terms. Before initiating a marketing budget program, certain aspects of the organization should be studied.

Advantage of Budgeting

Through the budgeting process, members of management are made aware of the problems that others in the organization face. A budget is an organization's coordinated comprehensive plan for the future, expressed in financial terms. There should be one master plan for the entire organization, and from this plan segmental budgets should be drawn up. The budget provides the means for coordination between activities of the various segments of the organization. Otherwise different segments of the business might follow courses of action that are beneficial to them only and not to the overall company. The marketing budget is but one facet of the plan for the firm as a whole.

Budgeting forces management to express objectives in a written form. Often members of the management team have different views as to what the company plans are for the future. The budgeting process forces them to get together and come to some compromise. Many times managers do not give much thought to where the firm will be next year or five years from now. They are so concerned with solving day-to-day problems that planning is laid aside. As a result, the firm can get caught in undesirable situations.

Top management may establish certain objectives such as a desired net income or return. In turn, segment managers must transfer these goals into budgets for their segments. Budgets spell out objectives and give direction to the firm. If constructively used, they can guide management throughout the accounting period by serving as a continuing reminder of predetermined objectives.

Top management's philosophy toward budgeting greatly affects how the budget will be received by middle and lower management. This philosophy can range from a positive view of budgeting as a means of planning, to a negative attitude that uses budgets as inflexible mechanisms to threaten employees. Marketing managers must be convinced that budgeting has many advantages, because if they are unwilling to give budgeting their wholehearted support, it will probably fail. All too often top managers pay only lip service to the execution of budgets. When they are uninterested in the budgeting process or view the budget negatively, the budget can become a costly scapegoat for many of the problems that plague the organization.

The accounting system must fit the needs of the budget program. There must be clear lines of authority and responsibility so that there will be accountability for expenditures. The chart of accounts and the organization chart should form the framework for the control aspect of the budget. The cost centers that correspond to divisions of responsibility should be included in the chart of accounts. The organization chart gives the functional responsibilities for each executive whose activities justify a budget.

Behavioral Aspects of Budgeting

When the budget is an effective cost-control tool, responsibility for planning and control coincides from top management levels down to middle and lower management. Since a budget should be established on the postulate that authority and responsibility go together, those people responsible for meeting the budget should participate in its initial development.

Participative budgeting. The organization is likely to achieve better acceptance of its budget if it is not imposed. Employees should be allowed to participate in preparing the budgets that affect them, and the data for the organization budget should originate at the lowest level of operating management. This participation in the budgeting process enables individuals to become personally attached to the organization's goals. They can feel that the budget is theirs, not one that is handed down by management.

Sometimes management does not really desire employee participation, but thinks it should lead employees to believe they are assisting in the budgetary process. Such an attitude is soon detected by employees, and strongly resented. This approach is no better than imposing the budget; perhaps it is even worse because of the subterfuge.

Participative budgeting is not the answer for all organizations. The personality and history of employees is a major factor to consider before soliciting their participation. Before they can plan their own operations, they must be told the basic constraints under which they are to function. They should be provided with accurate and pertinent information, and informed of important influencing factors. They should be asked to use their experience in evaluating the data supplied by the marketing research department. If the people responsible for meeting the budget do not understand its objectives, they will be less likely to improve their performance in order to meet the planned operations.

Employees participating in the budgetary process will try to make the budget less demanding to meet. Often they will bargain about the yardstick by which their performance will be judged. They may even intentionally create a slack so that they will have a buffer in case their performance does not meet the criteria established. For these reasons the data supplied at low levels must be refined and combined at successively higher levels. If participative budgeting is encouraged, top management must be willing to accept these refined decisions jointly made by employees and managers; they must be open to flexibility.

Top management, in turn, often views the budget as a means of increasing production and sets it so tight that it is almost impossible to meet. Employees resent unrealistic budgets because they reflect management's belief in Theory X, which states that workers are motivated solely by economic forces, and are naturally wasteful and inefficient. Unrealistic budgets tell employees that management believes they are so lazy that they will perform only if tight controls are established. With this approach, accounting will be strongly perceived as an instrument for reducing and controlling costs.

The comparison of actual performance against the budget influences the next budget. If employees performed efficiently, with the result that expenditures were lower than the amount budgeted, management will likely revise the next period's budget downward without checking out fully the reasons for the favorable variance. After this kind of experience, supervisors will reason that it is best to engage in a spending spree the last few weeks of the budgeted period to make sure the entire amount budgeted for their departments is spent. If, on the other hand, expenditures exceeded the budget, the supervisor and his or her employees will be criticized and often penalized.

Constantly increasing pressure on employees can lead to negative results in the long run. Employees will become suspicious of any move management makes, and be ready to justify any actions of their own to counteract this pressure. They may, for instance, develop ingenious methods of falsifying their reports. Morale will deteriorate if employees believe that the reporting system is unfair and they must perform in a climate of fear and distrust. The budget should serve as a means of communicating to employees how well their actual results match with budgeted results. Therefore budget departments should not merely communicate the results to management; employees should be frequently informed of their performance. All too often employees do not know if they are performing effectively until they are asked to discuss their variances from the budget at the end of the accounting period.

The manner in which unfavorable variances are reported can cause further breakdowns in the working relationship between employees and supervisors. The reasons for the unfavorable variances are usually omitted from the report, and this is especially detrimental if the factors causing the variance are not controllable at this lower management level. Often only exceptionally high unfavorable variances are reported, with no mention of significant favorable variances. This is an incorrect use of exception reporting because it emphasizes punishment only, rather than a combination of punishment and reward.

The better approach is to help employees see what mistakes caused the unfavorable variance. Their participation in finding reasons for not meeting the budget will foster good management-employee relations. The more rapidly results are communicated, the more likely that an employee will be able to see his or her mistakes and take corrective action. Cooperative attitudes toward budgetary control must permeate all levels of management.

The budget director serves in an advisory capacity. He or she should provide executives with information they can use to prepare new budgets. The budget director's responsibilities also include obtaining revenue and expense estimates from segment heads. This is a difficult task because it requires creating the goodwill that is essential to the success of the budget program. Since many administrative problems evolve from budgeting, the budget director must recognize human factors.

The budget director may find it difficult to see why marketing executives do not think highly of budgets and fail to view them as a proper means of improving their efficiency. The reason is that all too often the budget director's own success depends on finding things that are wrong. He or she must guard against trying to single out guilty parties and publicizing their failures. Rather, the budget director's project should be to find accurate explanations of unfavorable variances.

Budget Committee

Even though line managers are encouraged to participate in the development of individual segmental budgets to the full extent of their interests and capabilities, the organization needs to establish a budget committee that will be responsible for compiling the budget in its final form. This committee should review the segmental budgets for evidence of overoptimism, excessive conservatism, and padding. Normally the budget committee is made up of the president, vice-president, controller, and top line executives from all segments of the organization. Often the budget director is the controller or someone who is responsible to the controller. The committee's purpose is to coordinate all the planning of the firm. The budget director or committee should evaluate the reports prepared when the budgetary system is installed. Often the best procedure is to prepare the reports that the budget director feels are necessary, and then ask executives if these supply all the data needed. It is easier to eliminate duplication of reports under this approach than by asking each executive if he or she needs a specific report. If asked this question, the executive may think of reasons why he or she needs the data. Though the information exists in other (voluminous) reports, marketing executives are not usually eager to read through a mass of data to find what requires their special attention. The budget director should therefore use the exception principle and emphasize situations that are of most importance. It will also be of great assistance if the budget committee prepares a budget manual to serve as a reference in the implementation of a budget program. The manual will document procedures that might otherwise never get written down.

The budget committee should continue in an advisory capacity after the budget is finalized because it will be necessary to review the budget periodically and possibly to revise it as conditions warrant changes. There should always be a review throughout the period of the actual expenses and revenues with the budgeted data. This not only allows corrective action to be taken quickly but also is of help in forecasting and revising future plans. The committee may decide that conditions have changed so much that the budget is no longer realistic, or that it was not valid from the beginning. The review may take the form of periodic reports and meetings of the budget committee. It is of little value to determine merely that there is a difference between actual and budgeted performance. The significance of the review is that it can identify the *causes* of the variances.

Length of Budget Period

Usually the budget is prepared to correspond with the fiscal period of the accounting system. Many companies have both long-range and short-range budgets. The long-range budget provides guidance without being as specific as the short-range budget. The normal procedure is to prepare detailed budgets for each segment for the short run only, typically no longer than one year. Detailed long-range planning is seldom feasible. Since long-range budgets are usually only broad guidelines and are subject to many changes, they do not have to be circulated among middle and lower management.

Short-term budgets have the advantage of being more accurate. However, since they are prepared for brief periods, they are not in existence long enough to foster satisfactory solutions for the problems anticipated. Long-range plans are imperative in such fields as product development. Normally they are broad and cover a time period as long as 15 years, and their purpose is to anticipate long-term needs and opportunities that require definite steps in the short run.

Some long-range budgets deal only with specific areas such as financial requirements, future marketing conditions, and product line sales. The preferred approach is to budget marketing costs by months, and then sum the total. This is more desirable than preparing an annual budget and then breaking it down into months, because the number of business days in a calendar month will vary by more than 10 percent. Additional fluctuations in the monthly sales figure result from seasonal variations, holidays, and vacations.

Some organizations prepare their annual budget in two phases. For the first half of the year the expenses and revenues are detailed by months; the remaining six months are summarized in less detail by quarters. Every six months a new short-range detailed budget is built, partly on the basis of earlier summarized data and partly on the results from the previous six months. Other organizations prepare in detail an annual budget under a continuous or rolling budget approach. For example, under a rolling or progressive budget, at the end of March a budget for March of the next year will be added. As each month is passed, the next twelfth-month is added. Thus the organization always has a 12-month budget detailed in advance. Rolling budgets may be realistic because changing economic conditions can be incorporated into the plans each time a new month is added. Budgeting is a thus continual process rather than a once-a-year task.

Sales Budget

The sales budget is usually the first budget prepared because it supplies the raw data for production costs and other expenses; other budgets are contingent on the sales budget.

The amount of sales and the sales mix budgeted set the level of volume for the company's operations. Exhibits 10-1, 10-2, and 10-3 illustrate the process involved in arriving at the total sales forecast and budget. It is assumed that three products, A, B, and C, are sold for the organization's three territories X, Y, and Z. Exhibit 10-1 contains the monthly forecasts for each product line by retail and wholesale customers. These forecasted sales could be further detailed as to channel of distribution or any other appropriate segment. Each territory should prepare a similar type of analysis so that Exhibit 10-2, showing the forecasted territorial sales dollars by month for each product line, can be prepared. Exhibit 10-3 illustrates the total monthly forecasted sales broken down by territory. These forecasts, untouched, can become the organization's sales budget, or management may decide to revise them before they are adopted as the sales budget. It is assumed in Exhibit 10-3 that no revisions were made and that the sales budget represents the forecasts from Exhibit 10-2.

Advertising Budget

The advertising budget is difficult to establish because many factors affecting the success of the advertising campaign cannot be separately identified. A consumer may buy a product because of the availability of money or credit, the sales clerk, or some other influence. In addition, the effectiveness of advertising may depend more on economic conditions than on the advertising approach. The time lag between advertising expenditures and sales further complicates the picture. The extent to which the effectiveness of different advertising media can be measured varies. Local advertising is more easily measured than national advertising. Media advertising that contains

Exhibit 10-1. Territory X, unit sales forecasts by product line for the year 19___.

	Product A			Product B			Product C		
	Retail	Wholesale	Total	Retail	Wholesale	Total	Retail	Wholesale	Total
January	1,000	2,020	3,020	500	700	1,200	100	300	400
February	700	1,800	2,500	510	775	1,285	110	250	360
March	600	1,640	2,240	535	825	1,360	130	275	405
April	550	1,575	2,125	590	860	1,450	85	310	395
May	675	1,590	2,265	610	890	1,500	95	330	425
June	700	1,680	2,380	685	890	1,585	115	350	465
July	800	1,730	2,530	697	850	1,547	130	350	480
August	850	1,790	2,640	725	825	1,550	120	370	490
September	900	1,835	2,735	760	780	1,540	112	320	432
October	1,000	1,910	2,910	785	850	1,635	123	290	413
November	1,050	1,985	3,035	810	900	1,710	135	325	460
December	1,400	2,010	3,410	850	910	1,760	140	340	480
Total units	10,225	21,565	31,790	8,057	10,065	18,122	1,395	3,810	5,205
Unit price	45	40	—	30	27	—	10	8	—
Total sales	$460,125	$862,600	$1,322,725	$241,710	$271,755	$513,465	$13,950	$30,480	$44,430

Exhibit 10-2.   Territory X, dollar sales forecasts by product line for the year 19___

	Product A			Product B			Product C			Territory
	Retail	Wholesale	Total	Retail	Wholesale	Total	Retail	Wholesale	Total	Total
January	$ 45,000	$ 80,800	$ 125,800	$ 15,000	$ 18,900	$ 33,900	$ 1,000	$ 2,400	$ 3,400	$ 163,100
February	31,500	72,000	103,500	15,300	20,925	36,225	1,100	2,000	3,100	142,825
March	27,000	65,600	92,600	16,050	22,275	38,325	1,300	2,200	3,500	134,425
April	24,750	63,000	87,750	17,700	23,220	40,920	850	2,480	3,330	132,000
May	30,375	63,600	93,975	18,300	24,030	42,330	950	2,640	3,590	139,895
June	31,500	67,200	98,700	20,550	24,300	44,850	1,150	2,800	3,950	147,500
July	36,000	69,200	105,200	20,910	22,950	43,860	1,300	2,800	4,100	153,160
August	38,250	71,600	109,850	21,750	22,275	44,025	1,200	2,960	4,160	158,035
September	40,500	73,400	113,900	22,800	21,060	43,860	1,120	2,560	3,680	161,440
October	45,000	76,400	121,400	23,550	22,950	46,500	1,230	2,320	3,550	171,450
November	47,250	79,400	126,650	24,300	24,300	48,600	1,350	2,600	3,950	179,200
December	63,000	80,400	143,400	25,500	24,570	50,070	1,400	2,720	4,120	197,590
Totals	$460,125	$862,600	$1,322,725	$241,710	$271,755	$513,465	$13,950	$30,480	$44,430	$1,880,620

Exhibit 10-3. XYZ Company sales budget by territory for the year 19___.

	Territory X		Territory Y		Territory Z			
	Monthly Sales as Percent of Total	Total Sales	Monthly Sales as Percent of Total	Total Sales	Monthly Sales as Percent of Total	Total Sales	Total Organization
January	8.7	$ 163,100	9.5	$ 150,000	7.1	$ 75,000	$ 388,100
February	7.6	142,825	9.1	144,000	7.7	81,000	367,825
March	7.2	134,425	8.2	130,000	8.6	90,000	354,425
April	7.1	132,000	7.2	114,000	8.8	93,000	339,000
May	7.4	139,895	7.5	118,000	8.2	86,000	343,895
June	7.8	147,500	7.6	120,000	8.5	89,000	356,500
July	8.1	153,160	7.8	124,000	8.9	94,000	371,160
August	8.4	158,035	8.1	129,000	9.2	97,000	384,035
September	8.6	161,440	8.4	133,000	8.7	92,000	386,440
October	9.1	171,450	8.6	136,000	8.6	91,000	398,450
November	9.5	179,200	8.8	140,000	8.0	84,000	403,200
December	10.5	197,590	9.2	145,000	7.7	81,000	423,590
Totals	100%	$1,880,620	100%	$1,533,000	100%	$1,053,000	$4,516,620

reply cards or coupons can also be measured easily. Budgets are the primary accounting tool used by marketing management for controlling advertising and sales promotion costs.

The advertising budget should be determined jointly by marketing, financial, and accounting personnel so that the problems of each are given weight. Because of the nature of advertising, intuitive judgment is used more in establishing the advertising budget than in other marketing budgets. However, organizations have generally followed one of these approaches: a percentage of sales, an amount per unit of product in budgeted sales, business climate, or a specified objective (which may be to obtain a desired level of customer acceptance for the company's product).

Setting the advertising budget as a fixed percentage of sales is a popular approach. Many executives feel this method is advantageous because additional funds are made available for following a favorable market. However, the method does have serious weaknesses. Sales are supposed to be the end result of advertising, not the reverse. Also, this approach is inflexible. Advertising appropriations should be correlated with *anticipated* sales if the percentage of sales method is used. This is more logical because it assumes that advertising precedes sales rather than the reverse.

The advertising appropriation may also be based on a unit cost per ton, per product grouping, or customer. This method is easily used with flexible budgeting. The cost per unit is preferably a scientifically predetermined standard cost. In arriving at the cost per unit of measurement, the market population and past penetration should be considered.

Often the amount of funds available for advertising automatically becomes the budget; if there are excess funds, the advertising budget is increased. There is no logic in this method.

Management may consider the business climate in which it is operating. The extent to which the company can predict competitors' actions in regard to advertising will affect the advertising budget. The organization then attempts to relate its expenditures to those of its competitors. However, it is difficult to predict what the selling promotion activities of competitors will be. This approach is not logical if the appropriation is set before the tasks the advertising function is to perform are defined.

The sales objective approach studies the market and determines who the organization's potential customers are. The advertising necessary to achieve the desired level of customer acceptance for each product line is budgeted; the advertising budget becomes the total of these amounts.

Many organizations use a combination of these approaches.

DIRECT SELLING EXPENSE BUDGET

Before budgeting expenses for sales personnel, the organization must set a policy on what types of expenses will be reimbursed. Generally an organization considers out-of-town meals and lodging, transportation, tips, and telephone and telegraph charges as legitimate business expenses. Company policy may vary concerning gifts and entertainment. The method of reimbursing salespeople, or of advancing them funds, should be simple and economical to administer. It is very important that all salespeople fully understand the expense plan so there will be little controversy over expense items.

Compensation Plan
The organization should have a compensation plan that will attract and keep good salespeople, but one that is not so expensive that the organization cannot afford it. The company cannot afford a plan that forces it to raise its prices to a noncompetitive level. The cost of administering the plan must also be taken into account.

Salespeople obviously prefer a compensation plan that gives them some control over sales factors. Even though the organization may design such a plan, market potential could change because of factors beyond the organization's or the salesperson's control. Sometimes two salespersons will have worked to earn the same sales, and it will be difficult to reward each one justly. The compensation plan must stimulate salespeople to make more profitable sales. However, the organization needs to remember that there are important nonmonetary motivators. The marketing manager who takes a friendly interest in the salesperson and his or her family will have a more efficient, loyal sales force. The manager should also look for ways to publicly recognize efficient performance.

Compensation Methods
Many salespeople prefer a compensation plan that combines a stated amount with an opportunity to earn additional income. This provides enough security to cover basic living expenses regardless of the sales volume, and the incentive element of the plan works

as a reward for specific achievement. Above all, salespeople want to be assured that their salaries are determined objectively. They must be able to fully understand each element making up the plan. Otherwise they may feel they are being treated unfairly. There are several compensation methods.

Fixed salary. Under the fixed-salary compensation method, salespeople are paid the same wages regardless of sales volume and performance. This method gives the sales manager more power to direct and control his or her staff than the other compensation methods, and salespeople gain a sense of security since their income is stable. Fixed salary is appropriate if sales personnel are required to perform tasks other than selling, such as education and public relations. It is also appropriate when there are new salespeople, products, or territories. The strong disadvantage of the fixed-salary compensation plan is that it does not provide incentive. This means that the sales manager must supervise his or her staff more closely. Since sales salaries under this method are a fixed cost, unit selling costs vary inversely with sales volume.

Straight commission. This plan is a great motivator because the pay is determined strictly by accomplishment. The plan may be tailored so that different rates are assigned to different customers or products. The salesperson enjoys much flexibility and freedom of operation under straight commission, and the sales manager has little control over his or her staff. It is also difficult to set equitable commission rates. This method may be easier to budget than the straight-salary method; since the compensation is a variable cost, sales compensation goes up or down as sales or contribution margin vary.

Straight salary with variable commission. A combination plan of salary plus incentive is often installed. The salary is generally set at a minimum to cover living expenses, and the commission may cover all sales or be expressed as a percentage of contribution margin. It is also possible to tailor the commission to meet certain company objectives. Since this type of plan can become complicated, it may be costly to administer.

The straight salary with variable commissions is appropriate for the salespeople who are responsible for selling and servicing. It has the advantage of providing an incentive for the sales staff, while still allowing the sales manager some control over the staff's activities.

Salary with bonus. Some organizations give a bonus or lump sum payment to their sales personnel for a specific level of performance. Since they often do not commit themselves in advance as to the basis on which a bonus will be given, salespeople view this plan unfavorably.

They may perceive partiality or favoritism in the organization's plan for distributing bonuses. There is little incentive value in the bonus because it is indefinite and not related directly to specific achievements.

Sales Quotas

The marketing manager can use forecasts to establish quotas for his or her salespeople. Management may assign sales goals or quotas for each organization segment; these are management's expectations in dollars or units for a given future time period. Sales quotas are often expressed by product line for each territory. In a thickly populated metropolitan area served by several salespeople, these calculations do not give weight to all factors. When the boundary lines of each sales territory do not correlate exactly with the geographical limits of the territory, the calculations will be less accurate.

Salespeople should know what their sales budget is; they must approve and accept their quotas. If they feel the quotas do not reflect territorial potential but rather a marketing manager's prejudice, they will resent them. Often the sales forecast for each segment is increased some, and this becomes the incentive quota for each salesperson. If the increase is too large, the quota is unrealistic and will be detrimental to morale and performance.

Measurement of sales quotas. Sales quotas can be expressed as a dollar volume of sales. While this has the advantage of being simple and specific, it overlooks the fact that some products with low contribution margins may be easier to sell than others. Instead salespeople should be encouraged to sell the most profitable items.

A better way of expressing sales quotas is to determine the desired contribution margin each salesperson is to achieve. The accounting staff should be able to determine the contribution margin for each product line, so that the marketing manager will know which products contribute the most to fixed and indirect costs and income. Once salespeople gain an understanding of contribution margins, it should be apparent to them that quotas expressed in contribution margin dollars are more significant for organization profits than quotas expressed in total dollar sales. Often the product items with higher contribution margins are more difficult to sell, and salespeople should be rewarded for this extra effort.

Salespeople also need extra promotional aids to sell these products. Assume an organization has three products, X, Y, and Z, having contribution margins of $3, $2, and $1, respectively. The company will obviously try to sell more of Product X because it has the largest contribution margin. In order to plan for the future, it must forecast

how many units of each product it will sell. The sales mix ratio
is needed not only for budgetary purposes but also for breakeven
analysis. Suppose the company decides that it will be able to sell
100,000 units in the forthcoming period, consisting of 20,000 X, 50,000
Y, and 30,000 Z. The sales mix ratio is 20:50:30. The average
contribution margin is then 2($3) + 5($2) + 3($1) = $19 for 10 units =
$1.90 per unit. This $1.90 per unit can be used if a breakeven point
is needed for the entire organization. With fixed costs of $380,000,
the breakeven is $380,000 ÷ $1.90 = 200,000 units, consisting of
40,000 X, 100,000 Y, and 60,000 Z.

Some marketing managers object to this approach because they
do not want to reveal contribution margin figures to salespeople for
fear of misinterpretation. They are afraid that their sales staff will
identify the contribution margin with net profit, and forget that there
are many indirect costs the contribution margin must cover before
a net profit is earned. In addition, marketing managers know that
the quota must be understandable, and the simpler the computation,
the more comprehensible it will be. But with proper education,
salespeople will not misinterpret contribution margin, and this approach is more rewarding in terms of higher organization profits.

VARIABLE BUDGET

Under the fixed-budget approach, a budget is prepared for a single
estimated volume of activity and is not adjusted when actual volume
differs from estimated volume. Actual results are compared with this
fixed volume. A fixed budget is satisfactory if a company's activities
can be estimated accurately in advance and are based on certain
definite conditions.

Since most organizations experience drastically changing market
conditions (there are few completely predictable situations in our
economy), a fixed budget is not adequate. A variable budget more
readily serves management's purpose because it is used in comparison
with actual results and is therefore based on the actual volume
obtained.

A variable or flexible budget consists of a budget formula that
can be used for a series of possible volumes, all considered within
the range of probability. A budget can be calculated for each volume,
ranging from a possible 60 percent to 100 percent of capacity. However,
this duplication of effort and time in preparing so many budgets
is unnecessary. Instead, once the budget formula is known, a budget

can be prepared for any volume. Items may be different in different months because of seasonal variations or because of management's plans for certain expenses such as advertising.

Normally market expenses are not budgeted at 100 percent of capacity (theoretical capacity). This high a volume is unrealistic because interruptions in the distribution process are inevitable. A lower-volume level (often referred to as practical capacity) allows for such unavoidable delays as time lost for repairs, vacations, and holidays. If the marketing conditions are of a seasonal nature, a short-run approach (expected actual capacity) should be used in the variable budgeting process. A longer-range approach (normal capacity) is used most often because it levels out the highs and lows in volume and bases computations on an average sales expectancy.

In order to have a successful flexible budget program, the relationship of marketing costs to sales volume must be studied. If all costs varied in the same pattern with changes in sales volume, there would be no need for this analysis. However, costs are either variable, fixed, or semivariable. Total fixed costs do not change as sales volume increases, and vice versa. Unit variable costs remain the same, while total variable costs increase or decrease directly with changes in sales volume. Semivariable costs fluctuate intermittently or at different stages of volume. There is some similarity between the fixed-variable distinction and the controllable-noncontrollable classification. However, some fixed costs *are* controllable. For example, rent on the sales office building is controlled by the manager who has the authority to lease the facility.

Exhibit 10-4 illustrates the discrepancies that can result from using a fixed budget. Only a few marketing costs are included for illustration purposes. These budgeted figures represent scientifically predetermined standards if a standard-cost system is in operation. If 800 units were sold and the actual results were as given in Exhibit 10-5, there would be a net favorable variance of $300.

Management may be satisfied with the results based on the fixed-budget approach, since there was a net favorable variance. However, Exhibit 10-6 gives the formula that is used in a flexible or variable budget.

The basic ingredient is $10 per sales unit plus $2,600 a month. This is used in Exhibit 10-7 to correctly show the unfavorable variances, which total $1,700.

The fixed costs were included in Exhibit 10-7 so that the flexible or variable budgeting approach could be illustrated. If the territorial manager had no control over these fixed costs, or over some of the

**Exhibit 10-4.   XYZ Company, Territory X;
fixed budgets and marketing costs for January 19___.**

	SALES UNITS: BUDGET 1,000
Salaries and wages	$ 3,000
Sales commissions	4,000
Warehousing	1,000
Traveling	2,000
Total variable expenses	$10,000
Office rent	500
Advertising	600
Sales manager's salary	1,500
Total fixed costs	$ 2,600
Total marketing costs	$12,600

**Exhibit 10-5.   XYZ Company, Territory X;
comparison of actual with fixed budget for January 19___.**

	SALES UNITS		
	ACTUAL 800	BUDGET 1,000	VARIANCE
Salaries and wages	$ 2,800	$ 3,000	$200 Favorable
Sales commissions	4,000	4,000	—
Warehousing	880	1,000	120 Favorable
Traveling	1,920	2,000	80 Favorable
Total variable expenses	$ 9,600	$10,000	400 Favorable
Office rent	550	500	50 Unfavorable
Advertising	600	600	—
Sales manager's salary	1,550	1,500	50 Unfavorable
Total fixed costs	$ 2,700	$ 2,600	100 Unfavorable
Total marketing costs	$12,300	$12,600	$300 Favorable

variable costs, these noncontrollable costs could be omitted. There is one advantage of including such noncontrollable costs on this performance report: it emphasizes the services and benefits received from other sources.

Though they have many benefits, variable budgets can consume much effort and time. Data processing techniques can assist in their preparation. The basic ingredients of variable and fixed costs for each expense classification can be fed into the computer. Once the actual volume is obtained and entered into the data processing system,

Exhibit 10-6. XYZ Company, Territory X; variable-budget formula for the month beginning January 19__.

	Cost per Sales Unit
Salaries and wages	$ 3
Sales commissions	4
Warehousing	1
Traveling	2
Total variable costs	$10
Office rent	$ 500
Advertising	600
Sales manager's salary	1,500
Total fixed costs	$2,600

Exhibit 10-7. XYZ Company—Territory X; comparison of actual with flexible budget for January 19__.

	Sales Units			
	Actual 800	Flexible Budget Based on 800 Actual Units		Variance
Salaries and wages	$ 2,800	$ 2,400	($3 × 800)	$ 400 Unfavorable
Sales commissions	4,000	3,200	($4 × 800)	800 Unfavorable
Warehousing	880	800	($1 × 800)	80 Unfavorable
Traveling	1,920	1,600	($2 × 800)	320 Unfavorable
Total variable costs	$ 9,600	$ 8,000		$1,600 Unfavorable
Office rent	550	500		$ 50 Unfavorable
Advertising	600	600		—
Sales manager's salary	1,550	1,500		50 Unfavorable
Total fixed costs	$ 2,700	$ 2,600		$ 100 Unfavorable
Total marketing costs	$12,300	$10,600		$1,700 Unfavorable

the computer can prepare a flexible budget based on the actual volume obtained. The system can be programmed to list variances over a specified amount.

When standard costs have been established, it is necessary only to translate the sales budget into the marketing requirements needed to obtain the stated goals and apply the standards. Standards are closely related to budgets because they serve as building blocks for the construction of the budget. This method is particularly suited to costs of a variable nature. Semivariable and fixed costs can be estimated with little difficulty once the sales budgets are known. For order-filling functions, planning is based on the services required by the projected sales volume. For order-getting functions, planning involves determining the costs necessary to apply this method to each detailed function rather than the function as a whole.

Exhibit 10-8 illustrates the flexible- or variable-budget formula for some marketing expenses. Exhibit 10-9 is an extension of this budget formula; the number of work units is multiplied by the variable expense rate to arrive at the total variable budget. The marketing expense budgets shown in these two exhibits illustrate only a few

Exhibit 10-8.   XYZ Company, Territory X; variable budget of marketing expenses for January 19___.

FUNCTION	FIXED EXPENSES	VARIABLE EXPENSES	
		BASE	RATE
Warehousing			
Packing and wrapping	$1,000	Order	$ 1.00
Receiving	600	Purchase invoice line	.10
Transportation			
Gasoline and oil	—	Mile	.20
Drivers and helpers'. wages	500	Truck-hour of operation	5.00
Credit and collection			
Preparing invoices	700	Invoice line	.08
Making street collections	1,500	Customer	1.00
General distribution activities			
Sales analyses	1,800	Order	1.50
Mail handling	300	Number of pieces in and out	.05
Direct selling			
Sales personnel training	500	Number of salespeople	10.00
Entertainment	—	Customers	15.00
Advertising and sales promotion			
Newspaper	—	Newspaper inches	1.00
Radio and television	—	Minutes of radio or television time	50.00
	$6,900		

Exhibit 10-9. XYZ Company, Territory X; market expense budget for January 19___.

Function	Work Unit	Fixed Expense	Variable Unit Cost	Number of Work Units	Total Variable Expense	Total Fixed and Variable Expense
Warehousing and handling						
Packing and wrapping	Order	$1,000	$1.00	550	$550	$1,550
Receiving	Purchase invoice line	600	.10	1,800	180	780
Transportation						
Gasoline and oil	Mile	—	.20	3,000	600	600
Drivers' and helpers' wages	Truck-hour of operation	500	5.00	120	600	1,100
Credit and collection						
Preparing invoices	Invoice line	700	.08	1,900	152	852
Making street collection	Customer	1,500	1.00	90	90	1,590
General distribution activities						
Sales analyses	Order	1,800	1.50	300	450	2,250
Mail handling	Number of pieces in/out	300	.05	300	15	315
Direct selling						
Sales personnel training	Number of salespeople	500	10.00	10	100	600
Entertainment	Customers	—	15.00	20	300	300
Advertising and sales promotion						
Newspapers	Newspaper inches	—	1.00	1,000	1,000	1,000
Radio and television	Minutes of radio or television time	—	50.00	50	2,500	2,500
		$6,900			$6,537	$13,437

marketing functions and subgroups. The unit cost would preferably represent a standard cost; otherwise it would be based on a less scientifically determined basis. The budget is for Territory X only; a similar budget could be prepared for each territory or other segment group. The overall marketing expense budget for the year would be the sum of these individual budgets.

REPORTS TO SALES PERSONNEL

Salespeople need information on their sales volume, as well as details showing the scope of their performance. They are usually eager to know how they compare with others in the sales force. Since the competitive spirit motivates many salespeople, the smart marketing manager provides regular feedback to stimulate them. The manager also knows that what motivates one salesperson will not motivate another. The sales reports can employ various techniques to suit each salesperson's personality.

The effective marketing manager communicates with his or her sales staff more frequently than once a month. It is worthwhile to forward weekly performance reports to each salesperson concerning his or her achievements in selling the preferred products (those with higher contribution margins). Naturally the salesperson is interested in his or her take-home pay. Earnings should be specified—that is, show what portion is salary, what is commission or bonuses, and so forth. The salesperson's record on special items and lines should be detailed. In addition, he or she should be given segmental information showing sales and contribution margins by customer, product lines, and promotional items.

Segmental information by customer should show sales for the current month and sales for the same period last year. This enables the salespeople to know if they are gaining or losing business with each customer account. Customer purchases for the current period should also be reported on a quarterly and semiannual basis, along with comparable data for previous periods.

A variety of detailed information utilizing the exception principle can be obtained from the data processing system. The demands for effective, prompt reporting can be better met if the organization's computer facilities are used in the budgeting process. However, the marketing manager should be cautious about printing multiple reports, because after the salesperson has determined his or her own achievements, he or she may discard the other reports. Only to the degree that the staff is receptive to additional data should the marketing manager go to the expense of communication.

LIMITATIONS OF BUDGETING

While budgets have many advantages, it must be remembered that they are at best an educated estimate of what will happen in the future. Their value will be greatly reduced if management views them as something more than estimates. This is not to imply that the estimates cannot be improved upon; as more time and effort are exerted in developing these estimates, more reliance can be placed on the results.

The marketing manager must recognize that the budget is a series of estimates that appeared to represent good yardsticks for the organization when the budget was established. If conditions change and/or these estimates later prove incorrect, management should revise the budget. If no deviations are granted, the budget will become a straitjacket and management will be too inhibited to take risks for fear of not meeting the budget. Budgets are not a panacea for all management problems; certainly they are no substitute for skilled managers.

SUMMARY

Forecasting is a highly creative process in which management is expected to evaluate and compare alternative courses of action. The social and economic factors that make up the environment in which the organization functions must be considered. Some of these conditions are predictable enough to be incorporated into the forecast. Others are subject to intangibles that cannot be quantified with any degree of exactitude.

Marketing managers of today have more types of information available for use in forecasting sales than did their counterparts of several years ago. Various government agencies supply large amounts of statistical data that is often broken down into small geographical units. Marketing managers use these four types of information in preparing sales estimates: general business conditions, market conditions, conditions within the industry, and plans and policies of the organization. The increasing use of computers in forecasting sales and market potential means that information is available more quickly and in greater detail. While sales forecasts are not exact, if a careful analysis of factors affecting sales has been made, they certainly are better than an uninformed guess of what may happen in the future.

The important thing to remember in developing a marketing budget is that the results must fit the needs of the particular organization. The budget should be complicated or simple, depending upon the complications or simplicity of the problems it is designed to control. If the company operates an elaborate distribution organization, the budget should be prepared along detailed lines.

Before a budgetary system can be successful, it must be accepted by the employees whose activities are affected by it. People whose performance will be directly measured by the budget should be encouraged to participate in the budgeting process to the full extent of their interests and capabilities. The budget committee should be available to provide useful advice and assistance. The budget should follow the lines of authority and responsibility within the organization. It is also useful to designate which items are controllable and which are noncontrollable for each segment manager. Proper use of budgets will promote higher morale and a better working relationship between employees and management.

11

Marketing Communications

MARKETING is often viewed as a whole network of communications that involves both public relations and advertising. There is obviously an overlap between these two. Public relations identifies the organization's policies with the interests of the public; it is concerned with the organization's image within the community. On the other hand, advertising is a controlled means of persuasion through the use of mass media.

ADVERTISING

Though *marketing communications* can be considered a broader term than *advertising*, the terms will be used interchangeably in this chapter.

Costs

Some people argue that marketing communications increase the prices of articles. This is a difficult contention to prove, however, because there are so many factors (such as supply and demand) that affect the prices of goods. It is true that advertising costs, like all other expenses, are passed on to the consumer. But advertising affects sales volume, and increased production volume usually lowers the manufacturing cost per unit. Similar advantages in distribution and financing may result from advertising, and these also result in lower per unit costs. The real question about advertising is whether it fulfills its function more effectively than some other method would.

Social Role

Newspapers, magazines, television, and radio play a vital part in distributing news and providing entertainment. In countries like the United States, advertising expenditures are the major source of support for these mass media. Advertising exists only because the public tolerates this interruption in its entertainment. Therefore advertisers recognize that they depend upon the goodwill of the public, and this encourages them to develop messages that do not offend audiences—that is, they are less tempted to present low-quality sales messages. The one danger inherent in this approach is that advertisers may be so concerned with possible offenses to the public that the sales messages will all become dull and similar.

Objectives

For all communications programs, certain objectives must be defined initially. Some of these will relate to the type of image the program will seek to portray, the market audience the program is geared to, and other qualitative factors. What financial returns are expected in relation to the amount of funds spent must also be established. Every communications program must coordinate these two types of objectives: the qualitative and the financial. It is unrealistic to select a large market audience covering a wide geographical distance if the organization does not have the funds to support the necessary marketing communications.

While the purpose of marketing communications is to influence the attitudes and actions of consumers so that ultimately a sale is made, the communication process itself is more complex than it often appears. Marketing communications can be designed in various ways to fulfill other immediate objectives. For example, one objective can be to make potential customers aware of the organization's products or services. This awareness can be economically created through the use of mass media. If, instead, the organization wants to build a desired image, it may do this by running a single ad in a magazine such as *Playboy*. It can then use this association on product displays: "As advertised in *Playboy*."

Classifications

Primary and select-demand advertising. If a marketing executive chooses to use primary demand, it means that his or her objective is to create demand for a class of products. This type of advertising is often used by trade associations. Individual firms also use it when introducing a new product. Select-demand advertising is intended to make the consumer aware of one specific brand and thus create brand loyalty.

Product (service) and institutional advertising. Advertising can also be classified as product or institutional. If the objective is to increase the sale of a product or service, product or service advertising is undertaken. If, instead, the objective is to establish favorable consumer attitudes toward the company or to build a more favorable reputation for the firm, institutional advertising would be more effective.

When new products or services are introduced, a communications program that informs the public of their existence is needed. An organization may adopt the marketing strategy of first introducing the product to a specific market segment, and then advertising to make potential customers in other segments aware of the product. Merely making the public aware of the product or service is usually not enough to generate sales; information must be supplied so that potential customers can evaluate the product in relation to their needs. The objective of this type of advertising is to create favorable attitudes toward the product.

Organization of the Advertising Department

The location of the advertising department within the company varies, depending upon the size of the organization, the type of advertising the organization plans to use, and the involvement of top management in advertising plans. Often the advertising department reports directly to its own top executives, or to the top marketing or sales executives within the organization. But a large company with several divisions may decide to decentralize advertising so that it operates at the division level. Decentralization may prove better because the sales message can be prepared by people working in the local area who are familiar with the geographical environment.

Generally product managers have the responsibility for several products—unless one product's volume is sufficient to justify their spending all their time on this product. Product managers have the responsibility of determining how to best spend the communication dollars allocated to their product. However, in many firms product managers do not have control over the sales personnel for their product. Instead, the sales force is shared among several product managers. In this situation the product manager has limited input into the decisions regarding the division of the communications budget between media advertising and sales promotion.

While the firm may have organizational reasons for not giving the product manager responsibility for the communications efforts promoting his or her product, still there should be close coordination between the product manager and the sales manager. Admittedly this can be difficult. Responsibility for the use of mass media advertising is usually assigned on a companywide basis, while the sales force is ordinarily set up on a geographic basis. A sales manager is assigned to each region, and salespeople report directly to him or her. All regional sales managers report to the firm's national sales manager. This contrast in responsibilities makes the necessary coordination difficult. Yet it is important to achieve a close working relationship if the firm is to obtain the maximum benefits from its communications efforts.

Advertising Agencies

If the company relies on advertising agencies for the creation and production of its sales messages, its advertising department does not have to be large. Firms use advertising agencies in the belief that they will produce more effective advertising than their own people would. Agencies do introduce a fresh approach and have greater independence than an internal department. They also offer the firm experience gained from other accounts. The company has more flexibility if it uses an outside agency, because if it becomes dissatisfied, it can change agencies.

Types of agency. Advertising agencies are organized along several different lines. The larger agencies are usually organized according to either a group or a departmental system. Under the group system, the artists, writers, and other specialists are assigned a group of accounts. They then concentrate their efforts and skills solely on these accounts. Other advertising agencies group their specialists in the same department; for example, all artists in one department, all copy writers in another room. Everyone works on several accounts. The departmental system gives each specialist a broader background.

Compensation. Many agencies receive a media commission as compensation for their services. For example, suppose an agency prepares the copy for a newspaper advertisement that costs $10,000. If the agency charges 18 percent, it would keep $1,800 before forwarding the remainder (net of discount) to the publisher.

The agency may also charge its client a percentage of the additional costs, such as for artwork, filming, and taping, that it incurs. This would be over and above the cost of space or time. Some advertising agencies charge the client a flat fee. This practice is used especially if there is no agency commission involved, or if the media rate is so low that the commission would not compensate the agency for its efforts.

MEDIA SELECTION

The selection of the proper media for marketing communications may be a simple decision for a small industrial products manufacturer, but it is a major problem for a larger consumer products manufacturer. The industrial goods manufacturer will likely have only a few practical media alternatives. Usually his choices would range from advertising in the one trade publication to direct-mail communications. He would have to determine how appropriate personal selling would be.

Push Versus Pull Strategies

The relationship between mass communications and personal selling is referred to as the push versus the pull strategy. With the push strategy, personal selling is emphasized. Salespeople actively solicit orders from retailers, who push the products to consumers. The salespeople must explain the benefits of the product to retailers. In order for them to be interested enough in the product to push the sale, their economic incentives must be large enough to justify the necessary time and effort. Thus the push approach is appropriate for items with high profit margins.

The product must have several differentiating features to give the salespeople something to stress in their sales talks. These unique features will become the basis of the selling approach. Salespeople soon become tired of trying to sell just an average, nondescript product.

Products that require demonstrations are ideally suited to the push strategy. Many industrial goods fall into this category. Products that can be set up to meet individual needs, such as health and life insurance, are also effectively sold with the push strategy.

A very important requirement for the effective use of the push strategy is that the product be of high quality, and this usually means a high sales price. The combination of high prices, high profit margins, and large personal selling expenditures means that little money is left for advertising. The mass media advertising that is used is designed to support the salespeople's efforts and to create awareness of the product.

At the other end of the continuum is the pull strategy. Here the emphasis is on mass media advertising. The idea is to generate such great consumer demand that the products are pulled to the customers—that is, consumers demand that retailers stock the merchandise.

While products sold with the pull strategy have relatively low profit margins, their turnover is high and little effort is required to sell them. Salespeople assume the role of order takers rather than order seekers. Most consumer packaged goods, such as food, health and beauty aids, and cigarettes, are sold using the pull strategy. National advertising is used to create brand loyalty.

Factors Affecting Media Selection

The following order shows the degrees of effectiveness of the various advertising media: (1) face-to-face, (2) television, (3) radio, and (4) print.

While this order is a guide for marketing executives, other factors must be considered, including the characteristics of the product, the market audience, the firm and its competitors, and the content of the message delivered.

Product Characteristics

Before deciding whether the emphasis should be on personal or on mass communications, management should evaluate the product itself. As mentioned in the discussion of the push and pull strategies, a low profit margin almost prohibits extensive personal selling. Instead mass media advertising must be relied on. Product items that require some training to use must be sold under a personal selling approach. If the benefits of the product are not readily apparent—as, for instance, an investment in a mutual fund—a sales representative must be available to point these out.

Certain products are more effectively advertised if they are shown being used. For food products, the buying impulse is best motivated if they are shown, in color, being eaten. Therefore a newspaper is not the best medium in which to advertise food products.

Television can be effective for demonstrating products that require motion. Here, filmed or video-taped commercials are usually required.

Certain media tend to change or modify a product's image. If the product already has a specific image the firm wishes to keep, these media should be avoided. For example, a product with a very sophisticated image would not be advertised in a family-oriented magazine—unless the firm wanted to change the image. Thus the characteristics of the product will be a strong influencing factor in media selection.

Potential Market

The characteristics of the potential market are so important that one of the first steps in choosing a communication medium is to identify the potential consumer market. Not only do the product's features affect the strategy used, but also the type of customer that the organization is trying to reach plays a significant role. The socioeconomic and demographic characteristics of potential consumers should be investigated. The audience plays an active role in the communications process because it must assign meanings to the symbols used by the advertiser. It is the audience that determines which advertising stimuli it will respond to.

In appraising the different types of mass media, the marketing executive should study how people use an advertising medium. The extent to which people rely on television, radio, and the printed word varies according to their levels of income and education. Living environment, whether urban or rural, also helps determine people's usage of the various mass media.

Some classes of media can more accurately depict their audience characteristics than others. For example, the print media can provide advertising executives with more information on their readership than can radio or television. Since radio and television stations have different programming formats, they attract different types of audiences. Because of this, marketing executives should conduct their own research on what kind of audience each station attracts. This research will provide them with the data needed in choosing a station.

In evaluating a mass medium for advertising use, its ability to reach the potential market should be studied. If the product or service will appeal to only a specific market segment, it may be difficult to find a medium that reaches this group. However, if the product is normally sold to a trade or professional group, there may be industry journals that would reach these people. There is a danger here if the number of potential customers is small. It may prove unprofitable to use any mass media under these circumstances. This is why the number of potential customers should be estimated before the market strategy is chosen.

Company Capabilities

The financial and managerial capabilities of the organization cannot be neglected in selecting an advertising medium. The sales staff available also directly affects the marketing strategy chosen. It may appear that personal selling will generate the highest sales volume; however, before hiring additional sales personnnel, the organization must determine if it has the resources to pay the necessary compensation if the desired sales volume is not attained during seasonal slumps. If the company's resources are not large enough to incur this expense, this would not be the proper strategy to use.

The amount of funds available for marketing communications is always a limiting factor. Often the budget alone rules out the use of certain media, such as quality national television. Demonstrations are also costly, and may not be practical because of cost constraints, even though they would be the most desirable approach. The marketing executive also has to decide whether it will be more effective to advertise on a limited basis in a national medium, or to use a less expensive regional or local medium more frequently. The national medium might not give enough coverage to achieve an effective program.

Many small organizations do not have the managerial expertise to compete in a large market. Their market research departments are inadequate to gather the data needed, and not knowledgeable enough to use the available research findings. In addition to inadequate managerial knowledge, some firms may have limited distribution systems. It is foolish to advertise products in a geographical area where consumers are unable to obtain them.

Industry Use

Organizations often use the same medium their competitors use. They feel that these competing firms have chosen the medium wisely, and have continued to use it because of successful experience. A small firm, however, may not be able to afford the medium its larger competitors are using. It will then be forced to find the alternative that suits its budget. It may find that rather than using small infrequent advertisements in its competitors' medium, it will be better off with a different medium.

DIRECT ADVERTISING

Direct advertising is one of the oldest marketing communications. It is a very flexible method because there are various forms that can carry the message. The message may be delivered in person, placed on doorknobs of residential homes, put under windshield wipers of cars, or sent through the mail. Several forms of direct advertising can be used simultaneously, ranging from letters and postcards to inexpensive gifts and novelties.

Direct advertising permits the message to be delivered within a short time. This means that the advertising can be released to take advantage of current business, market, and social conditions. With direct advertising, it is easy to personalize and adapt the message to the audience being solicited.

Product Literature

Regardless of the form of direct advertising used, product literature is fundamental. This is especially true with the introduction of new products. The decision should not be *whether* to produce literature, but *what message* to include and what its scope should be. Salespeople need literature to leave with prospective customers. Suggestions to buyers as to where or how to use the product may be included in the literature. The kind of literature to produce depends on the product and the market situation.

Direct Mail

Advertisers have much flexibility in their use of direct mail. Not only can they design the content of the mailing to suit their needs but they can also choose a mailing list that will reach a selected market audience. Critical to the success of any direct-mail advertising campaign is the mailing list—the material must go to the right people. When the marketing executive has confidence in the accuracy and selectivity of the mailing list, waste circulation is limited. If direct mail is used, the sales message can be kept hidden from competitors.

Direct mail allows the introduction of new products and subsequent advertising to be concentrated in a narrower area than would be possible with the use of trade publications. A tight mailing list can be developed so that high-priority prospects are contacted. The cost of this list may be less than the cost of advertising in a trade publication, only a small percentage of whose readership are prospective customers. It is often quite difficult to separate media audiences into those who are good prospects and those who are not.

There are a number of sources for mailing lists. An existing firm's best choice is usually past and present customers. Manufacturers can obtain names of potential customers from their dealers and salespeople. Some firms exchange lists with other noncompeting firms. Before a firm decides to develop its own list, it should know the time and cost required to keep the list up to date. If the names and addresses are not accurate, the message will probably not reach the intended party. If, however, the firm is not appealing to a select group, the direct mail message can be addressed to "Occupant" of a street address in cities, and "Box Holders" on a rural free delivery route.

Many magazines sell their subscriber lists. There are also companies whose major revenue-generating function is the compilation of direct-mail lists. These lists may be rented or purchased. If rented, the advertiser will never actually see the list but will be told to send the cards or letters to be addressed to the list-holding company. Some of these firms classify their lists according to various characteristics. With this procedure, the advertising firm risks using a mailing list that does not fit its needs, because the list firm's notion of what kind of consumers will be receptive to the new product may be wrong.

The cost of direct advertising in relation to the effectiveness of results obtained is usually quite high. Much direct mail is wasted because many people dislike it and automatically destroy it unread. If the mailing list is carefully chosen, the chances of this happening will be reduced.

In designing the direct-mail items, an incremental cost analysis should be made. If these items are relatively simple, so the extra or incremental cost of printing and mailing an additional volume is not great, the organization does not have to spend so much time and money developing a select mailing list. It could use instead whatever lists it feels are appropriate.

Salespeople

Both push and pull strategies require salespeople. Personal selling is the characteristic form of communication in a push strategy. Salespeople also play a vital role in a pull strategy by setting up displays that provide a point of purchase coordination with media advertising. Whether a push or pull strategy is used, the salesperson is responsible for gaining the cooperation of the retail trade.

Salespeople are a very effective means of communication when new products are being introduced. They can carry information about the product directly to potential customers. They can also seek out the customers they feel will be most amenable to buying the product. However, salespeople are an expensive means of communication. They incur considerable traveling expenses, and waste much time waiting for a convenient moment to call on prospective customers.

If an organization expects its salespeople to communicate at maximum efficiency, it must be sure they are provided with product information. Sales manuals are a ready source of information salespeople can refer to in dealing with potential customers. Reference materials are especially important when new products are being introduced. Information ranging from possible product applications to prices and terms can be included in the sales manual. The materials should be arranged so that the salespeople can efficiently communicate all the features of the product. They should also be trained in effective sales techniques.

Sales meetings are another common way of providing the sales staff with sufficient information concerning the organization's products. For new products, it is especially important that salespeople be able to anticipate questions from potential customers. This kind of preparation can often best be done during discussions at sales meetings.

Reseller's Sales Staff

If the reseller's salespeople are to be able to answer customers' questions and problems, they must be supplied information about the product. It is also economical to train these salespeople in other aspects of the sales function, such as market and customer analysis. Manufacturers who realize the opportunity that the reseller's sales staff offers are quite willing to establish training sessions or provide some other form of assistance for these personnel. A knowledgeable salesperson can favorably affect sales, especially if competitors have similar products. This training and communication is an ongoing task. It is necessary to continually update and motivate reseller's sales staff.

Missionary Selling

A manufacturer may employ a salesperson whose function is to set up displays, refill the retailer's shelf, and in general assist the reseller's sales force. This individual is referred to as a missionary salesperson. Pharmaceutical firms employ missionary salespeople (known as "detailmen") who call on physicians to inform them of new drugs. Many of these people are pharmacists, so they have a command of the technical language and can converse intelligently with physicians. The objective of missionary selling is to create goodwill for the organization. In some companies any orders that the missionary salesperson receives are turned over to a reseller's salesperson.

INDIRECT ADVERTISING

Rather than use direct mail or salespeople, the firm may choose to advertise in newspapers or magazines. If it feels that the print media do not best serve its needs, it may choose to use television, radio, or outdoor advertising. Point-of-purchase displays and premiums are other possibilities, along with matchbooks, pencils, music and athletic programs, and other products. The advantages and disadvantages of each of these media will be discussed. Since the characteristics of specialized media vary considerably, it is difficult to make general statements concerning their effectiveness.

Newspapers

When a marketing executive uses newspapers to advertise, he or she has fairly precise knowledge of who is receiving the messages. A newspaper's circulation can be more accurately determined than a radio or television station's audience. The management of each newspaper knows which issue appeals to men and which to women. Generally the morning issue is read more by men, while evening papers are read by women.

Cost. Since several newspapers are usually available, the marketing executive should calculate the effective cost of each paper if circulation and rate charges differ. Suppose Newspaper A charges 60 cents per line and its circulation is 120,000, while Newspaper B charges 80 cents per line and its circulation is 200,000. The best way to compare these publications is to calculate the milline rate. The milline rate is the rate per line of a publication per million circulation.* For Newspaper A, this would be:

$$\frac{1,000,000 \times \$.60}{120,000} = \$5$$

For Newspaper B, the calculation is:

$$\frac{1,000,000 \times \$.80}{200,000} = \$4$$

According to these computations, the best choice is Newspaper B. In determining what circulation figures to use, only the effective

*This approach was suggested in Charles G. Dirksen and Arthur Kroeger, *Advertising Principles and Problems* (Homewood, Ill.: Richard D. Irwin, Inc., 1973), p. 307.

circulation, (not the total) should be considered. The waste circulation, or portion that is considered undesirable, should be eliminated.

Newspapers offer the advertiser flexibility. Intensive coverage of one geographical area can be made, and the advertisements can be tied in with the sales appeal in that area. The advertising message can also be slanted to the local newspaper reader. Besides providing intensive coverage of a geographical area, newspapers reach all economic classes. Almost every member of the family looks at a newspaper received in the home. In addition to these advantages, newspapers are a relatively inexpensive form of advertising.

Newspaper advertising has the strong disadvantage of being short-lived. A specific issue of the paper does not provide much opportunity for repeated exposure. Many times readers of newspapers glance hurriedly at the news items, and even more hurriedly at the advertisements. There are so many advertisements in newspapers that some readers don't bother looking at any of them. If the product appeals only to a certain group, much of the newspaper's circulation is irrelevant. Scheduling and contractual problems also present problems in arranging newspaper advertising. Lastly, newspapers are unable to show products that require special color.

Magazines

Unlike newspapers, which are designed for a broad spectrum of the population in a specific geographical area, magazines appeal to special-interest groups. While newspaper readers are of almost every economic class, magazine readers are usually middle and upper class. This selectivity is one advantage of advertising in magazines and periodicals: the advertiser is provided an audience with a specific set of characteristics. If the marketing executive has a definite market audience in mind, he or she can choose among various types of magazines to meet this objective. Many magazines conduct research on the characteristics of their readers and their reading habits. The advertiser should use this data, along with the comparative cost ratios, before choosing a magazine.

Magazines have repeated exposure and a longer life than newspapers, since they do not become out of date as quickly and are often passed along to other readers. Because magazines are printed on higher-quality paper than newspapers, the advertiser is able to use a variety of color and mechanical techniques. Magazine advertising is good for food and other products that are best presented in color. If the organization is trying to develop inquiries, placing ads in trade publications may be the most effective means of communication.

Marketing executives can take advantage of such advertising devices as coupons, pull-out gimmicks, and dramatic illustrations. National advertising in specific magazines lends prestige to the products. Since these magazines realize this, they offer endorsements for products they have advertised. This endorsement has value if readers place confidence in the magazine.

Cost. The unit of measure for comparing costs in magazines is cost per page per thousand, because most rates are quoted on the basis of a page or fraction of a page.* For example, suppose Magazine C costs $13,000 per black and white page and net circulation is 2.6 million. The cost per page per thousand would be:

$$\frac{\$13,000 \times 1000}{2,600,000} = \$5$$

Care must be used in comparing the cost per page per thousand. The figure indicated as net circulation is not the same as the number of people who will read the advertisement. The cost per page per thousand also varies between magazines. It is usually greater for magazines that appeal to certain interest groups.

Magazines do not have a wide distribution relative to the total population. Neither do they offer the advertiser the flexibility that newspapers and other media do. Copy must be prepared well in advance of distribution. The magazine's editorial and news material is somewhat dated because of the time schedule required in publishing and printing, though the weekly news magazine have overcome this scheduling problem and are able to report current events fairly rapidly.

A few magazines issue regional editions, but the majority do not possess geographical or market selectivity. A limited number of magazines allow firms to advertise different products in different regions. There is a charge for this special service.

Television

Television makes use of both sight and sound. It requires less effort to absorb a message delivered on television than one advertised in the print media. The human voice is more effective than printed material, and motion can be used to show the product or service. A salesperson demonstrating a product on television approximates the personal sales approach.

*This approach was illustrated in Charles G. Dirksen and Arthur Kroeger, *Advertising Principles and Problems* (Homewood, Ill.: Richard D. Irwin, Inc., 1973), p. 316.

Even though the cost of network time is high, television may actually be the most economical medium to use because of audience numbers. In addition, television stations often offer a cumulative quantity discount rate based on the number of time units the advertiser uses during a given period. Since virtually all American homes have at least one television set, and it is on several hours a day, television enables the advertiser to reach huge numbers of people. Television is the mass medium par excellence, which is why so many firms use it. Sometimes they don't even use motion on the screen to demonstrate their products.

Since the message advertised on television must necessarily be brief, the executive is forced to decide which details about the product will convey the message in a very short time. Television's unique features—such as zoom shots and closeups—make the viewer feel part of the overall production. However, these sophisticated production techniques (and color) are costly.

Television advertising can be geared to the desired audience, since the size and makeup of viewers vary throughout the 24-hour cycle. For example, prepared breakfast cereals are most often advertised on children's programs. As more television channels become available, there will be increased selectivity. Another factor that will affect selectivity is the continuing increase in the number of television sets owned by each family. In multiple-set homes individual family members can choose the program they wish to watch.

Timing is important for television advertising and often creates a serious problem. Prime-time hours are limited, and an increasing number of advertisers desire prime time. The marketing executive must also consider that there are different time zones in the United States. A message telecast at 8:00 P.M. (prime time) on the East Coast would be seen at 5:00 P.M. (children's program time) on the West Coast. Delayed broadcasts can, however, overcome this limitation.

The marketing executive is faced with some disadvantages if he or she chooses television advertising. If the viewer walks away from the set during the commercial, the message is lost. In fact, many viewers take advantage of the commercial break to change stations or temporarily leave the room. In the print media the message is available for a longer period of time.

Advertisers must choose a specific television program to carry their commercials. Tastes and preferences for the various television programs vary widely according to geographical area. A very popular show in one area may rarely be viewed in other places. The firm is faced with the decision of choosing the most logical program. Since there is so much risk involved in selecting a popular show, few advertisers now sponsor programs. Instead they are following the safer approach of using spot announcements or participating with other companies in the sponsorship of several programs.

Radio

The advent of television changed the role of radio. No longer is it the primary form of family entertainment. The function of radio is now to provide local and national news and a music format. A large share of radio listening is done outside the home, in cars and on beaches.

Even though television has changed the radio-listening habits of many Americans, the radio is still an important medium. Radio advertising concentrates on the human voice, and can effectively convey warmth and feeling. An additional advantage to radio advertising is that people often listen while performing other tasks such as household work or driving a car. Radio demands little time or concentration from the listener. Since almost every household has at least one radio, radio advertising can reach a large number of people.

If speed is important, radio or television advertising is superior to other forms. Radio advertising also offers flexibility in timing and market audiences. The firm can choose in which markets it will advertise. The type of listener varies by the time of day and the program being aired; this fact enables the marketing executive to obtain great audience selectivity. In larger cities certain radio stations appeal to ethnic groups—for example, Afro-Americans. Such stations are good to use if the product or service has special appeal for these specific audiences. Even though few advertisers sponsor radio programs, the same considerations that apply to sponsoring television programs apply to radio. Football and basketball games are often sponsored by advertisers wishing to appeal to a large listening audience with certain characteristics.

Radio advertising has the same perishability that television advertising has. If the message is missed when it is aired, it is gone forever. That people tend to turn on a radio while performing other functions often means they do not listen closely. They especially tune out commercials. It is impractical to use radio as an advertising medium for products that are more effectively shown than talked about.

Before the advent of television, lyrics were written and set to music for use in radio commercials. Television changed the focus to the visual, and decreased the use of music in advertising. There is some question among marketing executives whether music can be considered a form of marketing communication. While it is readily agreed that music can produce a strong emotional response, it does not carry a consistent message. Music evokes highly personal experiences in listeners. On the other hand, written and spoken language can give in detail a message that is understood by most people. Even though music causes individualized responses, it can be used effectively by the marketing communicator who has had musical training.

Outdoor Advertising

In evaluating the use of painted displays and billboards as a means of advertising, a prime consideration is what percentage of the population will see this communication. The display or billboard must be placed in a high-traffic area. Another important consideration is the message itself—it must attract attention. Time is a big factor because motorists driving down an interstate highway at 55 miles per hour cannot take the time to read details. The message must be short and identify the product.

Outdoor advertising is relatively inexpensive and does offer much flexibility in regard to location. But an effective outdoor display requires creative effort, since brevity is imperative. Also, there is pressure against outdoor signs from concerned citizens because they destroy people's view of the countryside. Some states have outlawed all advertising along major highways.

Demonstrations and Exhibits

For some products one of the best forms of advertising is to show it in action. The organization may demonstrate a product at a booth at a trade show, take movies of it in action, or arrange a special showing. A trade exposition is often a good place for exhibiting new products. This is especially true if the product is too large to be moved. Even if the product can be carried to customers' plants, it may be less expensive to bring it to one location than to demonstrate it at several different sites. If the demonstration is well planned but given to a less than capacity audience, the company's assets are being wasted. The company should try to ensure that prospective buyers attend the demonstration.

Much attention should be devoted to the design of the exhibit. The demonstration should be set up so that it best communicates the advantages of the product. The approach will vary according to the product; the best combination of communications strategy should be used. Portable demonstration units are a possibility, but these are usually very costly because a driver and technicians must be employed, and the equipment will have to be purchased or rented. Portable demonstration units have one major advantage: the demonstration has to be set up only once. There are many extra costs involved in exhibits and these should be reflected in the budget.

A movie film that shows the product in action may be produced; though a live demonstration is usually more effective. In some cases, however, motion pictures are better than a live demonstration because of film techniques such as slow motion and animation. Before deciding to produce a film, management should analyze the cost and time involved, which is usually higher than for a live demonstration. And if the motion picture introducing the new product does not approach the sophistication of the modern films the public is accustomed to viewing, a shabby product image will result.

Point-of-Purchase Displays

Displays are often set up in retail stores to create a "buying atmosphere" for the customer. Various forms of visual material can be displayed at the point of purchase. These displays are often combined with a sales promotion deal to serve as a further inducement. Another purpose is to spur selling efforts by resellers. The overall objective is to increase the turnover of stock by inducing both the consumer and the reseller to take action.

Sales Promotion and Deals

Organizations frequently use sales promotions and deals to counteract a competitor's actions. They are designed to generate action in the short run. Promotions and deals are often offered to retailers in connection with packaged goods that are currently sold through self-service stores. They may take the form of a reduced price or trade buying allowances for the retailer who agrees to buy a certain quantity of the goods.

Temporary price reductions are often offered to consumers as an inducement to try the product. Retailers' customers may be given reduced prices on other products if they bring in a certain number of the product's labels. Two-for-one offers and cash allowances to consumers or retailers are also used as temporary means of promotion.

If the promotion is in the form of reduced prices to the consumer there is a real danger in keeping it for too long. Customers may become so accustomed to the new lower price that they will resent any change back to the original higher price. Promotions may attract new customers only temporarily; once the price is raised to its initial level, the customer may switch to another brand. It is difficult to create brand loyalty if promotions are constantly offered by firms in the industry.

The accountant and the marketing executive can fairly accurately assess the future cost of promotions and deals. Once this cost is estimated, it can be applied against the expected benefit. Deals and promotions can be controlled if they are offered through specific retail chains or apply only to geographical regions.

Even though the extra cost of deals can be closely determined by the accountant, few firms bother making the calculation. Some neglect to include all costs associated with the promotion, such as the special printing of labels and coupons, extra displays and advertising, and the additional effort and expense of the salespeople.

Premiums

Premiums can be an effective means of sales promotion if the market audience is appropriate. Producers of prepared dry cereals that appeal to children can use toys as premiums to good advantage. The prize may be included in the product, or may require several boxtops and a small amount of money. Dishes, towels, and kitchen utensils can also be effectively used as premiums. Other companies enclose coupons or bonus points that can be redeemed for merchandise on their products.

It is often quite difficult to choose a premium that appeals to a wide range of consumers. The cost of the premium product is another factor for consideration. If the premium is very expensive, or very cheap and readily available to consumers, it will not attract many people. At the same time, the premium should not be so appealing that consumers are buying the premium as opposed to the product being pushed. It is usually more effective if the product and the premium are closely associated. For example, a marketer of ground coffee could offer an attractive coffeepot.

The accountant and marketing executive should work together in deciding what price to attach to the premium. The approach commonly used is for the consumer to pay the wholesale cost of the premium, plus the costs of shipping and handling. The organization may decide instead to require more boxtops or proof-of-purchase coupons from their own product and no money. The approach chosen depends upon the price of the merchandise involved, as well as the marketing strategy being used.

Contests. Instead of going directly to the consumer, the company may set up contests for its resellers and salespeople. Care must be used in deciding upon the premium. For example, a vacation for the salesperson or reseller alone would have little appeal; they should be allowed to take their husband or wife. The vacation spot chosen should be an attractive place the winner would not otherwise visit.

Advantages. Premiums, coupons, and contests are most effective in product lines that do not evoke strong brand loyalty. The extra savings or chance to win may be all the incentive necessary to get the consumer to buy the product. There is a danger in the overuse of coupons and premiums; consumers will grow to expect them, and their value as an incentive for buying will be lost. These forms of sales promotion are most effective if they are used infrequently.

Dangers. Before introducing premiums, management should investigate the short- and long-range effects. If the sales promotion causes an abnormal percentage of sales in one time period rather than actually increasing total sales, the premiums cannot be considered effective. For example, a reseller who wants to win the European vacation offered may buy several weeks' supply of a product during the contest period. With an inventory so overstocked, he will not make additional purchases for several weeks after the contest period ends.

The increased sales during contest periods may have an effect on the organization's physical distribution system. Temporary personnel may have to be brought in to handle the increased workload, and additional storage space may be needed for the large inventory levels.

ADVERTISING BUDGET

In Chapter 10 the various methods of establishing an advertising budget were discussed. The percentage of sales method is easy to apply, but there is little logic in its application. Sales should be the end result of advertising, whereas this method assumes the reverse by calculating advertising as a percentage of sales. Under the objective task method, the first step is to decide on an objective for the program over the next year. Then the advertising necessary to achieve this objective is estimated.

Approaches

Budget planning can be done from the top level down to the lower levels, or it can be built up from below. The top-down approach prevents suboptimization, which occurs when a segment's attempts to realize its own objectives prevent other parts of the organization from achieving the highest level of accomplishment. Top management may be in a better position to consider the financial aspects of each communications program. It may be more aware of the quantity discounts available so that the most profitable mix of advertising can be used.

The bottom-up, or buildup, approach starts on the lower management levels and solicits the participation of the people whose activities will be judged by the budget. The argument for this approach is that information is gained from people closer to the marketplace. In addition, the active participation of the people involved should be good for motivation. Since other aspects of budgets are discussed in Chapter 10, the material will not be repeated in this chapter.

Cooperative Advertising

Manufacturers of packaged consumer goods may cooperate with retailers in advertising. This form of marketing communications is used for several reasons. The retailer often receives lower rates in newspapers because he is a local advertiser, whereas the manufacturer would be a national advertiser. The usual arrangement is for the manufacturer to pay 50 percent of the amount spent by the retailer for local advertising when the manufacturer's products are featured in the advertising. Generally the maximum amount the manufacturer will reimburse the retailer is specified. The retailer should provide the manufacturer with proof of the advertisement before any reimbursement is made.

Cooperative advertising has distinct advantages, yet it often results in problems. Some manufacturers find it difficult to secure proof the retailer has actually placed the advertisements, but rather than refuse to reimburse him, they will give the allowance because this is what their competitors are doing. This kind of advertising expenditure is unjustified and wasteful. The best policy is to draw up a contract between the two parties specifying what type of advertisement is reimbursable. The contract should also state the maximum amount that the manufacturer will pay and what proof will be needed for reimbursement.

EVALUATING COMMUNICATIONS MESSAGES

In evaluating the effectiveness of communications messages, several factors must be considered. The message must not only attract the consumer's attention; it must also develop some bond to which the potential customer can relate. Some messages develop this bond by arousing some basic need and showing how the product or service can fulfill it. Some of these needs are physiological, while others are psychological or social. In addition, a person is born with certain of these needs, while others are acquired in the environment in which he or she is reared.

Maslow has suggested the following hierarchy of needs:

1. Physiological—for food, water, sleep, sex, and physical activity.
2. Safety—for protection and security, for the familiar and the comfortable.
3. Love—for affection, belongingness, and acceptance by those one respects and loves.
4. Esteem—for self-respect and the respect of others, in the form of reputation, recognition, and prestige.
5. Self-actualization—for accomplishment and unique personal achievement.*

Maslow's hierarchy suggests something important for marketing executives: the needs at the lower level must be satisfied before the higher-level needs become effective motivators. Once a need is fulfilled, then it no longer serves as a motivator.

It is difficult to receive 100 percent satisfaction, but once a level of needs is fairly well satisfied, then the next order of needs becomes a motivating factor. At any one time several needs will influence a person's behavior. A person who has highly developed self-actualization needs will still be motivated by the most basic safety and physiological needs; however, a person whose major concern is to find enough food and shelter will not be motivated by self-actualization needs.

The most effective communication techniques first arouse needs, and then show how the particular product or service can satisfy them. This is why it is very important that the specific needs of the market audience be known before any form of market communications is attempted. The nature of the product or service determines the type of need to which an appeal can be made.

Emotional and Rational Appeals

Marketing executives can use emotional or rational appeals to satisfy certain human needs. The potential customer must be aware

*A. H. Maslow, *Motivation and Personality* (New York: Harper and Row, 1954), pp. 80–106.

of these needs before an appeal can be made. Emotional appeals usually rely on sentimental language, while rational appeals use reason and logic. The characteristics of the market audience to whom the appeal is directed help determine whether the emotional or rational approach is appropriate. If the targeted audience is highly intelligent, the rational approach is usually best. Persons of lower intelligence are less likely to respond to logic and arguments for using a certain brand. Most marketing executives find that emotional appeals are effective in attracting attention to the message, but rational appeals result in better acceptance.

The type of product involved is also a determining factor. High-fashion merchandise and jewelry are best advertised through emotional appeals, while machinery requires a rational approach. Threat appeals are a form of emotional appeal; they suggest unpleasant consequences if the receiver does not follow the actions suggested by the communicator. Life and health insurance companies are extensive users of threat appeals.

An effective use of group pressure can be made in marketing communications by stressing the opinion that "everyone is using the product, why don't you?" This type of message appeals to a person's need for social approval. Often it can cause someone to adopt an opinion even in the face of opposing evidence.

EVALUATION OF MARKETING COMMUNICATIONS

Most organizations spend a significant part of their communications budget on media advertising. Because so much money is invested in this form of communications, efforts should be made to judge the effectiveness of the media used so that comparisions between different media can be made. The market audience and the impact of the message are two important factors in evaluating media.

Marketing communications are difficult to measure because the consumer's buying response is variable. However, all tests of effectiveness should be based on whether consumers' buying habits were changed. This is a difficult measurement task because it is hard to separate long-term from short-term effects. In addition, some advertisements are designed to perform only part of the selling task, such as creating fraud awareness. Thus in evaluating marketing communications there is always the question of *what* to measure.

One measurement technique is to determine the number of individuals exposed to the medium being used or to the specific advertisement. Some firms, such as A. C. Nielsen Company, provide regular services for measuring television and radio audiences. But their surveys measure how often and how long people tune in a radio or television program rather than whether or not they were viewing or listening to the advertisements. (As mentioned earlier, many television viewers stop watching or listening during commercials.) These firms usually employ one of three basic approaches: diary, personal interviews, and mechanical systems.

Several methods,—recall, recognition, perception, and inquiry counts—measure individual print advertisements. Some of these methods are often criticized because they measure only readership and not selling power. The relationship between reading and buying is not clearly established.

Under the aided recall method, the investigator builds parts of the original impression and then asks the respondent to fill in the missing parts. With the pure recall method, no aid is given to the respondent. The aided recall method is more practical. In some forms such as the identification test, it is similar to the recognition method.

In the recognition method the reader reports if he or she saw a specific advertisement in a specific publication. The advertiser or agency may use organizations that provide recognition tests, or it may conduct its own tests. One big weakness of the recognition method is that many interviewees will, intentionally or otherwise, give incorrect answers. They may have seen the advertisement, but in another publication. They may confuse the advertisement with one that closely resembles it. Still, if the correct sizes of samples and techniques are used, the recognition test can be useful because it measures interest and attention.

Perception measures can be made almost immediately after exposure. The advertisement can be placed in front of the respondent to measure what changes in attitudes it has caused. It is difficult to get very accurate results from perception measures because respondents' answers are influenced by other advertisements they have seen.

Inquiry counts provide an ideal check on the effectiveness of individual advertisements, when they can be traced to these advertisements. It is crucial to be sure a tracing can be made back to the specific advertisement. Some firms accomplish this by using a different post office box or department number on coupons. The limitation of this approach is that it does not measure the long-term effects of the advertising program.

Evaluating Salespeople's Efforts

It is more difficult to evaluate and allocate sales force resources than advertising resources because people are involved. A salesperson cannot be temporarily switched from one geographical area to another. His or her feelings, as well as family attitudes, affect his or her effectiveness. The response to the salesperson's effort is the sum total of the individual customer's reactions. If customers dislike a salesperson, they will not hesitate to complain or stop buying the product. Thus it is quite difficult to objectively evaluate a salesperson.

Summary

Marketing executives can choose among several media in communicating the organization's product or service, and the messages used can be combined in several ways. Marketing communications decisions cannot be made without first considering their impact on other factors of the communications mix. The salesperson is aided by advertising, coupons, and premiums. It is not economical to incur the expenditures for mass media if the number of prospective buyers is limited. All alternative means of communication should be looked at carefully and impartially. Each may have its place in advertising an existing product or introducing a new one.

Both quantitative and qualitative factors must be considered before a communications medium is chosen. Audiences are growing more sophisticated. The overriding consideration is to choose a message that will attract and hold the receiver's attention. The receiver's needs must be aroused to the extent that he or she will try to satisfy these needs by taking the action suggested by the advertising message. The trend is toward more media specialization.

Marketing communications strategies must be coordinated with other elements of the marketing mix. Each medium of marketing communications should be evaluated for its contribution to the total communications system. Marketing communications dollars not only have a favorable effect on the operation the year they are spent but there is also a carryover to other years. In later periods the firm can receive benefits from effective marketing communications conducted in prior periods.

12

Accounting During the Product Life Cycle

IT is difficult to look ahead when the existing product lines are producing a net income, but companies must be constantly on guard for new product innovations. They should be evaluating consumers' reactions so as to anticipate what the consumer and industrial demand of tomorrow will be. Introducing new products is a gamble; not doing so is a greater one. Competition forces organizations to develop new products in order to maintain or improve their position. When one company achieves a breakthrough product, it is almost imperative that others in the industry develop products that can serve as substitutes for this new product.

A products management program needs the backing and participation of top management. It should establish broad guidelines for the program, including budget, timetables, and objectives. A mere statement by top management that the company plans to develop new products and appraise existing product lines is not adequate. The director of products management should develop a strategy that solicits potential buyers *and* the cooperation of management.

MARKET RESEARCH

Market research involves determining the feasibility of introducing new products and improving the performance of existing products.

Industry trends, competitors' activities, pricing, and changes in marketing methods or distribution channels are but a few of the activities that market research is concerned with. The acceptability of new products or new markets is evaluated. Once it is determined that they will be accepted, marketing research provides the strategy for selling the new products.

In reviewing each product there is always a temptation to gather more information than is necessary, and the gathering of unnecessary information is very expensive. This temptation can be partially avoided by defining the objectives of the study in detail before it is undertaken. The accountant and the marketing executives should establish a budget for each major product review project in order to discourage the collection of excessive data. Resources should be allocated to the project on the basis of expected benefit. As a useful guide, the budget could be set at one-half the annual expected increase in net income. Because the more accurate the research, the more expensive it will be, management may set minimum degrees of accuracy. Typical objectives of a product review would be:

1. To examine past trends so that short-term future trends can be forcasted.
2. To identify major competitors and their market share.
3. To estimate total market size.
4. To examine the different segments of the market, from sales territory to user.

These objectives would not be appropriate if management wanted to test different pricing policies or the effectiveness of its advertising and sales promotion. In these cases other marketing research techniques should be used.

Information Sources
There are two kinds of basic information sources for marketing research. One comes from internal company records and published material, and is referred to as desk research. Field research comes directly from individuals within the market such as customers, suppliers, and distributors.

Desk research. In market studies for new products desk research may be the most important. National statistics are now being published by government and international bodies. National economic indicators such as gross national product and population figures are given, and detailed surveys of principal industry sectors are also included. Financial and trade journals are other good sources for desk research.

Competitors may publish brochures and catalogues, which can be obtained and studied.

Field research. Since field research is generally quite expensive, the market researcher should avoid the temptation to start field research projects without first planning for the activities involved. There is a danger that he or she may begin interviewing people without fully realizing what questions should they be asked. Consequently repeat interviews may be required, and these generally annoy the people originally interviewed.

There are alternative sources of research that may answer the same questions as field research. These should be investigated first, so the researcher will be certain that field research is necessary before it is attempted. If it is decided that field work is required, the most appropriate method of research must be determined. Specifications, such as the size and structure of the sample, must also be decided.

Interview Methods

There is a tradeoff between the reliability of information obtained and the cost and speed involved in obtaining it. With samples, the higher the degree of accuracy required, the larger the sample size must be. It should also be noted that the more detailed the data is, the more expensive it will be to gather.

For example, personal interviews are highly reliable, but cost more than other kinds. At the other extreme, mailed questionnaires are not expensive, but their reliability is unpredictable. The detail obtained from a mailed questionnaire is usually scanty because the interviewee's prime concern is usually to check off answers as quickly as possible. Telephone and group interviews fall somewhere between these two extremes.

New Products

New products can be developed within the organization or purchased from outside. There are both advantages and disadvantages in developing products within the organization. The initial investment in a research and development department is high; and technical competence is required if a viable product is to be produced. The research department must be organized, and this sometimes creates management problems because its activities are so different from the organization's other functions. The risks are higher for developing products within the company, but often they are justified because they result in greater earning potential.

At the other end of the continuum are licensing and joint ventures. The initial investment is low; however, internal management, manufacturing, and marketing skills are needed. A viable product can be produced much more rapidly, so the risk is much lower than it is for product development within the firm. Acquisition of new products by this method is necessary if speed is important; however, the earning potential is less than with internal development.

Licensing is most appropriate if a product line needs supplementing or if time is a big factor. Licensing usually takes the form of a franchise or other form of sales agreement, so market penetration is immediately achieved. The joint venture method of acquiring new products is most appropriate if both parties want to get involved.

Joint ventures are different from license agreements because both parties contribute financial and physical resources on a continuing basis. Neither orgainzation has to have a complete combination of management, marketing, and manufacturing skills since the "product" partner will supply the missing parts.

Launching New Products

When new products are introduced, a certain chain of events should occur. The organization has some choice in setting up the sequence of events; however, there are some ground rules that should be followed for the best results. One is that sales personnel should be trained before the new product is publicly introduced. Another is that literature describing the new product should be available either at the time of introduction or soon afterward.

The characteristics of the new product help determine the sequence of events. If the market is well defined in advance (as is the case when the new product is related to existing ones), management may want to contact present customers before announcing the product to the general public. This will not only make current customers feel important but also may be a rapid way of making sales. Competitors' major customers should be contacted too.

Before public announcement is made and competitors are aware of the marketing strategy being used, a sales presentation could be made to these potential customers by scheduling an industrial show. However, marketing strategy is not the only reason for not making a public announcement first. If the new product has service requirements and these cannot be satisfied all over the country, the product cannot be introduced on a nationwide basis.

If the new product's market is not well defined, the initial introduction would probably be made through a press conference, news release, trade show, or some other form of public announcement. Public announcement of a new product is a major occurrence, and the way it is handled plays a role in the product's success. Therefore it should not be decided upon lightly. The accountant should provide marketing executives with the cost of each feasible alternative way of making a public announcement. Then the costs can be matched against the advantages of each alternative. For example, a news release to a trade publication may be the least expensive alternative. But if the readership of the publication is not properly alerted because the advertisement is too small to be seen, it is of little benefit. Conversely, the trade press may prove very helpful by devoting special articles to the new product that can reach potential customers other than those already known.

Once public announcement occurs, the company loses control over its customers; it no longer can choose who can buy its product. The press can praise or criticize it. At the same time, the company should feel compelled to provide the public with details concerning the product, emphasizing its innovations and advantages. The idea is to overcome the tactics of competitors' salespeople, who will be pointing out the product's flaws to potential customers.

There is considerable pressure to make the public announcement introducing a new product before competitors do. If several companies are all known to be developing a similar product, the one that first announces it to the public has gained an advantage. This company can stress the innovations of the product. (Often the trade name of the company first introducing the product becomes almost generic— the trade name "Coca-Cola" is an example.) Any successive competitors must stress their product's benefits over those of the first company. The company that first introduces the product sets the pace and assumes an image of leadership.

All too often this kind of pressure causes a company to launch a new product before enough tests have been conducted to ensure that it performs according to its specifications and is free of technical deficiencies. Or it launches a product without giving enough attention to the pricing policy. If company executives find the price is too low after the product is introduced, it will be difficult to raise it except over a long period.

The right moment to introduce a new product is a matter of opinion, not fact. Different people within the organization will have varying opinions as to the correct time. Marketing executives are anxious to release the product as soon as possible in order to jump competitors. Production and technical people generally prefer more time for testing.

If an organization waits until it is sure that all "technical bugs" are out, it may find that a competitor has gained the advantage of product introduction. Thus most solutions are compromises, and organizations usually introduce new products before their technical performance is completely assured. The decision should be made by executives who have studied the factors involved and who have had experience in making such judgments.

Effect of Company Size

Small companies do have some obvious disadvantages in introducing new products. Their resources, whether management personnel, cash funds, or other assets, are usually limited, and they cannot afford the elaborate research department and production facilities necessary for the new products. Their handicaps become readily apparent when they are trying to beat a larger company in introducing a new product first.

Small companies do have more flexibility and can move faster than large companies. Instead of having to fight the red tape that permeates the typical large organization, small company managers can make a joint decision and move quickly. Since the vested interest they have in existing products is smaller, they may be more willing to take risks.

Competition

It is certainly unrealistic to expect that a new product will not be faced with competition for several years. With increasing technological advancement, the time span between product introduction and competition is narrowing. The best protection an organization has against competitors attracting its customers away is to develop such brand loyalty that it will be both expensive and difficult for customers to switch. Customers need to be so convinced of the superiority of the product that they will question whether any other product is a suitable substitute.

Budget for Product Launching

Product planners often do not realize how expensive the introduction stage will be. In the consumer goods field, where the launching and successive advertising costs are so significant, the accounting and marketing executives should be considered members of the project team from the beginning. The planning phase should be thought of as part of the marketing strategy and given an appropriate budget.

A high initial budget for launching the product increases its chances for success because it allows extensive market penetration. Obviously most companies cannot afford as high a budget as the product could utilize. A budget less than this ideal amount has to suffice.

Mortality Rate for New Products

The mortality rate for new products is very high. The reasons for this high failure rate can often be traced to inadequate market research. Errors may have been made in estimating the need and market segment for the product. The manufacturing capability of the company may be at fault, or the price placed on the product may not have been the proper one.

Some of the blame can often be laid to inadequate monitoring of the new product, either in the launching process or after it was introduced. Management often does not realize the significance of the launching step to the total profitability of the product. It must be admitted, however, that if the product is poorly structured or if the timing is poor, it cannot be saved by any amount of monitoring. An adequately planned and financed launching stage is no guarantee of product success.

Product Inquiries

Once mass communications have been in effect long enough, the next sequence probably will be to provide answers to the inquiries generated from introduction. Many marketers feel that the responsibility for follow-up rests with the sales department. This is not feasible for a firm whose market is wide because it places too great a burden on the sales force. In most organizations the number of sales personnel is limited. Additionally, many of the inquiries will not be from potential buyers, but the salespeople will not know this until after they make the sales call. Even if they find the inquiry has come from a potential buyer, they will have to spend more time selling a new product than a mature one.

The follow-up of product inquiries should be handled by someone less qualified than the salespeople. Steps can be developed that will apply whether the inquiry comes from a potential buyer or not. Most of the steps to the point of determining if the prospect is a potential buyer will be routine. This procedure frees the salespeople to deal only with prospective buyers.

PRODUCT LIFE CYCLE

Once the product becomes a reality and is made public, it begins its life cycle. The stages in a product's life cycle are known by different names, but basically they are market development, market growth, market maturity, and market decline. Each stage has its own distinct characteristics.

Market Development

In the market development stage sales are low because the demand for this specific product has not been stimulated. Income will be low or nonexistent. The strategy here is to create demand for the product by convincing consumers to try it. The advantages of the product should be emphasized so that consumers will overcome their innate resistance to change. As the product reaches the end of this stage, management must be prepared with adequate distribution facilities to meet the demands of the market growth stage.

Market Growth

The transition from the introductory stage to the growth stage is usually difficult to define. It is at the beginning of the growth stage that short-range income goals begin to be realized. Product income will reach its peak during the latter phase of the growth stage. Sales revenue should continue to increase in the growth stage, while contribution margin should peak out. By the end of the growth stage, the contribution margin should be less than that experienced in the middle of this stage.

Since this profitability will attract other firms to the industry, management's strategy should be to create brand preference. This is usually best accomplished through advertising, other sales promotion, and effective pricing. Management should use several techniques to prevent the market from becoming saturated. One is to try to keep the product's success as secret as possible from competitors. Patents and copyright protection may also be of help.

The organizational structure of the introductory phase has to be kept flexible so it can be adapted to changing requirements. As the product cycle reaches the growth phase, the responsibility of duties should be clearly defined and the organization structure tightened. The emphasis on profitability requires that each department take advantage of cost control measures.

Market Maturity

If the new product is successful, sales volume and profit margin will increase during the development and growth stage. The maturity stage begins when the profit margin levels off, even though sales volume and net income continue to increase. The saturation stage is reached when sales volume and net income both level off. This indicates the beginning of price competition for a static or slowly growing market. Management should then try to find the special market needs that it can best fill.

Market Decline

When volume, income, and profit margin are all decreasing, this signals the beginning of the decline stage. The lengths of the various segments of the cycle do not follow any precise pattern; however, the first two stages (development and growth) are generally compressed. The last two stages (maturity and decline) are usually longer than the first two. Cost control is certainly needed in the market decline stage because this part of the cycle is not very profitable. It is possible that this stage will last for some time, if competitors gradually leave the field.

Unit Contribution Margin

One of the accountant's important roles in connection with product life cycles is to keep a close watch on the contribution margin. The unit contribution is an important figure to calculate because the point where it changes is significant. In the market development stage sales revenue should be increasing to a point where the contribution margin changes from being negative to becoming positive or at least zero. Conversely, a downward drop in the unit contribution trend may be the first sign of an impending market decline. Unit contribution margin analyses can be used for both existing products and new products.

Product Life Cycle Analysis

The product life cycle concept is of use in evaluating the future profitability both for existing products and for new ones. Analysis of product life cycles is helpful in planning for cash flow, advertising expenditures, and the introduction of new products. The ideal situation is to introduce a new product when an existing product reaches its peak. This will allow for a more steady flow of contribution margin, because as one product's contribution margin starts to decline, another product will begin to assume its position. This policy is especially important in the consumer-retail field, where a steady stream of products is common. It is not as important for industrial products, because to introduce new products in this field is usually more time-consuming and involves more drastic means.

The concept of the product life cycle seems very reasonable when it is discussed; however, it is quite difficult to apply. Managers often have insufficient data to be able to pinpoint what stage in the life cycle each product is in. It is also difficult to predict how long each of the stages will last and what problems will be encountered in each one. The length of the cycle may vary considerably. A product's life cycle may suddenly be shortened because of a scientific breakthrough or a technological advance. Conversely, new applications of the product can lengthen a product's life.

The limitation of the product life cycle concept is that few products behave the same way. However, despite the fact that the life cycle of two products is not the same, the concept does allow managers to study each product's basic pattern and to identify trends so that corrective action can be taken.

It is especially important for managers in a small company to understand the concept of product life cycles because they have more various responsibilities. They may forget to periodically evaluate their products to see where replacements are needed simply because of the pressure to meet daily operational demands. In a larger organization management personnel will be assigned the specific tasks of studying the life cycles of the organization's products and will be constantly looking for areas where new products are needed.

Even though most marketing executives understand product life cycles, too few of them use the concept to their advantage. It is most important that executives forecast the intensity and duration of each stage for new products. They should also know what stage existing products are in, and how long the cycle will probably last. Product life cycles are becoming shorter and shorter because of increased competition, substitution, and obsolescence. Today it is more important than ever to match the correct marketing strategy with the product's stage in the life cycle.

Difficulties in making the transition from one phase of a product's life cycle to another should be anticipated. Some of these problems may be alleviated if the project team members associated with the product in the introductory phase are assigned a permanent role in product management. This approach has the disadvantage of not permitting a carry-over of experience gained in the introductory phase from one new product to another new product. When another product is designed, a different team may be assigned to work on it.

RESEARCH AND DEVELOPMENT

Once management decides to undertake the necessary research and development to design a new product or improve an existing one, a budget must be established. There usually is little difference between actual and budgeted expenditures; rather, the phase most concerned with cost control is the one where the appropriation of funds is made.

In trying to decide how large the research budget should be, managers often rely on some basis they have used in the past, such as a certain sum per year or a specified percent of sale. The overriding question is whether the appropriation will produce enough income to justify the expense incurred. This is often difficult to answer because of the uncertainty of income forecasts. However, the accounting and marketing executives should work closely in matching even rough income estimates to budgeted expenditures. This is a much better approach than trying to guess what competitors are spending on product development. Most organizations follow a flexible approach in regard to their research and development activities. If they are hit by unfavorable economic conditions such as high interest rates or a decrease in operating income, they will postpone research.

Budget results should be detailed by projects. Within each project, the budgeted costs should be broken down into phases; if several departments are involved, this means that separate departmental budgets should be established for each project. Exhibit 12-1 illustrates one form of detailed budget for the development of new Product X. The total budget is broken down by expense items for the three different departments involved. Overhead is allocated on the basis of the estimated hours necessary to complete the different phases. The charge in Exhibit 12-1 is $20 per hour. The completion dates for each phase are also given.

Exhibit 12-2 illustrates the status report that should be prepared for all phases or departments. A summary for all departments working on the project should also be made. The budget for the expense item is matched against the expenditures incurred to date and the commitments made. The unexpended amount should be studied by the project director to determine if it will be sufficient to complete the phase. While the project director should be cost-conscious, he or she should not hesitate to ask top management for an additional appropriation if it seems the planned results cannot be achieved with the remaining unexpended amount.

Even though budget appropriations are made for individual

Exhibit 12-1. Budget for a new product.

Project Director: Mr. John Doe
Project Number: 111

| | Total | Phase or Department | | |
Expenses	Budget	Planning	Production	Promotion
Labor cost	$ 23,000	$ 7,000	$13,000	$ 3,000
Consulting fees	18,000	10,000	3,000	5,000
Supervision	2,000	500	1,200	300
Direct materials	18,000	1,000	16,300	700
Supplies and other indirect materials	10,000	1,500	5,900	2,600
Equipment	21,000	—	21,000	—
Overhead allocation	8,000	1,100	6,100	800
	$100,000	$21,100	$66,500	$12,400
Estimated hours	400	55	305	40
Completion date		May 31, 19X1	Feb. 10, 19X2	April 15, 19X2

Exhibit 12-2. Status report for new product X, March 30, 19__.

Planning Department
Project Number: 111

Expenses	Budget	Expenditures to Date	Commitments	Total Expenditures and Commitments	Unexpended
Labor cost	$ 7,000	$ 5,000		$ 5,000	$2,000
Consulting fees	10,000	8,000	$2,000	10,000	—
Supervision	500	300		300	200
Direct materials	1,000	700	100	800	200
Supplies and other indirect materials	1,500	1,200	200	1,400	100
Overhead allocation	1,100	800	—	800	300
	$21,100	$16,000	$2,300	$18,300	$2,800

projects, top management needs to periodically review all research projects underway. Exhibit 12-3 contains a form for this summarization. Only three projects are given for illustration purposes. The costs incurred in prior periods are listed, along with the current year's expenses. To these two figures are added the estimated future costs.

Exhibit 12-3.   Research and development cost summary, December 31, 19X1.

Project No.	Project Description	Costs to Jan. 1, 19X1	Current Costs	Future Costs	Total Costs	Annual Forecasted Income
111	New Product X	$3,000	$16,600	$1,500	$21,100	$6,000
121	New Product Y	5,000	4,000	3,000	12,000	4,000
131	New Product Z	1,000	15,000	2,000	18,000	5,000

Annual forecasted income is also given so evaluations of the project's success can be made.

ANALYSES OF TIME

Considering the competition for markets, time may be even more important than dollars. The incremental income to be gained by introducing a product several months earlier and beating competition should be balanced against the incremental cost of stepping up production and market tests. These figures should then be compared to the income estimated if the original time schedule is followed. After having made this analysis, and with these figures available, management is in a better position to make the correct decision.

Management should assign some dollar value to time so that it will have a basis for investment and expense decisions. Some type of timetable scheduling should be used, whether a simple method of making up calendars or a more sophisticated computerized Program Evaluation and Review Technique network. A detailed timetable is essential to new product introduction.

Program Evaluation and Review Technique

Program Evaluation and Review Technique (PERT) is a network analysis that may be used to time the sequence of events in the introduction of new products. The critical path technique is a variation of PERT that can be employed in analyzing the interdependence of the various elements. A PERT system involves diagramming the various steps that make up the project; each block represents a specific activity. PERT has an advantage over timetable techniques because it recognizes that certain steps of the sequence can be performed concurrently. Both PERT and the critical path technique are effective planning and control tools.

Most PERT programs require high-capacity electronic computers. Once the steps are determined, the various events can be fed into a computer and stored. When progress or completion of the individual events is fed in also, periodic reports will indicate what segments are falling behind schedule. The networking techniques can be applied to simpler tasks without using computers. Exhibit 12-4 illustrates a simplified network of the steps that must be completed when new products are introduced.

In Exhibit 12-4 the events leading to C (Marketing Strategy), D (Financial Plan), and E (Production Tests) can begin only after A (Product Plan) and B (Market Research) are complete. F (Test Marketing) can begin only after Events C, D, and E are finished. The project can be completed with G (National Introduction) only after Events C and F are finished. The estimated times needed to complete each step are given. The critical path of the series of steps that determines the time limits for completion of the project is: Events A, B, E, F, G, which would take 11 time limits. By determining the time limits involved, management can focus attention on the more critical steps and possibly shorten them.

Exhibit 12-4. Network for new product introduction.

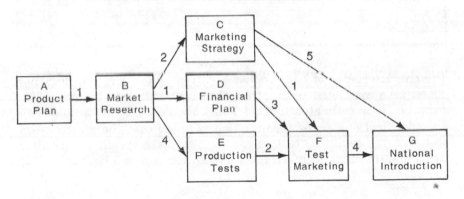

Time Budget

A time budget can be prepared as illustrated in Exhibit 12-5. Only a few of the typical functions under each phase are listed. The times budgeted for each operation are given so that the actual time can be compared with the estimate to arrive at a variance. The time allocated for each phase will vary between projects, depending upon the advance planning completed before the project is initiated and

Exhibit 12-5.   Time budget analysis.

Phase	Hours Budgeted	Actual Hours	Variance
Planning			
Product specification	24		
Personnel involved	5		
Research	7		
Market analysis	10		
Finance	9		
	55		
Production			
Personnel training	30		
Purchasing	15		
Control functions	10		
Test runs	200		
Product revisions	50		
	305		
Promotion			
Sales training	10		
Field testing	15		
Advertising	15		
	40		
Total hours	400		

the characteristics of the product involved. The operation does not have to be completed in order for the comparisons to be made. For example, it is estimated that 24 hours should be spent in planning the specifications of the product. If it is found that the project team is halfway through its task of arriving at these specifications after 15 hours, the current unfavorable variance becomes 3 hours.

BUDGETS AND ANALYSES

If a company must choose the one management tool that is of greatest importance in new product management, it would have to be the budget. Budgets vary in their complexities; therefore they can be prepared without much additional cost to the organization. Top management is accustomed to thinking in terms of budgets and does not have to be sold on them as a planning and control device.

Budgets force managers to quantify their ideas and estimates regarding expected costs and revenues for the product. If there is no formal budget, these figures could be carried around in the head of the project manager for quite a while before it is realized that the product could never be made successful because so much expenditure would be required to get it off the ground.

A well-prepared budget can serve as a basis for outside funding. Banks and financial institutions will be able to study the forecasts of revenue and expense and thus be in a better position to supply the necessary financial backing. Budgets help ensure that these dollars will be controlled and effectively spent. Comparison of the actual and budgeted expenditures can reveal areas where there have been cost overruns, and these variances will provide the springboard for study into the source of the problem. It could be that the original budgeted figures were established in a different economic environment. If prices in general have risen, the budget should be revised.

Budget preparation forces the people concerned with the new product to exchange ideas. Together they can plan not only in terms of dollars but also in terms of time. The budget for each phase can include deadlines, as illustrated in Exhibit 12-1. The budgeting process is a means of communication between parties within the organization; without it, each person might work in his or her own area of specialty and never grasp the whole picture of product management.

Research and Development Costs

Once a reasonable budget is set and research begins, the accounting department must collect costs for the new project. FASB Statement No. 2, issued by the Financial Accounting Standards Board, specifies the correct accounting for research and development costs.* Research is defined in the statement as planned search or critical investigation aimed at discovering new knowledge, with the hope that new products or services will be developed or that improvements will be made to existing products. The statement defines development as the translation of the research findings or other knowledge into a plan or design for a new project.

The activities identified as research and development for financial accounting and reporting purposes are also discussed. The statement does not apply to costs of research and development activities that are conducted for others under a contractual arrangement, or indirect costs that are specifically reimbursable under the contract terms.

*Financial Accounting Standards Board, Stamford, Conn., October 1974.

Research activities in the extractive industries are also not covered by the statement.

The statement discusses the elements of costs that should be identified with research and development. These include the materials, equipment, and facilities that are acquired or constructed for these activities. Those assets that have alternative future uses should be capitalized as tangible assets at the time they are built or acquired. The depreciation of such equipment would then be considered a research and development cost. Salaries and related costs of the personnel engaged in research should be included in research and development costs.

FASB Statement No. 2 indicates that all research and development costs that are encompassed by the statement are to be charged to expense when incurred. The financial statements must also disclose the total research and development costs charged to expense in each period for which an income statement is presented. The objective of Statement No. 2 is to reduce the number of alternative accounting and reporting practices followed, and to provide useful information about research and development costs. The requirement of expensing research and development costs when incurred must be applied retroactively by prior-period adjustment. FASB Statement No. 2 is effective for fiscal years beginning on or after January 1, 1975.

Appraisal of Existing Products

An appraisal of the organization's existing products will give management the opportunity to evaluate what stage in the life cycle each product is in. The review should be detailed enough so that a comparison between products can be made. An analysis of what the future market will be, as well as an estimate of the returns to be obtained from alternate product policies, should be made.

In estimating what the return of each product line will be, only direct costs should be considered. Careful attention should be given to determining the cost of the factory space used. Only direct costs that do not require an allocation should be considered because an allocation of indirect costs will be misleading. Exhibit 12-6 illustrates some of the common direct product costs.

Incremental Cost Analysis for Product Lines

Once the stage in the life cycle of the product line is determined, opportunities in the existing market should be evaluated. This is where incremental analysis will be helpful, because it will not be wise to incur a larger expense in advertising than the additional

Exhibit 12-6.   Product line analysis.

Sales revenue of product line		$XX
Direct costs:		
Direct material	$X	
Direct labor	X	
Supplies	X	
Depreciation or rent on machines used in product line	X	
Product line supervisor	X	
Direct cost of factory space used to make product line	X	
License royalties	X	
Total direct cost		XX
Income attributable to product line		$XX

sales revenue will be. For example, suppose marketing research shows that $9,000 of extra advertising will result in increased sales of 100 units, or $15,000. Before deciding that the organization will earn an extra $6,000, management needs to perform the type of incremental cost analysis illustrated in Exhibit 12-7. Only a few incremental cost items are considered in the illustration. The results show that the organization should not incur that much advertising expense because it will not generate enough additional contribution margin. A less expensive means of advertising or sales promotion should be used.

Exhibit 12-7.   Incremental cost analysis.

Incremental sales revenue (1,000 units)			$15,000
Incremental cost			
Variable costs of products:			
Direct material (1,000 units X $4 cost)	$4,000		
Direct labor (1,000 units X $3 per unit)	3,000		
Variable overhead (1,000 units X $1 per unit)	1,000	$8,000	
Advertising		9,000	
			$17,000
Incremental loss			$ 2,000

PROBLEM AREAS

Management must be realistic and plan ahead for possible problems, especially in the introduction of new products. A large number of new products (from 50 to 80 percent) run into difficulties and are cut. Some of them are doomed from the beginning because they have inherent problems. Other products may fail because market conditions have changed. Then, too, the cost of production may have been grossly underestimated, and the price that must be charged may lower the demand below what is needed to manufacture the product. These are but a few of the problems that may arise.

Product Design

The problem may stem from faulty design. This is usually first noticed on the product's initial entry into the market. Depending upon the severity of the deficiency, it may or may not be possible to change the product by reengineering it or by altering its properties. The accountant should work closely with management in this stage because the cost of such changes should be weighed against the alternatives available. If the product's deficiency is so severe that it cannot be sold, management must decide either to abandon the product or correct the faults.

Production

In addition to the problems directly associated with product design, management will likely encounter production, marketing, and/or financial problems. The plant may not have the necessary facilities to produce the product at the capacity level anticipated. Problems in securing the correct type of material or labor skill may have arisen. The delivery of production equipment may have been slower than promised, or this equipment may not be operating correctly.

Marketing

The organization may face a number of marketing problems. When a new product is introduced, unexpected resistance may arise because the market is slow to recognize its advantages. More time may be needed to make a sale than was originally anticipated. An analysis of the problem should be made so that it can be determined if changes in the marketing strategy are needed.

Historical information concerning repurchase rates can usually be gathered on consumer goods; it will indicate whether the product can be made viable. It is more difficult to obtain historical data in the industrial goods field. The people involved with the project must study the growth pattern of the product to determine if it will be sufficient to yield income levels that will justify the investment.

CUTTING PRODUCTS

The question of cutting products should arise during the introductory process If the product has no hope, it is a costly mistake to extend it beyond this stage. Conversely, the product manager does not want to cut a product that will become successful. Since this is such a crucial decision, data should be gathered throughout the introductory cycle to allow the organization to make a better and more objective decision.

During this introductory stage the marketing department should be developing its strategy and obtaining an idea of what the reaction will be in the marketplace. Then a more realistic return on investment (ROI) can be made than when the funds were first allocated. This revised ROI can be used to decide if the project should be continued. The ROI evaluation should be an important aspect of product review, because as the project proceeds, more funds will be required and the expected return should be closely studied. However, the decision to cut a product should be based on more factors than ROI. Management has a sunk cost that must be considered in a go, no go, decision concerning the new product. The company often finds after the product has been developed and is being tested in the factory that it has spent more on research and development than it had anticipated. If the marketing research department predicts that more market resistance will be encountered than was originally thought, the result will be a lower ROI than was hoped for. Management must then consider that the amount spent so far on the product is sunk cost, and no decision made at this point can change this cost. If the expenditures fell into the research and development costs classification as defined under FASB Statement No. 2, they have been expensed in the accounting period incurred.

The revelant costs in this decision are the additional expenses that will be incurred before the product becomes marketable. These incremental costs should be used in connection with the lower, revised ROI to compare the product with alternative projects available. If alternative new products are expected to earn a much higher ROI, the best decision may be to scrap the original project. There is no point in spending additional resources on a project that is doomed from the beginning. However, there is an additional uncertainty; the initial ROI may prove to be overoptimistic on this new project also.

The corporation's tax status as well as competitors' activities should be considered when cutting product lines is being contemplated.

If it is known that competitors are planning to introduce a similar product, their time schedules should play a strong role in the decision. If the organization knows that it can beat its competitors in introducing a product, this should be weighed in favor of continuing with the product. If, on the other hand, the organization knows it will have to introduce the new product after its competitors, this will certainly be to its disadvantage. Another factor to consider is whether the new product will be a complementary good to some of the firm's existing products and increase the sale of these products.

When insufficient funding becomes evident, the organization must be careful in choosing the correct course of action. Faced with this problem, organizations often begin cutting out unprofitable product segments of the business without first determining what stage of the life cycle these product lines are in. It is generally understood that few new products are extremely profitable during the introductory stage. In fact, the emphasis in this early stage should be on market penetration. However, when faced with financing problems, the organization should reevaluate the objectives originally planned for the new product. New short-range goals must replace the long-range goal of maximum market penetration. All too often a product has been cut because it was never given the necessary support. Many research projects have failed because the organization found in midstream that it did not have sufficient capital to finish them. Another possibility is that the original plan did not provide for enough advertising. Then later, when the choice is made to continue the product as opposed to killing it, the cost of the necessary advertising will likely be much more.

SUMMARY

An income goal for a new product should be established on the basis of what could be earned by the company in other types of alternative investments available, such as expansion of the present product lines. This will help management set a more realistic goal. The goals of each phase of the product's cycle vary. In the introductory stage the objective is to ensure the product's life by maximizing market penetration. During the growth and maturity phases the goal is to achieve optimum short- and long-term income. While profitability is a concern in the introductory stage, it should not be the prime emphasis. If too much emphasis is placed on profitability when the product is first introduced, the product may be forced to maturity too soon. It will then be difficult to optimize income in the later stages of its life. Before spending a large sum of money on research and development, several factors should be considered. The overriding factor, of course, is whether the cost will be worthwhile. An evaluation of existing products in the market should be made so ideas regarding new product innovations can be obtained. Many business failures have occurred simply because marketing executives failed to determine that there was a real need for the product and that proper opportunities existed in the marketplace. This should be done in the beginning, before the product becomes a reality. The accountant should work with the marketing executive in estimating expected returns.

Production management will continue to be a means of achieving organization growth in the future. However, the planning necessary for success will be more significant. The costs required for the development of new products will increase. More and different types of special skills will be required for research activity. Product lives are expected to become even shorter.

In a world of continuing economic pressures and income consciousness, the role of product management must be repeatedly studied. It must be remembered that in almost all new product introductions, greater demands on resources are made than was anticipated at the project's beginning. The secret in production management is not to rest on past laurels. A past success in introducing a new product is no guarantee of future good results.

Index